retirement for
two

everything you
need to know
to enjoy the rest
of your lives together

Dr Maryanne Vandervelde

PIATKUS

In memory of
Bertha Wiersma Vandervelde
My mother. Always with me.

Contents

Acknowledgments

The personal stories that appear in this book have been gathered over many years from a variety of sources—some of whom I can't remember because they have become part of my storytelling folklore, some of whom do not want to be mentioned here. Nevertheless, I am grateful to all of these people, and I'd like to specifically thank the following, in alphabetical order: Rosalie and Daryl Adrian, Mary Ann Barnes, Glenda Burkhart, Jill and Dick Davis, Jim and Erna Davis, Dorothy and Ed DeVries, Craig DeSilvia and Becky Poulson, the late Dr. Monte Jan Dray, Susan and David Dykstra, Dr. Jean and Jay Entwistle, Kay Enokido and Tom Crouse, Carol and Chuck Farrell, Nancy and Haines Gaffner, Jim and Pam Going, John and Gloria Kasonic, Harmon and Nita Killebrew, Teri and Bill Looney, Larry and Arma Looney, Dr. Norman Looney and Dr. Norah Keating, Peter Looney and Patricia Ostrander, Jack and Laurie McHale, Jane and Bob McKibbon, Barbara Meyer, Judy and Henry Miller, Dr. Rhoda Mintzer, Claudine Paris, Ilka and Dr. Jim Priest, Mike Schaefer and the late Dr. Colleen Coyne-Schaefer, Carol and Norman Schnall, Larry and Annemarie Storey, Madeleine and Bob Swain, Bill and Petty Taylor, David and Sandi Vandervelde, Margie and Paul Versaw, and Diane and Dave Zaharias.

Now to my "main men": My husband of forty years, H. Ray Looney, encouraged the writing of this book even when I was uncertain about it, and he fed me many stories of retiring couples during his years as a corporate executive. Of course, he also provided fodder through his half of our relationship issues! My son, Spencer Velde Looney, the most creative and deepest thinker in our family, was (and is) a great sounding board.

Professionally, I am indebted to my terrific agent/attorney, Gail Ross, and her talented colleague, Jenna Land. And my joyful relationship with Bantam Dell/Random House is attributable to Philip Rappaport, as well as Barb Burg and Nita Taublib. Many thanks to all five for helping my future retirement by making this book a reality.

Part One: Personal Partnerships—in Retirement

1.
The Issues

My Story

When I was thirty-six, I moved across the country because my husb and was offered a great new job. I eventually landed on my feet, but I couldn't find any books about what was happening to me—my career, my friendships, my relationship with my child, my house, my life—while I was helping my husband up the corporate ladder. So I did a survey of the Fortune 500 CEOs and their wives, and I wrote *The Changing Life of the Corporate Wife*. My research showed, for example, that the quality valued most in a corporate wife was her sense of humor. Certainly, humor is a wonderful quality in any human being, but I doubt that this would be first on the list for a CEO. I found that both men and women were hungry for better ways to manage their lives—at a time when our culture was just starting to examine the rigid, traditional expectations that businesses placed on executives and their partners. The questions continue to this day for all kinds of leaders and their partners, and I believe that my book played a small part in the dialogue. That book sold well, and many couples told me how much they were helped by it.

Now I'm sixty-two, and my husband has been retired for five years. We have faced some challenges that seem to be typical of people our age, and we frequently find ourselves in discussions with like-minded friends. At this point, we have sorted through most of our angst about retirement, but our forty-year marriage is still a work in progress.

This Book at This Time

I decided several years ago to gather information about this stage of life because the subject has interested me for a long time—in my clinical practice with couples and families as well as in my observations of friends and family members. This book is, therefore, based on:

- Stories I've jotted down over many years from family and friends as well as from therapy clients

- Issues that came up over the last twenty years in corporate human resources training sessions about people facing retirement

- Interviews conducted, by phone or in person, over the last five years with a network of acquaintances around the world

- Perusal of the professional and popular literature

This is *not* a book about money or finances. There are hundreds of those to be found in bookstores and libraries. This aspect of retirement should never be minimized because a secure retirement clearly is built on a sufficient financial base—however that is defined by both partners. But the people I've queried say that most of their financial planning took place years back. Decisions they made a long time ago have determined their financial status now. They've come to terms with what they have and don't have in monetary resources.

Money, per se, is rarely what current or about-to-be retirees want to talk about—the emotional implications of money, yes; the decisions that couples must make around money, yes; apportioning assets in a second marriage, yes; but whether one has enough money or how to get more, almost never. Rather, it's the emotional turmoil and the relationship stuff that hits them unexpectedly when they anticipate retirement or when they actually retire.

What *do* couples in their fifties, sixties, and seventies want to talk about? Relationship issues—psychological and emotional struggles that are causing conflict. Single retirees often mention loneliness, but coupled retirees say things like "I never imagined it would be so hard to be together 24/7" or "I am with this person for better or worse, but not for lunch!"

Freud said that work and love are the two major ingredients of life, and it seems logical that the loss of one will have major effects on the other. Retirees whose identity was found largely through work have a lot of soul-searching to do as they look for identity elsewhere. And people whose close relationships have been neglected will have to do a lot of work in order to establish a basis that will be satisfying for the rest of their lives. This has always been true, but there are three major reasons why we need to pay more attention to retirement now than ever.

One is that the first baby boomers turned fifty-five in 2002 and technically became senior citizens. Fifty-nine million people born before 1946 are already retired or soon will be retiring, but they are being joined over the next few years by seventy-seven million boomers—those who were born between 1946 and 1964. Because the boomers are a huge population cohort, they are already starting to redefine retirement, and this stage is attracting as much focus as all of their other stages have. As they have always done, boomers will look for—indeed, they will expect—answers.

Two, age discrimination is a fact of life, and many people are finding themselves out of work earlier than they had planned. Furthermore, we seem to be living longer and longer—seventy-seven is now the life expectancy for men, eighty-four for women. So, many of us will find ourselves coupled—without our usual routines—for many, many years. We'd better find mechanisms and systems to make it a happy time.

Three, retirement is more complicated now than ever because of the many choices we have. Only a few years ago, gender and age roles were strictly defined. Now the options are wide open. With fewer and fewer prescriptions, we all need to figure it out for ourselves. And better late than never! It becomes very clear to most of us at retirement that life is not a dress rehearsal.

Retiree Differences and Similarities

Not all retiree couples are alike. The following are just a few of the differences:

- Some are age sixty-five or older when they hang it up; others take early retirement in their fifties or even forties.

- Some choose retirement when they are ready; others are forced into it by organizational downsizing, ill health, or other factors.

- Some partners come to retirement simultaneously; others want to retire at different times, in different ways.

- Some are in long-term marriages; others are in long-term but unmarried homosexual or heterosexual relationships; still others are in relatively new unions—married or unmarried, heterosexual or same-gender.

- Some have had high salaries, retiring with lots of money and choices; others have just enough to live comfortably; still others are financially strapped.

- Some couples have been on two-career, fast-track treadmills; others have both held jobs more than careers; many have had more traditional roles, with one person home-based.

- Some have looked forward to retirement; others have dreaded it.

But every couple will have to face certain types of decisions, such as:

- Where they will live

- How they'll spend their time

- How they'll spend and/or save their money

- What kind and quality of sex life they'll have

- What their relationships will be like with children, grandchildren, other relatives, and friends

- Whether they'll have pets and how they will deal with them

- The emotional closeness or distance of their relationship

- What they will do when they want different things

- How they will both deal with aging and the future

- How they will cope with medical issues

- How they will make legal decisions

Most important, if retirement is to be a happy time, there will have to be some resolution of conflicts. Both partners may have to learn some new attitudes and behaviors because they will be facing some new realities:

- They need to fight fairly—perhaps becoming more equal than they have ever been in the past.

- If they can't communicate on a somewhat adult level, there's big trouble ahead. The squabbling adolescent model of communication will not work very well in retirement.

- Some couples will need counseling, and they will have to choose the counselor carefully.

- If divorce is the best solution, it should be done well.

- When one partner dies, the remaining one needs excellent coping skills.

- After divorce or death, new relationships can be extremely challenging.

- Getting clear about hopes and dreams can help. Giving up some of them can bring peace. Finding new hopes and dreams can be a truly exciting adventure.

- Growing whole, individually and together, is the most important task of this stage of life, and it is not easy.

The Bottom Line

These are serious issues, but we also learn at this stage of life that there is no better time to laugh! If we didn't have much sense of humor before, now is a great time to develop one. If we are fortunate enough to have wonderful options, we need to finally figure out who we are and what we want out of life in order to make our choices wise ones. On the other hand, if life has presented us with lemons, now is the time to make lemonade.

For most of us, love and meaningful relationships are more important as we age than ever before, but getting and keeping the love we want is always a challenge. This book lays out the issues that are unique to couples as they retire and proposes principles by which most partners should live.

The vignettes of real people suggest solutions that may be emulated—or, in some cases, avoided. The questions at the end of all the following chapters offer ways to clarify thoughts, personalize the process, and formulate next steps.

2.
Retirement Is Wonderful

Anticipation

One of the reasons that so many couples have problems in retirement is that they don't anticipate the changes accurately. It is optimistic and rather charming that so many people think retirement will be wonderful. For example, Prudential Securities did a survey of 826 married Americans between the ages of forty and sixty-five, reported in an article called "Happily Ever After? How Baby Boomers Envision Retirement."[1] Their findings include the following:

- Eight-nine percent believe that they and their partner will become better friends.

- Seventy-four percent think that their relationship will become more romantic.

- Eighty-five percent say that both will agree on where to travel for vacations.

- Eighty-five percent think that they will agree on where to live.

- Most expect to agree on how much time to spend with family members (76 percent), how to spend leisure time (75 percent), and how to spend their money (71 percent).

  But there are also some concerns:

- Fifty-four percent of the husbands who are the sole breadwinner say that it will be hard for them to adjust, and 61 percent of them expect to have a hard time developing new routines.

- Both men and women agree that the men will have a harder time finding new friends.

- Eighty-one percent feel that they need to plan better for what they will do in retirement.

- Seventy-nine percent think they need to prepare better financially.

It would be interesting to see surveys of the same group a year or two after they retire, and perhaps five years later, in order to compare expectations with reality—as well as to understand the effects of time. It is possible that their optimism about relationship issues will be warranted, but it's more likely that the 81 percent who say that they need to plan better, especially for what they will do, will find that this segues into partnership problems.

Maybe the optimists' satisfaction in relationship areas *will* be very high, but that still leaves room for many couples who will struggle. Indeed, the evidence below suggests that the adjustment process takes time and that anticipations need to be examined.

The *Wall Street Journal* recently featured a survey of one-year-retired adults done by Joel Savishinsky of Ithaca College, which looked at the rewards and challenges in that first twelve months.

Expectations in the relationship areas were generally not very accurate; many psychological hurdles were not anticipated. But the study also found that by the end of the first year, life really starts to get comfortable if couples are working through the problems.[2]

Many of these surveyed couples found happiness especially in "drift time," and this is a lovely, graceful idea. For example, they could start out on a bicycle trip but never make it to their destination because they had the luxury to digress, to slow down, to change directions. They could go to the grocery store at any time of day. If plan A for their time didn't feel right, they could divert to plan B or C or D.

The adjustment may take some time and effort, and retirement will never be perfect, but many of those surveyed after one year said that it was wonderful.

The Fun-and-Games Picture

Most of us keep our noses pretty much to the grindstone as we move through life. For those of us who are achievement-oriented, this pattern probably started when we were very young children. From about age twenty to sixty—a long and, with luck, productive forty years—we jump through a lot of hoops. We build our careers, raise our children, take care of our parents, tend a few friendships, and try to save some money.

This should not imply that life is a straight line to retirement. Most people have some periodic existential crises that propel them into course corrections—a different educational path after becoming bored, a change in career or financial goals after being fired or getting a promotion, a new approach to relationships after a painful breakup, an altered lease on life after becoming a parent.

Some of us have major early-life or midlife crises, during which we drastically alter our directions—getting a divorce, completely changing our lifestyle, dealing with an addiction to alcohol or drugs, sometimes buying the proverbial red Porsche.

But most of us chug along through those forty years like the little engine that could. Our diversions from the straight and narrow are few; our obligations and commitments are many. We know our roles within our primary relationships, and we try to be a good, supportive partner.

If we're smart, we also have some fun along the way, but we usually find ourselves reacting more than acting. We have many opportunities to make choices, but we also have a lot of life simply thrust upon us. In fact, people in business careers say that their lives have become exponentially harder in the last twenty-five years. "There are a lot more demands on the schedule, we're all expected to be quick, and we're all playing on a bigger stage because it's global."[3]

It's no wonder, then, that most people look forward to retirement—or *jubilado,* as the Spanish so elegantly call it. Those forty years may not have worked out exactly as we wished or in the ways that we expected, but now we will finally be free of most constraints. If the world will not totally be our oyster, there is at least a shiny new shell waiting to be opened.

In the most optimistic view, potential retirees think that the times ahead will all be fun and games. They'll play. If they have their health and a small financial cushion, they'll be home free. Their working years may have been complicated and interesting, sometimes even fulfilling, but it will feel so good to be free of time constraints and office politics that they'll never miss work at all. They really look forward to the more simple, direct, secure, comfortable years in their future.

And if they have a partner, either long-term or recent, they don't expect to be lonely. They'll have someone with whom to share this wonderful time. Even if their relationship has a few kinks in it, free time will be a panacea for any problems. Whether retirement looks like a grand adventure or more of the same minus work, this'll be good. It might even be awesome! Nothing to worry about. They'll figure it out as they go along. It's no big deal, is it?

For optimists like this, retirement *may* turn out to be wonderful, but their lack of thoughtful concern can also get them into big trouble. The most successful retirees seem to balance the fun-and-games view with a realistic picture of the adjustments required.

Freedom, Choice, and New Opportunities

For many of us, this is the first and only time in our lives that we can make really significant choices. We may not have youth any longer, but we likely have gained some wisdom. If we want to, we can reinvent ourselves. We can live wherever we want. If we have enough money, we can work—or not. We can volunteer and give something back—or not. We can take classes and learn something new—or not. We can ski or play tennis or golf—even on weekdays, when access is easier. We can travel for short or long periods of time—or not at all. We can strengthen old friendships or make new friends—or neither. We can spend more time with our children and grandchildren—if they will have us. We can take care of pets—or not. We can spend quality time with whomever we wish. We can improve, or at least conserve, our health. We can sleep as much as we want, staying up late or getting up early. We can pay more attention to our investments. We can finally relax.

One couple described retirement as freedom from ties and dresses. My own husband has a closet full of suits providing sustenance for the moths. (He says he has to keep a couple for weddings and funerals.) At the same time, he has acquired a huge wardrobe of shorts and golf shirts. To my chagrin, he has been known to wear shorts to the finest restaurants! I too have a lot of business suits in my closet, but I seldom wear anything these days except comfortable pants, cotton shirts, and sensible shoes.

Clothing issues are frivolous, but bigger, more important questions must be addressed in the context of this new freedom. The overall, most interesting question is "What do I want for the rest of my life?" And behind that question is "What will bring me pleasure and peace?" While these questions suggest wonderful opportunities, they can be terrifying as well.

New Images and Role Models

There has been a dramatic shift in most people's thinking about retirement. This stage of life used to be seen as sad and even slightly embarrassing—old people waiting in the wings before the final curtain call, people who have been put on the shelf, out to pasture. Now, however, younger people often sound jealous of their elders. Advertisements show retirement as sexy and older people as upbeat. The shrewd marketing of one retirement chain says: "It's a time for boundless fun with friends old and new."

It has been said that retirees are the new adolescents. They play sports, drive fast cars, travel to exotic locales, and have romantic dates with each other. In the words of Neil Young's song, a lot of retirees would rather burn out than rust.[4]

Our role models have changed too. A lot has been written, for example, about Jimmy and Rosalynn Carter in their post-presidential years. They both were out of jobs early—he at age fifty-six, she at fifty-five. They had some adjusting to do, but they have become examples par excellence for many. He plays softball. They are both physically fit. They build houses for Habitat for Humanity in poor neighborhoods and do other volunteer work. They both write books. Together they run the Carter Center—a forum for resolving international disputes and pursuing health issues. She hosts a yearly symposium on mental health. He travels around the world to monitor elections and mediate conflicts. They have taken up new recreations and hobbies. They have helped each other try many new things. They also make their family a priority.[5]

There is some conjecture that the Carters have worked so hard at retirement because their record in the White House leaves a lot to be desired. If this is true, it is an option that is available to all of us. That is, if we are not happy with what we accomplished at work, we still have many years to do other things well. If we have been victims of difficult bosses, they are no longer in charge. If we have made some poor choices in the past, the slate is now almost clean again. If our parents and grandparents provided negative models for retirement, we can make up our own rules. This is a wonderful time for new beginnings.

Happiness

Retirement may be a bigger deal than we had thought, and doing this stage well, especially as a couple, may take more effort than we had planned. Transferring our focus away from work can have unexpected ramifications, and learning to maneuver around new barriers may take some new skills. But all of this can be a wonderful experience for couples who are determined to find the best path—for them.

Jacqueline Bouvier Kennedy's oft-quoted advice about relationships was "Stay loyal to those who love you." If we are lucky enough, or resourceful enough, to have a partner in this retirement adventure, we'd be wise to listen up!

Anna Quindlen's graduation speech at the Collegiate School in New York City, now a book called *A Short Guide to a Happy Life*, suggests this simple prescription for happiness: Pay attention to relationships. Ms. Quindlen wrote short, elegant vignettes about her own role as a spouse, a parent, and a friend, and each paragraph ends the same way: "I show up; I listen; I try to laugh."[6]

None of these three behaviors is particularly easy because most of us are very selfish about our time and energy. We don't always want to show up when others ask; we have more important things to do. Then, because our minds are occupied with our own, more significant issues, it is hard to calm down enough to really listen. That is, it's difficult to not only hear the words but also use our "third ear"—the one that searches for context and meaning. And finally, it is not always easy to keep one's sense of humor, especially in relationships that have been strained over the years by anger or disappointment. But the effort to laugh and not take life too seriously will bear magnificent fruit in both oneself and one's relationships.

Most of us take little time to ponder philosophical matters as we struggle to make a living and raise our families, but retirement is finally the time to focus on meaning! Happiness does not come out of the clear blue sky, and it seldom comes to very selfish people. Happiness involves relationships with others and activities that have some meaning for us. The examined life is still the best one, and retirement—especially with a partner—can be wonderful because you now have the time to make happiness happen.

Questions to Ask Yourself and Your Partner

1. If I (you) have not yet retired, am I (are you) anticipating retirement accurately and with reasonable complexity? What tools am I (are you) using for the relationship part?
2. If one or both of us has retired, to what extent were our expectations accurate?
3. Did anticipation versus reality change over time? How were the first two years? After that?
4. To what extent did we keep our noses to the grindstone in midlife? Too much or not enough?
5. To what extent did either or both of us have a midlife crisis or existential event?

6. To what extent did we have fun along the way? Why or why not?

7. Now, to what extent do we expect to have total fun and games in retirement?

8. What type of adjustments do I (you) expect, or have I (you) experienced, in retirement?

9. Do I (you) expect to ever be, or have I (you) ever been, lonely in retirement?

10. What will be, or what have been, the best parts of having freedom, choice, and new opportunities?

11. Do I (you) expect to acquire, or have I (you) acquired, any new feelings of contentment in retirement?

12. How loyal am I (are you) to those I (you) love?

13. How well do we "show up, listen, and try to laugh" in our relationship?

14. What is my (your) definition of happiness at this stage of life? How happy do I (you) feel individually, and how do we feel as a couple?

15. Does either (or do both) of us need a sense of humor tune-up?

16. To what extent are we living "the examined life" in order to be happy?

17. What are the advantages for me (you) of facing retirement as a couple?

3.

's Also Difficult

The Day Comes

To many people, retirement comes as quite a shock. One recently retired executive described his experience this way:

> You've made it through the office farewell party, and Retirement Day was last Friday. Now, you have no job to go to, no morning coffee break with co-workers, no business lunches, no tough-but-familiar routines to give your day shape and purpose. You're on your own. What do you do next?

And Lee Iacocca put it this way in an interview with Tom Brokaw:

> [Retirement is] one hell of an adjustment. After going at full tilt, you're going to go through the windshield if you slam on the brakes. . . . Money does not bring you the happiness you think it will 'cause you've

*got a third life to lead. . . . Your mind starts to atrophy if you
don't use it. . . . Life involves work. Retirement is for the birds.*[1]

Expectations from Others

There are good lessons for the rest of us in all of the positive
role models touted by the media, but there is pressure in these
images too. People now want to know what you are *doing*—or will
be doing—in retirement, and they expect to hear about something
productive. You will be measured in social conversations by how
you are filling that newfound free time. And it will be hard to one-
up all of the media stories about eighty-year-old skydivers and
ninety-year-old Nobel Prize winners.

Your grown kids may have even higher expectations than your
peers, partly because they want you to be happy and perhaps
because they know how capable you are. However, they also
don't want the responsibility for your happiness on their shoulders, and they probably don't want you on their doorstep at this
stage of life. So they too put pressure on you to be productive and
interesting.

The survey done by Dr. Savishinsky at Ithaca College con-
cluded that most retirees seek out role models without even realizing it, but they are more likely to fixate on negative examples
than positive ones. They are very concerned about not blowing it!
They talk more about the people and places and pursuits to avoid
than they do about what they really want.[2]

The Couple Factor

Facing retirement as a couple is comforting in many ways, but
it really compounds the issues because every couple must deal
with two sets of reactions, agendas, priorities, and needs. The

retiree must cope with his own feelings of loss and confusion as well as his partner's.

A very common realization after the big day comes is that one or both parts of the couple have no idea what the other is thinking. Both people may have been so set in their prescribed roles that they have not thought much about their relationship in retirement. They have probably been taking each other for granted for a very long time.

Most couples are experienced at this phenomenon, and some are experts at not paying much attention to each other. When they do try to communicate, partners frequently say or hear things like:

- How come you never told me that?

- You never asked.

- I told you last week—at least twice.

- How come you never listen to me?

- I don't have to listen to you all the time [one of my husband's favorites].

People often express disappointment that their post-retirement relationship is much harder than they thought it would be. Suddenly the old patterns get shaken up, and communication becomes more difficult. Figuring out your own wants and needs is hard enough, but you have to be aware of your mate's preferences too.

Furthermore, your friends and children often have a picture of how you should act as a couple, so you feel pressure from those around you to handle it—to keep it cool. You should not fight too much; you should not rock the boat to any great extent. These well-meaning people are sometimes not very empathetic about your problems because they do not want their relationship with you to change. Real trouble in your relationship at retirement can seem threatening to those who care about you, and consequently you may feel very alone.

In this environment, power struggles ensue, and people often feel depressed or angry. Divorce may be considered when one person or both people begin questioning what they really have together. Indeed, divorce statistics for this age group are rising (see chapter 18). Loose ends and freedom can turn out to be tricky for a couple.

In the best of circumstances, partners recognize these dangerous situations as an omen. Rather than letting small annoyances fester, they figure out what the issues are and hone their problem-solving skills, as in the following example:

Josie and Tom had cofounded an executive search business and sold it when they were in their late fifties. None of their friends worried about them when they decided to leave New York City and move to Tucson because they are both gregarious and make friends easily. They would surely find a new life while keeping their old friends too.

They had discussed their needs for privacy, and they organized the new house with work areas at opposite ends. Josie paints and does volunteer work with arts organizations; Tom consults and serves on business boards. However, after a few months in their new routine, Josie became concerned that they were bumping into each other, literally, in the kitchen, and she became exasperated one day when they reached into the fridge simultaneously. After some high-decibel accusations and denials, Tom admitted that when he hears the kitchen door open, he heads there. And he admitted that he often feels lonely.

They talked at length about how separate their lives used to be. Even though they worked together and raised three children together, they had separate roles at both work and home and quite a few separate friends. Neither of them had any doubt that they could re-create fulfilling lives for themselves in Tucson, but it wasn't happening as quickly as they had assumed it would. For example, Tom had tried to get himself appointed to a sports-related volunteer board, had been rejected, and had taken it harder than Josie had realized. They talked about strategy to get both of them on the boards they wanted to be part of, and they agreed on their level of contributions to these organizations. They reminded each other that they are newcomers here and reassured each other that they simply needed to be more patient. They had to slow down a bit from the pace they had lived in New York.

Tom and Josie are gradually making terrific new lives for themselves in Tucson. They have some separate friends and activities, but they also socialize with interesting new couples together. When they are working at home, Josie now calls Tom into the kitchen sometimes for a sandwich or snack, and Tom says he's trying to avoid his Pavlovian response of running to her. They joke about her various methods of attracting his attention with her culinary (and other) skills and his unsuccessful attempts at playing hard-to-get. They both enjoy the humor in their tales of "kitchen collisions."

"My World Has Changed"

Your world both inside and outside the home will have changed in at least three significant ways, and this can require a major adjustment.

One, after many years of busyness surrounding a relationship, it is often a shock to be left alone with each other most of the time. Maybe you've never really evaluated the relationship before. It worked while you were both doing your jobs. You never had time to talk anyway. Now you just hope that you have something in common—besides the kids, that is. You're already bored talking about *them*.

Two, you also may need to learn that the skills and behaviors that brought positive results in the workplace are almost the opposite of those that get good feedback at home. Whether you are male or female, your hard-nosed, kick-ass performance was probably rewarded at the office. You made decisions easily there. Perhaps you had secretaries and assistants at work. Well, toughness and quick command of the situation will only elicit negatives at home. Furthermore, you won't have any underlings at home for the rest of your life, and if you try to make your partner perform as one, you probably won't like the results. If the kitchen is foreign territory to you, you'd better learn some culinary tricks or you might starve to death. Now that you have more time, you will probably be expected to feed yourself more than you were before. In fact, very few retired couples include one person who loves making three meals every day. Chores such as laundry, bill paying, travel reservations, and yard responsibility may also be up for grabs and possible reassignment. You may even need to change your vocabulary.

Three, retirement usually affects the way people treat you, and that in turn affects the way you will interact with the outside world. Many workers think that they are widely and well loved by their colleagues, only to be shocked after retirement when they learn that those people are not really their friends. If you were a powerful person, you'll find that people will no longer suck up because you can't do much for them anymore. You'll see people around you change. If you were one of those who did the sucking up, you'll probably feel lost—without purpose. Either way, your ego will suddenly deflate, and you'll have to adjust.

Your partner will also be affected by your changing world because your status was surely connected somewhat to each other's. Those business or professional friends were people you probably saw and enjoyed as a couple. But now there may be social rejections or confusing signals from those you had thought of as friends. If you were a big shot at work, your partner may have enjoyed being Mrs. Big Shot, with lots of perks, and giving that up can be hard. Therefore, unless you are both in touch with feelings, your partner may have such a difficult time dealing with his deflated ego that there is little room left for tending to your sense of loss. It will take time for both of you to adjust your social life and find new ways of fitting into the world around you.

The positive side of this change is, of course, that you and your partner won't *have* to do certain things or suck up to particular people anymore. You won't have to go to the dinners with clients, holiday parties, and charity events that never really interested you, nor will you have to dress or act in prescribed ways. The negative side is that you'll have to work a little harder to make some *real* relationships.

The wisest people in powerful positions make sure, all along, that they have friends outside of work, but even these relationships might change when you can no longer provide business or professional contacts. It is truly hard to know beforehand who your real friends will be after retirement.

Loss of Work

Most of us are lucky because work provides us with so many positive things. Indeed, these factors constitute a major part of our lives:

- Satisfaction with our accomplishments

- Feelings of importance and usefulness

- Self-esteem and respect from others

- Status

- Awareness of our place in the world and in the work group

- Companionship and camaraderie

- A daily, reliable routine

- Income—important as a benchmark even if we don't need the money

- Medical and other insurance

These factors and feelings are extremely important to most of us. One retired professor says that even the women who cleaned bathrooms at his college seemed to be excited about their jobs. They had developed a close-knit group, and one woman said that she couldn't wait to go to work on Monday mornings. It obviously wasn't the work itself, toilets being what they are, but it was all the other factors mentioned above. Besides getting valuable paychecks and insurance, these women received emotional support from one another. They gave wedding showers and baby showers. They helped one another get through many trials and tribulations in their lives.

Not all retirees used work to identify themselves, but a lot of us are stuck in the work ethic. Since school days, we have had our self-worth tied up in our jobs. We judge other people by their jobs. It is not by coincidence, then, that cocktail parties resound with the question "What do you do?" We have all asked it and answered it hundreds of times.

Workaholics, especially, will have to do some real soul-searching if they are to retire successfully. Not the least of their issues is how they will answer that question at the next cocktail party. It is not pleasant to hear people pontificate about what they *used* to do, as though they have to justify their importance.

Neither is it comfortable to hear someone sheepishly answer that question with "Nothing." It seems that many of us who were so comfortable socially and had so much to say while we were working suddenly struggle to find words for the transition into retirement.

If we can't come to terms with the changes and verbalize the ways in which retirement is affecting us psychologically, the feelings can easily spill over into the relationship with one's partner.

Megan is married to Steven, a retired professor of philosophy. He always loved the classroom and his students. After he retired, however, Megan was expected to be his constant, eager listener. Steven felt compelled to editorialize on everything—from what they were watching on television (even commercials) to what he read in newspapers, roadside ads, and professional journals. In Megan's words: "His mind is in gear every minute, and he chooses to comment on everything."

There are times, like when they are traveling by car, that Megan enjoys batting ideas back and forth with him. She feels that she has gained a great deal of knowledge about books and issues from him by osmosis because he has shared so much of his excitement with her over the years. But being his primary audience sometimes became a bit much! At those times she tried to clench her teeth and breathe deeply. When her mouth is engaged in this way, she says, it is difficult to retort!

Since Megan retired at the same time, she decided to make a project out of becoming a nicer person. She tried to reply to her husband's comments in a positive tone of voice rather than with grunts, uh-huhs, or a nod. She says it wasn't too hard to start this habit, and it soon began to feel good. It also occurred to Megan that she had her own form of editorializing. When asked a question that seemed to have an obvious answer, she was prone to comments like "What a stupid question!" But that kind of reply was guaranteed to evoke harsh remarks and escalate any argument. She found that a more pleasant and engaged comment added a different slant to the conversation, and it seemed to be paying big dividends in their relationship.

Then, almost two years post-retirement, Megan saw a specialist for bowel and digestive problems, and she learned that her new approach might not be working as well as she'd thought. After extensive tests and a referral from her internist, she began weekly sessions with a therapist. She eventually agreed with the doctors that she was internalizing her feelings and making herself sick. When she first explained these conclusions to Steven, he didn't get it, so she had to be more forceful. She warned him that she would be telling him to shut up sometimes in the future because her own health may depend on it. To her surprise, he heard that, and he has been trying to limit his constant talking about meaningless things.

Megan now also finds ways of encouraging Steven to talk more about the loss of his teaching life, and she was shocked to see him in tears one day as he was cleaning out his files. He told her how much his students had meant to him and how much he missed them. She urged him to start teaching a philosophy course at their church, and he has enjoyed that immensely. She thinks that, with time, he will be able to stop pontificating so much, and she is, meanwhile, setting limits on her listening time. They are both trying to be more introspective about their feelings.

The luckiest people may be those who can taper off if they want to—artists, some academics, attorneys, physicians, small-business owners, and so on. They have the luxury of leaving their responsibilities gradually, but sometimes that is problematic too. Trouble comes when they continue to go to the office long after they have (or should have) handed the reins to others. This gradual-retirement idea can be a nightmare for other employees if the retiree butts in and gives unwanted advice, but it can also be a savior for retirees who cannot give up the work habit easily.

In reality, however, most jobs are all or nothing. Some people have tried job sharing, but it seldom works well. Other people make consulting or project arrangements with former employers, but they usually find the lack of authority frustrating. Jack Welch, former CEO of General Electric, says in his book *Jack: Straight from the Gut* that he was always a hard charger.[3] Writing his book served as a necessary bridge for him, allowing him to break free from his beloved GE and stay out of his successor's hair. My own husband jumped from a CEO's job into a demanding house-remodeling project. I was happy to have his help, and he says that being an assistant general contractor made for a great transition.

Retirement from paid work really *is* an ending, and some people have a hard time with endings because they carry the shadow of mortality. It is common for retirees to claim that they want no party and no gift when they leave, and this is often because it is so hard for them to face retirement, let alone talk about it. But usually, when some ceremony is forced upon them, they say that it was a happy experience. They learned that retirement is not death. They liked knowing that people wanted to honor them. They, and sometimes their partner, realized that they needed some closure to the working chapter in their life.

Many Are Pushed

The biggest adjustment of all is for those who did not retire voluntarily. Retirement is complicated enough when two partners have planned for it, but it seems like fewer and fewer couples are rewarded with their exact preferred timetable these days.

Many companies, as well as nonprofits and government entities, give pink slips every year to thousands, especially when the economy is down, and older people, with their higher salaries, are often the first to go. We have all heard stories of people who continued leaving home at the same time each morning for months or even years before their partner learned somehow that there was no longer any job. What pain that scenario expresses!

Even without doing anything bizarre like the pretend-job pretense, older workers have to come to terms with a lot of feelings when they are pushed out: rejection, inadequacy, guilt, shame, anger, and rage. Denial may help for a while, but those feelings will show up in health problems, unwarranted anger, alcoholism, or other behavioral issues if they are not dealt with. Eventually those feelings need to be worked through.

People whose work had been difficult or who had complicated relations with their employer may have retired voluntarily, but they can still struggle more than they had anticipated with feelings that they were pushed out. Even though they officially left on their own, they know that, in actual fact, they were not wanted. They wonder why they weren't appreciated more by their bosses. They wish they could have ended their career on a happier note— or with a better compensation package. Coming to terms with this could be simply a matter of adjustment; sometimes time does heal wounds. But there may be signs of a major depression or other problems. Either way, partners are affected every time.

By the time Ike turned sixty, both he and Janine were fed up with his banking career. The early years had been good ones. They had enjoyed living in Asia and were happy to be settled in San Francisco by their early forties. Ike made it to senior vice president by age forty-eight, and he expected to be the next president of his large division. But sometime in his early fifties, he began to get hints that he'd reached his limit. At age fifty-three, when his boss retired, the bank brought in a young hotshot as president. Ike was diligent and obedient the next seven years, and his boss was relatively kind, but there was no question that retirement looked attractive.

He and Janine talked about travel and volunteer work. When the bank asked what he wanted as a retirement gift, Janine suggested a trip, but Ike requested a top-of-the-line computer setup, and he spent many evenings before the big day getting it ready.

The morning after the party, Janine watched Ike descend to his office in the basement with an orange and an apple. At about six o'clock he reappeared for dinner and an evening of sports on TV. She knew he was tired and she didn't want to bug him, but after a couple of weeks she asked him if this was to be a pattern. He exploded in anger, saying that she would never understand.

You bet she doesn't! Two years have now passed, and they are both miserable. When she tries to get their kids to talk to him, he says she exaggerates. When she mentioned it to their family doctor, Ike demeaned her lack of work experience and suggested that she get a job for once in her life.

What has happened to their plans and their relatively happy marriage? There is no doubt that Ike was damaged

*by those years of sublimation and pretending at the bank.
There is also no doubt that he did not plan well for
change and free time. Is he clinically depressed?
Probably. Will he come out of it naturally? Not likely. Is
there a way to get him some help? Only, perhaps, if all
those who love him can do some kind of meaningful
intervention. Neither Ike nor Janine can currently see a
way out.*

Even in thriving organizations, ageism is so common—and so
hard to prove legally—that many workers in their forties and
fifties are now finding themselves unemployed or underemployed.
With laws on the books against a mandatory retirement age, some
employers seem terrified that they won't be able to push out
enough older workers to make room for the advancement of
younger ones.

Employers may honestly find, in this era of rapid technologi-
cal and cultural change, that the older worker simply is not
keeping up. Some companies believe that they need savvy
workers who are able to understand and accelerate the trends.
But they may also compare salaries and conclude that they can
get two younger people for the price of one old codger. Thus
bosses these days are finding the most creative and innovative
ways to get rid of older people. You can be out on your ear before
you know what's happening. And it is rare that a job-hunting
worker past fifty locates a *higher*-paying position. Another job is
frequently a step down.

One also hears more and more about early retirement for
health reasons. Maybe the employee's illness was prolonged.
Perhaps it was temporary, but the boss wouldn't or couldn't hold
the job open. A chronic illness may have left you with less energy,
and you are no longer able to work as hard as the job requires.

Perhaps age has simply made it impossible to continue to do

hard physical labor. For example, Andy is a food store produce manager who ruined his back over the years by lifting heavy boxes. He has never had a pension or retirement savings, and he is fifteen years away from Social Security eligibility. He can't get workmen's comp because there was no specific injury. He applied for Social Security disability, but they're training him instead for computer work that intellectually he probably can't do. Physical problems like this are also a common story for construction workers who were once strong but have weakened as they aged or sustained injuries.

In previous decades, when families were more united, older workers like this were probably folded back into homes where the wife went to work or the children supported their parents. And Social Security disability may have been more available decades ago because there was more trust from the system and less people working scams on the system. But disability is no longer easily available, and everyone now seems so financially stressed that adult children can barely fend for themselves. For people who lose work early like this, money may be very tight.

On the other end of the spectrum, some people retire young because they've made millions and have sold—or wanted out of, or been pushed out of—their company. It's a common goal of investment bankers, for example, to retire rich by age forty-five, and we in Seattle have grown accustomed to retired Microsoft millionaires in their forties. Even with big money, however, many of these retirees flounder. They did not grow up planning to retire so young, and they have few role models. They feel vaguely guilty about being home all day. Their partners are not eager to have them around. They're already sick of traveling. The nonprofits they so generously supported turned out to be just as mean and chaotic as business. They miss the intellectual give-and-take of the workplace. They miss their buddies. Even though retirement looked wonderful from a distance, it is not unusual for these young retirees to go back to work within a year or two.

Physical Health Losses

Aging will always deliver physical losses, and illness is a wild card. There are many things that we can do to enhance and preserve our health, but there is no doubt that older people are more likely to get sick than younger people are. As we age, a heart attack, stroke, or cancer diagnosis looms just beyond the horizon. Chronic illness is always a possibility. We do what we can to stay well, but we have little or no control over our genes.

Even with healthy aging, everyday functions become a little more difficult. He can't garden all morning without getting back problems. She hears her bones creak as she climbs the stairs. She gets black-and-blue marks when she bumps into a piece of furniture. His knees will need arthroscopic surgery soon. Their freezer contains more ice packs than food. Dinner parties often turn into information-sharing sessions about doctors and dentists.

Their friends are starting to die. They've been to more funerals than weddings lately. And the loss of those friends takes an emotional chunk out of their lives. It forces them to face their own mortality. Recently they've become very interested in learning the ages at which their parents and grandparents died.

Mental Changes

There is wide variation among people in how aging affects our minds, but I've never heard anyone assert that he is as sharp at seventy as he was at thirty. Does accumulated knowledge make a difference? Yes. Does wisdom help to compensate? Undoubtedly. But many things happen in aging brains that are just beginning to be understood—and about which there is still much scientific disagreement.

The experts used to believe that neurons were being lost daily in older brains, but most now say that any loss of brain cells is limited and that the older brain is capable of generating new cells. However, the brain does undergo significant changes:

- Starting at about age fifty, it shrinks, and most of the shrinkage comes from the cells' loss of water content.

- The frontal lobes, which are the seat of higher thought, can shrink 30 percent between ages fifty and ninety, so functions such as attention, impulse control, and focusing on several things at once can be impaired.

- Older neurons seem to process signals more slowly, so the ability to retrieve old information and learn new is often damaged.

- As dendrites (the fibers that grow out of the cell body of a neuron) decrease, the synapses that connect neurons become less efficient. Thinking is slowed as brain signals must travel along more circuitous pathways. The result is often hesitation as we search for pieces of information, and recent learning is often lost with the weakening of those newly formed synapses. This loss of connectivity, especially in the hippocampus, damages our ability to form and retain memories.

- Production of the stress hormone cortisol becomes irregular, affecting sleep and other bodily functions.

- However, brain function is closely tied to general health, so normal functioning of "the brain in winter" can still be very good.[4]

Lifestyle and Appearance

In terms of lifestyle, men seem to struggle with the loss of strength and virility more than women do, and denial is a common phenomenon.

A group of seven women in their fifties and sixties gathered for a reunion weekend recently. They had worked together in midlife, and individual relationships had been maintained, but they had not been together as a group for ten years. The four who were still married initially spoke well of their husbands, but when one woman mentioned some complaints, it was as if the floodgates had opened. The husbands, generally a few years older than the women, were aging fast.

One man, who had always seemed scary-smart to his wife and her friends, couldn't keep the bills and investments straight. He became belligerent when confronted about errors. His wife wondered if she would have to take over all the business details—and how in the world he would ever let go of it.

Another woman said that her husband, always a spiffy dresser, would no longer get dressed up. He still goes to his office but no longer wears suits or sport coats. He'll come out of the bedroom some mornings in dirty Dockers. He went to a friend's house for dinner in jeans. He colors his hair sporadically, but she wishes that he would just accept his gray hair rather than the half-and-half he sometimes exhibits. He used to be a social butterfly, but he can now sit for hours doing nothing. Of course, he too cannot stand to be confronted.

The third complaint was about driving. That husband, always an alert and careful driver, now has had his first accident and first-ever speeding ticket. He screams at other drivers, and his road rage is increasing. Sometimes when she rides with him and they are talking, he simply goes more and more slowly. Accused of not being able to drive and talk at the same time, he becomes furious. If she drives, he constantly tells her *what to do. As a passenger, especially in heavy-traffic situations, she is now consciously quiet.*

And the fourth man? He is fighting age like the devil itself is chasing him. He wants to go somewhere all the time, do something all day long. He has taken up running—both literally and figuratively. He brags about his loss of weight and his taut, "young" body, but his face is increasingly gaunt and lined. His hair has left or is leaving fast, although he buys new salon products every week. Despite Botox injections to try to stave off wrinkles, his age is evident.

This is not to suggest that aging is hard only on men. Indeed, women seem to struggle with it as much or more, but in slightly different ways. Perhaps because our culture judges women so much by their appearance, women tend to focus on changes they see in the mirror quite early—sometimes even in their thirties. Many older women get increasingly engrossed in their appearance, practically living at nail salons and spas. Some buy expensive creams and cosmetics. An increasing number go the plastic-surgery route—some using only Botox and collagen injections, others spending tens of thousands of dollars on face-lifts and liposuction. Some women want more and more clothes and jewels, as if designer labels and sparkles could take attention away from wrinkles and extra pounds.

Then there are the women—and men—who pay less and less attention to their appearance as they age. It is as if they finally have permission to look like slobs. They finally can be lazy.

Either extreme about appearance can create problems with one's partner. For example, a man may think his mate is crazy to go under the knife repeatedly—especially if she begins to get that obviously pulled look. (One man says his wife has had so many plastic surgeries that she has to lift her leg if she wants to smile.) He may resent the money his partner spends on all of her efforts to defy the calendar. Or, at the other extreme, he may be the one pushing her to ever-more-extreme procedures. As usual, honest discussions and moderate approaches are probably the best policies.

It is interesting to hear women talk about the day they realized that men were no longer noticing them. In a recent group, for example, all except one woman could remember exactly that moment of recognition—usually on a busy street or in a crowded store. Suddenly it became clear that the men around them were looking at younger, hotter babes! One woman described a time when she smiled back at a man on the street, only to discover that he was flirting with the chick behind her.

As hard as this is, especially for women who have traded on their looks for years, there can be great compensation in the new-found freedom from the pressure to focus on one's appearance. The loss of youth may be legitimately mourned, but the message for these women is that it is finally time to pay attention to other attributes besides looks. Nevertheless, it still is a loss.

Victimization Is a Waste

It's always tough to be really honest with ourselves and to take full responsibility for our actions, but there is no better time to face up to life than at retirement. What is life, anyway, but making choices and living with consequences? Very few things in life happen totally *to* us. If we've made good choices, the consequences will usually be positive. If we've made poor choices in our lives, we will have to deal with some negative results, but even those can be tools for learning. On the most basic level, we create our life. We write our own life story. Over the course of many years, life beats all of us up a bit, but we usually still have wonderful choices. We need to be resilient in order to be happy.

Among other things, we choose our own partner in this culture. Let's at least take responsibility for that! Let's focus on why we were attracted to this person and what the positives have been all these years. Arranged marriages may work in other countries, but few of us would want that—even though some of us might have done better that way.

Questions to Ask Yourself and Your Partner

1. What are my (your) images of retired couples? Where did they come from? How do we compare to these ideas?
2. To what extent am I (are you) affected by our culture's new, higher expectations of retirees? Do those images feel like pressure to me (you)?
3. Are our children's expectations of us relevant and reasonable?
4. What are the disadvantages for me (you) in facing retirement as a couple?
5. How are the skills and behaviors I (you) used to succeed in the workplace different from the ones I (you) must have in order to do well at home?
6. In what ways have people in the outside world treated us differently since we retired? Do we have any ego issues because of that?
7. How important was my (your) work to my (your) identity? What are the implications of this for me (you) now?
8. Was I (were you) pushed out of work, or did I (you) feel that way? If so, how does that complicate my (your) retirement?
9. Does either of us have any significant health loss at this point? How is that affecting our relationship?
10. What signs of normal mental and lifestyle changes are we experiencing? How are these affecting our relationship with each other? With the outside world?

11. Are we more supportive to or critical of each other as we experience these losses?

12. As a man, how am I dealing with the normal loss of strength and virility?

13. As a woman, how am I coping with the normal changes I see in the mirror?

14. Do I (you) fall into the trap of feeling victimized very often? How successful am I (are you) at climbing out of it and taking personal responsibility for my (your) life?

4.

Variations on the Theme of Relationships

Previous Power and Roles

Most people have ideas in their head about what a committed relationship should look like—both before and during retirement. Generally, these ideas came from childhood and the example set by our parents. Sometimes religion has been a primary influence. Furthermore, over the years of a long-term relationship, patterns have grown out of both personalities. For example, if both people tend to be traditional and passive, power has probably not been much of an issue. Or, if one person is passive while the other is aggressive, the stronger partner has probably been the primary decision maker. But if both personalities are strong-willed and not much affected by tradition, roles and power were probably more idiosyncratic.

Often people don't have much time to analyze these issues while they are busy earning a living and raising their kids. Then retirement comes, and something happens that starts you thinking about other possibilities.

Maybe the former breadwinner gets interested in gourmet cooking and pushes the other partner out of the kitchen. Perhaps the financial decision maker wants to get rid of all that responsibility. Or the driven career person, who had been easygoing at home, starts dictating new rules to family members.

During your working years, resentments may have built up consciously or unconsciously about roles, but neither one of you wanted to rock the boat. Life was hard enough without fighting over petty power issues. Now that you have a little less stress, however, those issues loom large. Or maybe those things are now exacerbated because you don't have as much physical and psychological space as you used to. You also have more time on your hands.

These realizations may come gradually, but often new retirees are shocked into the conclusion that they can't live with this person one more minute unless there are some major changes in the system. Then was then; now is now! Suddenly one of you realizes that you need to think and talk long and hard about your future relationship.

As difficult as this may sound at first, retirement really is a great time for a relationship shake-up because often, when you think about it, the old roles don't fit anymore. You both probably want to try new things, and you're willing to give up power over things that don't matter so much anymore.

This retirement event may just be the perfect catalyst for fighting the forces that are keeping you stuck as a couple. In fact, those forces might send you spiraling downward psychologically—consciously or unconsciously—unless they are stopped right now. If there have been mistakes in the past, try to avoid blaming yourself or your partner. Focus on the future. Take stock of your lives and figure out where you want to go. Redirect the new burst of energy that can come once the burden of work is lifted off your shoulders.

Everything Versus Nothing Together

The biggest decision retirees have to make is how much time they will spend together. Some couples seem joined at the hip. Either they both want it that way, or the one who wants it is so dominant that the partner must conform in order to keep peace. In the extreme, most of these couples have easy but boring lives. They may share every experience, but they have nothing new or interesting to bring to each other. Are these the couples whom one sees in restaurants eating dinner in silence? I, for one, would rather sit next to a couple who are arguing than one where both people seem bored, just staring at their food without speaking.

Other couples seem to disagree about everything. In extreme instances, these couples have no interests in common. They do nothing together. They fight all the time, or they hardly speak to each other. One wonders why some of these couples stay together, yet many of them seem relatively content with this arrangement. Perhaps they enjoy the freedom to pursue their own interests to their heart's content. Maybe they appreciate the times that they do come together because they can talk about their diverse experiences. It's possible that the ones who fight a lot find that stimulating.

But moderation between these two extremes seems to produce the happiest retired couples. With so much new time and freedom at retirement, most individuals want to spread their wings a bit. They often experiment in various directions before they settle on specific activities more intensively. They don't want to constantly worry about their partner's interests meshing with theirs—or with endless questions and criticism of their choices. But neither do they want to be lonely or alone all the time. They don't need a partner for that! In most cases, they want the fun of sharing their own excitement about their activities and the interest of hearing about their partner's world too.

That formula doesn't sound too difficult, but getting to the most satisfying spot on a togetherness continuum for both partners may take some work. On a scale of one to ten, for example, it's unlikely that you'll both be immediately happy at number five. It's more likely that one of you will prefer three while the other one wants eight. One of you, for example, may enjoy shopping all the garage sales together while the other wants to putter alone in a workshop or sewing room. In that case, you'll have to find ways to articulate and understand each person's feelings and needs, and you'll probably have to compromise.

In addition, the togetherness position that's comfortable for both of you may change over time. You might become more interested in the other person's hobby than you ever thought you would. Or after a couple of years of traveling extensively together, you may decide to stay at home and seek more separate outlets. Certainly, if one of you becomes ill, that person may need a period of dependence, while the partner will have to facilitate care—meeting the closeness needs of the ill person while, at the same time, developing enhanced independent coping skills.

Parallel Play

Watching children at play reminds us how happy humans can be when they are engrossed in separate but parallel activities. As toddlers, children frequently play side by side without obvious communication. Although they are not talking, they seem to enjoy the camaraderie. At this age, children cannot express their feelings very well in words, but they are showing feelings through physical action, storytelling, and art. While the process may look inconsequential to adults, these toddlers are solving problems, building skills, and overcoming physical or mental challenges. Kids can do some of this play-work alone as well, but they actually seem to be happiest in parallel play.[1] For instance, two little boys in a sandbox can be very content playing with different trucks next to each other, silent at times and babbling to themselves or each other at other times, whereas they'd probably be fighting if they tried to play with the same truck in that sandbox.

When three older girls play with their dolls, or when several boys play soccer together, they have some social interaction, but it is basically parallel play. Even in high school and college, study groups involve some conversation, but it is mostly parallel activity. In a college chemistry lab, two students might work intently on different experiments, perhaps even in different rooms, but enjoy the opportunity to check in with each other periodically. If they worked on the same experiment, they might be more likely to goof off or become competitive about the method and results.

This parallel-play model can work with retired couples as well because it meets our needs for both freedom and involvement. If, as a retiree, you find yourself wanting either extreme freedom or total involvement, you may need to examine your motivation. Are you too needy and insecure to manage your life separately? Are you too selfish and unwilling to share?

Some people crave total attention from their mate, but it really is foolhardy to be depressed or jealous if your partner wants to do things alone or with others, because those activities usually benefit you too. They make your life fuller when your partner talks about them, and they give you time to develop your own interests. Your mate's independence allows you to concentrate on things you really care about and obtain rewards in your own way. This arrangement forces you to make decisions that are right for only you, without being overly concerned about how your actions will affect others. In short, this pattern allows you to grow.

When Vince and Ellen retired simultaneously, he real-ized that he didn't have any friends except her. In the past he had always enjoyed saying that his wife was his best friend, but now it felt uncomfortable. The first couple of weeks, they both had errands and to-do lists to accomplish, but then Vince would say over breakfast each morning, "What shall we do today?" It eventually dawned on him that her answers usually contained the word I rather than we, and he became increasingly annoyed. She was seeing her sister or a friend or former coworkers for lunch. She was taking a computer class. She was shopping for groceries or clothes. She was babysitting a grandchild.

His resentment increased. This was not at all as he had imagined retirement! They took a couple of trips together, but when he went back to the hotel for a nap each afternoon, she chose to keep touring on her own. On one trip, where she had insisted on taking her divorced sister along, Vince really felt left out.

He complained about Ellen's neglect to everyone who would listen, but his family doctor didn't just listen. He told Vince it was time to grow up and get a life. He was sounding like a victim and sinking into depression. He'd better replace work with something other than Ellen or his health would suffer. Vince was shocked and angry initially, but he was able to hear this message because the doctor also tempered it with empathy and told him that many men have trouble with this transition.

The following week, Vince actually went to the local community college for career counseling. He had worked many years as an attorney, but he laughingly told the expert that he wanted to find out what he was good at. The tests showed that Vince was good at many things, indicating that he had a lot of options. When the counselor learned that Vince still had, in storage, every car he had ever owned, they both focused on what it would feel like to restore old vehicles. Vince realized that he had *always loved old fire engines, so he sold two of his cars and bought a 1952 fire engine, sight unseen, on the Internet.*

Ellen fussed a bit when Vince said that he intended to remodel the garage on their country property and hire a mechanic to help him, but she got kind of excited about the fire engine thing too. She started going to car shows with him, and they both realized that he was happier than he had been in years.

Some days they don't see each other until dinnertime. They've made friends with other car show couples; more important, Vince has some new male friends. They have achieved a balance between joined-at-the-hip and live-your-own-life that suits them both very well.

Expectations and Honesty

People are loaded with relationship stereotypes by the time they reach retirement. Because they've lived a long time, they assume that they know themselves and their partner very well, but the fact is that most people don't have a clue what retirement will feel like until it actually happens. They think they know what they'll do and how they'll feel, but there are usually many surprises ahead.

This phenomenon happens throughout our lives. Even introspective people are often surprised when our reactions to events and other people are different from what we'd expected. Sometimes our perceptions are just plain amazing to us, or events don't unfold exactly as planned and our reactions change from what we thought they would be. We should probably expect these surprises after living several decades, but in retirement they often throw us because we think we know it all. For example, you think retiring with money will make you feel powerful and secure, but the stock market falls apart and the board you're on gives you problems, and you feel worse than you did when you were working. Or you marry a man you don't really love because you're lonely since your husband died, and then over time you find that he's wonderful and you're really in love. Similarly, you think that losing forty pounds will make your partner happy and give you a whole new, exciting lease on life at age sixty, but nothing really changes in the relationship and you still feel lousy despite your skinny (or skinnier) life.

So it's also hard, as a couple, to predict what kind of relationship will work best for you in retirement. You may start out wanting to do everything together, but you become bored with each other's appearance and conversation within a week. Or you may have plans for lots of separate golf matches or yoga classes or volunteer work, but you miss your partner and decide to rearrange your priorities.

This is a moment of truth. You may decide that your relationship is terrific as is, or you may have to figure out a whole new path. Nevertheless, the process of honest examination is important. There are endless variations on the theme of relationships, but it is the clarity of the vision and the fairness of the decision making that will determine the success and happiness of a couple in retirement.

Questions to Ask Yourself and Your Partner

1. How do I (you) feel about our previous power and roles?
2. What would I (you) like to change about this now?
3. To what extent am I (are you) prepared to shake up our relationship in retirement?
4. What do I (you) fear about change in our relationship?
5. What position on a togetherness continuum, from one to ten, feels most comfortable for me (you)?

6. What is my (your) definition of healthy togetherness? If we differ, who feels strongest about it, and why?

7. Does either of us feel hurt or neglected when the other does things separately? What occasions have elicited those feelings? Why?

8. What needs to happen for resolution of our needs to be together versus separate? How might we compromise?

9. In what ways do we have parallel play? Do I (you) want more or less of this?

10. Am I (are you) able to separate my (your) own wishes from family or cultural stereotypes about relationships? Do we both understand where our stereotypes came from?

11. Have we clarified what we expect of each other regarding the closeness or distance—physically and emotionally—of our relationship? If not, how and when should we do this?

Part Two: The Challenges—Old and New

5.
Deciding Where to Live

A Very Big Decision

One of the most fascinating aspects of this stage in life, for me, has been watching what decisions people are making about where they will live. Although some couples have always been in sync about this, many partners come to verbal blows—and a few come to divorce—over this issue.

For some retirees, there is no problem. They will stay put. They will remain near their children or other family members or friends. They may travel a little more, or they may not even venture out of their comfort zone for travel. Some will say this immobility relates to money, but the truth is that one can always find places with a similar or lower cost of living. It is more a mind-set: "Let's not rock the boat. We're used to this place and this area. This is our home, where we've spent the best years of our lives, raised our children, buried our parents. Why take a chance on anything new and different?"

And this works fine if both members of the

couple wholeheartedly agree. But if one person is more adventurous than the other, or if one part of the couple really wants change, some compromise will have to be worked out. No couple can be in two places together at the same time, so these compromises can get complicated.

It is amazing that so few people come to retirement having really thought about this issue honestly. They may have felt that they were too busy. Retirement seemed far away, so they put off discussions about where they would live. One or both of them may have had pie-in-the-sky attitudes about retirement, and nobody took future decisions seriously. Or the subject may have started fights, so it wasn't raised very often.

But wise couples, as they moved up in age, had been watching their elders. Perhaps they explored some possibilities—reading about, asking about, or visiting various locations. They may have mentally tried on different places and lifestyles.

Even for people who have given retirement location a lot of thought, there is a continuum from people who want no change at all to people who want total change—from people who want to stay forever in their current house and town to people who want to forsake all the old and start everything anew.

There is surely nothing right or wrong about either extreme or any position in between. But problems come when ideas have not been thought through carefully and honestly, or when the couple makes a decision impulsively or irrationally. And the problems also appear when two people want to sit at very different places on the continuum between no change versus total change. And the problems definitely occur when one person forcefully imposes her decisions on the partner. This often happens when one partner has a stronger personality or because one person has taken the lead in previous decisions, but determinations about where to live never work well unless both people buy into them.

Influencing Factors

A great number of factors influence where we choose to live in retirement.

Climate

There seems to be a general longing for warmth as we get older. Maybe our brittle bones can't handle the cold as well when we age, or maybe we're just sick of shoveling snow and worrying about slipping and falling on icy streets. But there is no denying the fact that warmer places are full of retired people. Of course, those places also get very hot in the summer, so many people feel that they also need a way of escaping the heat during the warmer months.

Robin and Jenny love the cultural richness of Chicago, and they also have grown children there, so they always planned to stay in the middle of the city after retirement, with their cabin in Wisconsin for summers and week-ends. When the time came, they did sell their large town house for financial reasons, but they bought a small condo across the street, where they could still walk to all the places they loved.

They had no doubt about their plan for several years, but they worried a bit when their friends began moving to warmer climes. In the winter of his seventy-fourth year, Robin fell on an icy sidewalk and broke his leg. During the two months that he was on crutches, he never left the condo. It would have been too difficult to get in and out of either their car or taxis. When spring arrived and they both craved some time in Wisconsin, Jenny went to get their car out of the garage, but it wouldn't start. She rented a car, but when they got to the cabin, they found that the pipes had frozen and the place was flooded. For the first time in their lives, they began to feel that maybe they couldn't handle winter weather anymore.

They survived one more year in Chicago, but Jenny started complaining about arthritis, and their kids began urging them to move south. At first Jenny and Robin felt hurt and rejected. Although there were no grandchildren yet, they didn't want to miss out on future possibilities, and they dreaded being so far away from their children.

Facing seventy-five, they finally bit the bullet, sold their home, and then moved into an active retirement community situated, near some longtime friends. Their health has improved, and they love their new surroundings. The biggest loss is their pride, because they were so wedded to Chicago and thought they always would be. They are not sorry they stayed in the city as long as they did, but their feelings about climate turned out to be quite different at 75 than they were at 65.

Climate preferences are often intertwined with our health and our passions. For example, some people are really bothered by seasonal affective disorder (SAD). They need a certain amount of sunlight or they feel really depressed. Other people believe that arthritis is worse in cold climates. With real choices of location at retirement, some people want to head for the sun, even though their partner may not mind the winter darkness and cold at all.

Then there are the couples who differ on indoor versus outdoor activities. One person may want warm weather because he would play golf or tennis every day, but the other may not give a damn about sun because everything she loves is indoors. Retirees who love to ski are attracted to Colorado or Vermont. Those who love horses and the wide-open spaces buy a ranch in Montana or Wyoming. And those who like sailing or powerboating want to be near big water. The crunch comes, of course, when partners have different passions and, therefore, need to work out a compromise.

Cost and Type of Living

On a retirement income, many couples want to find a place with a lower cost of living. They may have needed to be in, or close to, large cities for their jobs, but they no longer need city or close-in suburban living, with its high costs. They may be more than happy to escape the traffic as well. They might be quite willing to drive an hour or more, or take the train, on the evenings when they do want to take advantage of the city, or they may not care at all about the things that cities offer.

Small towns, especially in certain parts of the country, can easily cut in half a city dweller's expenses. People seem friendlier in small towns and rural areas too; they greet one another on the street and are often more willing to help one another.

Of course, leaving the big city can be traumatic for those who love the symphony, ballet, live theater, art house movies, professional sports teams, or first-class shopping. To the surprise of many, big cities can be wonderful places to retire in because of easy access to taxis and public transportation; delivery service from grocery stores, restaurants, and dry cleaners; and personal help from doormen and building staff when older people become frail. Leaving the city can also mean inconvenience for those who want to travel into and out of a major airport, train station, or bus terminal.

Foreign or Domestic

Many immigrants return to their homelands when their working years are over because they have family members in the "old country" and feel more comfortable there. Some people move overseas because they want a more relaxed or exotic life; others want to stretch their retirement income further than they can if they stay where they are. For example, one former executive said that he had spent his entire life traveling the world, and he could not imagine a better place to live than New Zealand. Some people who have worked abroad as expatriates simply want to remain where they now feel at home.

There are currency issues for many of these retirees, and there may be tax issues as well, but foreign retirements seem to be increasing as the Internet shrinks distances.

Some foreign governments do not allow noncitizens to own property, and certain unstable governments have been known to confiscate the property of noncitizens, so retirees need to be careful about foreign investments.

Health care in other countries can be spotty, and it can be especially scary if you do not know the local language. Many retirees decide to come back home for medical care as they get older or if significant health problems occur.

Retirees also know that an adopted country will seldom really feel like home, so many older couples see foreign living as a temporary adventure rather than a permanent home.

It is suggested, in a book intriguingly called *The Grown-up's Guide to Running Away from Home,* that certain steps be taken before a foreign move. First, search the Internet by country name and "retirement." Second, talk to people who know that country well. Then move there for a year without too many commitments, and get serious about learning the language.[1]

Wanting a Bigger House

Surveys show that a lot of people over age fifty-five want homes that are bigger and more luxurious than seniors have desired in the past. This trend began in the early 1990s, when retirees started telling real estate agents that they don't want cheap little houses anymore. This does not mean that they want a bigger lot or more lawn care. They also do not want high-maintenance homes. But they do want space to have their children and grandchildren for visits. They want room to entertain friends graciously. They want to be able to spread out their projects and hobbies. They want upscale appliances and functional kitchens. They want big closets so that their seasonal clothes are always available for travel. And one agent said that she is hearing a lot of requests for his-and-hers offices these days.[2]

Downsizing from the Big House

The same surveys that reveal that some retirees want bigger homes also show that retirement can be the ideal opportunity to downsize from the place where one's children were raised. The kids are gone; the yard and garden are too big for the couple to take care of; the house is too big to clean; repairs are due or overdue; the taxes are sky-high. For many people, then, retirement seems like the ideal time to clear superfluous things and tasks from their lives.

Design

Those surveys of the senior market also show that empty-nesters have new ideas about design. They control 65 percent of the nation's wealth, so they can get what they want: both classic elegance and casual comfort.

Retiree couples are very mobile, and they spend a lot of money on out-of-home entertainment. Even meals at home have often been prepared outside. They prefer single-family houses rather than condos, but they want easy maintenance inside and out, large decks, no lawns, and security systems so that they can leave the house unattended. Good lighting is very important, and homes need to be wired to accept new technology. They want one-story places, or at least only one living level. Storage is important. They like a "mother-in-law" area where a live-in nurse could stay. Great rooms, consisting of living room/dining room/kitchen combinations, are very popular. Kitchens should contain an island or large counter. Dining tables should look good for two to four people or for ten to twelve. Master bedrooms can be fairly small but must have large closets. Bathroom hardware should be levers rather than knobs for aging hands. Amenities may include wheelchair-friendly door widths and countertops, raised toilets, nonslip bathtubs, skidproof tile, adjustable-height closet rods, and gently graded walkways.

The surge of new boomer retirees will not want to give up their active lifestyles. Whether they build/buy a new home or remodel the one they already have, they will want to manage their own housing in their own way. Nevertheless, they will also be planning and thinking ahead, and they will have a huge effect on what senior housing looks like thirty years from now.

Children and Grandchildren

This is the biggest factor of all in determining where many couples will live, and the decision can go either way. On one hand, one or both members of the couple may be so attached that they cannot imagine being any distance away from their progeny. On the other hand, one or both of them may feel the need to get far away from demanding or troubled offspring.

Partners frequently struggle with each other about this, and they often can't imagine sufficiently how closeness versus distance from children and grandchildren will feel.

One West Coast couple had raised their children in, California, and had assumed that their kids, who loved the area, would always be nearby. By a series of flukes and circumstances, however, all three children, two spouses, and four grandchildren ended up in Seattle. After much soul-searching, Chuck and Angela sold their big house on the peninsula, said their good-byes to a host of friends, and bought a condo in downtown Seattle. They seemed quite excited about their new adventure. They had both decided that their kids were more important to them than their friends were, and they liked the idea of city living. But they did wonder: How hard would the adjustment be? How much would they miss their old friends and surroundings? What would happen if their friends drifted away emotionally? Would their children sometimes wish their parents had more of a life? Would their kids feel the heaviness of future responsibility for them? What would it be like for both of them to restart their lives in a new place? What would they do if they discovered that this move was a huge mistake?

Chuck immediately missed his golfing buddies more than he had expected to. He also missed the business roundtable where he had heard interesting speakers at Stanford University every week. He got lost on the Seattle roads and cursed at the crazy drivers. They both hated the rain and cold, especially by contrast with the Bay Area sunshine. They had thought they knew themselves so well, but they were surprised at their feelings of loss. One night, after a long phone conversation with old friends back home, they both broke into tears.

After a year in Seattle, however, the complaints were coming much more from Chuck than from Angela. She seemed totally enthralled by her grandkids. Her conversation started to sound a little boring to Chuck, and he was increasingly irritable. He wondered how he could get her involved in other activities, and she finally noticed that he was drinking quite heavily. They had thought that they were united in this plan, but there were now cracks in their facade. Neither of them really wanted to return to Palo Alto, but it looked like some changes were in order.

They were embarrassed when their daughter confronted them about their relationship and suggested a counselor, but they agreed to go. After six sessions they saw each other's point of view much more clearly, and they decided to buy a small condo in Palm Springs for their own use in the winter. The first year, Angela would only go for two months, but Chuck stayed five and found some golfing friends. Last winter Angela went for three months, and she now says she is building up to more. Chuck hopes this is true, but he also admits that he is enjoying some separate time.

Friends

Some retired couples are very influenced by their friends. They want the comfort of people they know, or they are afraid of new situations, so they stay put near their circle of friends or buy a place wherever their friends go. This can work very well when people enjoy the same things and want to spend time together. And it works especially well when those friends also respect one another's privacy.

There was a recent article in *Time* magazine about friends who can't bear to separate in retirement.[3] One group of couples, in their eighties, all sold their houses and moved to an assisted-living facility simultaneously. Another group plans to buy a plot of land and build several houses on it or remodel an apartment building. A different group is executing a plan to co-own two houses in different climates. These people do not want to go to a lonely paradise; they want emotional fulfillment. Since their adult children tend to move around a lot, they've decided that friends are more important to them. As one woman says in this piece, when friendship has stood the test of time, it should be allowed to continue into retirement.

But following friends in retirement can also create a disaster:

> *Bill and D.J. found a neat little town for their retirement on the coast. They told several dear friends that there would be an invitation forthcoming to visit the following winter when the place was fixed up and ready for entertaining. Much to their surprise, they learned three months later that one couple had bought a place in the same small town. D.J. and Bill had wanted their choice to be unique; they wanted privacy and perhaps some new friends. They resented the interlopers. The newer homeowners, on the other hand, thought that their friends would be flattered that they wanted to live nearby. The two couples see one another occasionally, but their relationship has never been the same.*

Gay or Straight

The 2000 census was the first to attempt an accurate count of same-sex partners. The questionnaire did not ask sexual orientation, but people of the same gender could identify themselves as unmarried partners. So, with future censuses, there will eventually be more accurate statistics about gay couples at various ages in various locations. In the meantime, an article in *Time* magazine estimates that there are two million gays and lesbians age sixty-five and over in the United States and that population will double by 2030.[4]

The 2000 census also shows that gay couples are clearly an urban phenomenon. They still tend to cluster in certain areas of a city, but they can increasingly be found all over town. As society has less prejudice, gays of all kinds have gone more mainstream, living wherever they want to.

Jobs tend to determine location for working lesbians and gay men, as they do for straight couples. However, when they have choices at retirement, most gays want to live where they can be part of an accepting and interesting group. Many of them have experienced some kind of discrimination in housing, and they do not want to face that anymore. This generally means a major city or certain parts of the country have become known as havens for lesbians, gay men, bisexuals, and transgender persons (all four groups are sometimes collectively referred to as "LGBTs"). Some retirement facilities have denied access to gays, touting the rights of private organizations to have policies against same-sex couples living together, but the law is murky on these points, and discrimination lawsuits are difficult to win. This kind of bigotry appalls fair-minded people, but it remains to be seen whether we will see progress through laws or via societal changes.

The gay and lesbian population has every right to "grow old together, protected from vicious stares." LGBTs want to be seen as "average human beings who long for intimacy and emotional connection at least as much as the next heterosexual."[5]

Old or Young Companions

Whether one prefers to be surrounded by people one's own age or by more diversity is an important consideration. Many senior complexes, especially in sunny climes, exclude children and young couples. This may be an advantage to those retirees who dislike the noise and chaos of kids and prefer to focus on the activities of people their own age. But it is a disadvantage to others, who like to be with young people and are bored with seniors-only activities.

Planned communities for seniors aren't what they used to be. Ads for these places now refer to "the active adult market." One brochure for a 1,000-acre development says: "Act your age with abandon." And these complexes are springing up all over the country, no longer just in sunny climes. Rather, they are often down the interstate from affluent areas where adult children live. They are usually built around golf courses, and their community centers are huge. They may no longer have shuffleboard courts, but they have computer labs and health spas instead. Often gated, they provide fairly high security. People moving from two-story houses appreciate the one-level floor plans.

Seniors are a highly researched market, and developers say that about 20 percent of people between fifty-five and seventy-five would like to live in an active adult community, but that leaves 80 percent who want something else.[6]

Health Services

Some retiree couples want a facility that offers a range of health services, from independent apartments to assisted living to nursing home care. These are usually called continuing-care retirement communities (CCRCs) or life care retirement communities. Some couples are willing to pay large amounts of money to buy into such an arrangement because this will relieve any anxiety about their future health care needs. It also gives them security that their partner will be in a safe place if anything happens to one of them. Experts say that the things to look for when choosing one of these comprehensive arrangements include:

- The cost structure, especially the up-front deposit

- The operating philosophy

- The rules

- The facilities beyond the beautiful lobbies

- The level and type of staffing

- The type of residents and their level of energy and happiness

- Your potential for compatibility and friendship with these people

- The quality and type of meals

Any facility that is not open about all kinds of information is probably not worthwhile for you to consider. Make sure that you go for several visits, and realize that this is a complex and difficult decision.

But other people want to maintain control of their health care resources, perhaps buying long-term care insurance, self-financing through their own savings for the future, or believing that they will never need a nursing home. Nevertheless, these more independent retirees will generally want decent health care to be available near their place of residence. Clearly, some people will not consider rural areas where doctors and hospitals are sparse or nonexistent. Some couples look up the ratings of hospitals on the Internet before they even consider a given city, and some people interview doctors in a new place before they look at real estate.

Mistakes

Fortunately, place of residence is not one of those things in life that can never be changed. Mistakes happen. Learning about oneself and one's partner can result. The worst consequences may be some money lost and some pride hurt, but in most cases neither of these is life-threatening.

There may even be some advantages to making less-than-permanent decisions at retirement about where to live. Indeed, some couples run around the country or the world, trying out different options. Other couples do a "your turn–my turn" arrangement—perhaps each person chooses a new place every three or five years, or if one person wins the decision about the retirement location and things do not work out well, the other person will get to choose the next place. And if the couple retires relatively young, they may both get bored with any permanent decision and may still have several moves in them.

Mistakes like the following may be painful, but they usually force us to learn important lessons about ourselves.

———

Laurie and Larry had lived all their lives in New England but had always loved their vacation visits to Maui. They both dreamed of retiring there, and for years they bored their friends silly with their pictures and descriptions of the island.

In their mid-fifties they both took early payouts from their professional jobs in local government, and Larry made quick work of moving to Maui. Before Laurie knew what had hit her, he gathered lots of information on the Internet, contacted people they had met during vacations, and bought plane tickets. Laurie seemed a little shell-shocked as she told their family members and friends about the plan, but she went along with it. The idea was to rent in Hawaii for a year and keep their old house in Massachusetts while they looked for a permanent home. Reluctantly, Laurie organized a garage sale and gave her best friend permission to live in the house for a year. It took her two weeks to pack, she hardly slept at all that last week at home, and Larry had to physically push her onto the plane. She wondered how all this was happening so fast.

Within two days on Maui, they had found a condo to rent. Laurie expressed a lot of concern about adapting to a small, one-bedroom place, but the location was great, and neither of them wanted to spend extra money for a larger apartment. A few days later, Larry got a part-time position selling time-shares. He had never done anything like that before, but he loved the challenge and made some friends. Laurie tried to hide any negative feelings for Larry's sake, but she began to eat less and sleep a lot more. Her only happy times were during her increasingly frequent phone conversations with her children and parents. She liked hearing about the house from her friend, but she resented the small complaints about things needing to be fixed. She always begged for the details of what other people were doing and seldom would talk about herself. Months went by, but she simply could not adjust. She made few efforts to meet people and sank into her first-ever depression.

On those vacations to Maui over the years, Laurie had often verbalized her desire to get away from her friends, parents, kids, grandkids, and the place she had lived all of her life in order to feel free and to grow as a person. But, to her surprise, she missed those people and that place more than she ever imagined she could. She felt totally out of control in her new environment and insisted, after eight months, that they return to New England.

Larry had not seen this coming. They had never talked much about feelings, and he had been enjoying this adventure so much that he had barely noticed her depression. When he had picked up signals, he thought it would pass. Finally, when they talked at length, Larry wanted Laurie to give it at least a year, but she was determined to leave. He wondered if he should somehow force her to stay (if he could), hoping that time would help, and then deal with her resentment if it didn't. Or if he felt this happy in Maui, should they live separately? Or should he swallow his anger and return to their home-town?

No easy answers here, but Larry was convinced—that is, pressured—by their three adult children to go back home and keep the marriage together. This time Laurie actually packed in one day, and she paid through the nose to get herself a flight home pronto. Larry stayed a couple of weeks longer to wind things up, and on the flight back he wondered if he was now in a deep depression.

In the two years since, they have both gained a few new insights about themselves. Laurie realizes that she drifted along for many years without being very intro-spective or decisive. She says that she is trying to under-stand her motivations better. More than anything, she is facing her symbiotic relationship with her parents and her adult children. They demand a lot of her, but she evi-dently needs them too. She had thought, in Maui, that she felt guilty for not being available to them, but she is recognizing that she also benefits from feeling important in their lives. She has gone back to work part-time in her old social-work agency, and she has been thinking more about her needs vis-à-vis her colleagues and clients. For Larry's part, he realizes that he bulldozed this decision the way he did a lot of others in the past, but he also harbors considerable anger toward Laurie for messing up this opportunity. He loves his family too but doesn't feel so attached to them. He's not sure what he will do about the anger and how it will play out in their relationship.

They're both pretty sure that they won't be this impul-sive again without trying harder to predict the conse-quences. But they are also coming to appreciate the great adventure they experienced, and they now laugh about some of the fun they had in Maui. They intend to vacation there soon, and they joke about how long they might visit without catching the bug to move there again.

One Location or Two

Staying in one spot has many advantages. It is certainly cheaper than two residences, which may require double mortgages, double furnishings, double repairs, double gardening, and double everything else. Travel back and forth can be costly too. Any given couple, even if they can afford it, may prefer to save that money for luxuries of other kinds. Furthermore, it takes energy to keep two places going and to keep yourselves hopping between them. When you initially retire, you may have lots of energy, but at later stages in life this kind of frequent change may not be worth the effort.

However, if they can afford it, many couples are finding that their needs are well met by two locations. In situations where they can't pay much, that second home may be a trailer, a recreational vehicle, a rental apartment, a time-share, or a place co-owned with others. Or people may sell one substantial home to get two smaller ones.

One beauty of this arrangement is that it allows the couple to experience two climates. What a luxury it is to be able to be warm in the winter and relatively cool in summer! For people who like to be outdoors for sporting or cultural activities, or perhaps for long walks in the park, pleasing weather conditions can seem like heaven.

A second advantage is that change helps people to avoid boredom. Couples who have had lots of work stimulation in their lives often love decorating a second home, finding new friends and activities there, and even traveling between the two places. If the second home is in a desirable location, it can also be a great attraction for adult children and grandkids—a place to have quality time with your family that you might not get if you both live in the same city. Or the second home can be a place for relaxed time with visiting friends.

But most important of all for some retired couples, two homes provide them with a system for getting away from each other when they want or need it. It is really quite interesting how often people with two homes can be found in the separate locations. They usually don't verbalize their desire to spend time apart; instead, they have a myriad of reasons—golf, friends, house repairs, business interests, and so on. For example, one person goes ahead of the other to get a car fixed or keep a doctor's appointment. But occasionally they also admit that they need a break from each other.

Some partners never go to these different locations alone, and some are found in different places only once or twice a year, but a few couples seem to avoid each other most of the time. These situations are neither right nor wrong; the point is that two locations give a couple more choices.

After many years of work schedules that probably kept them apart much of the time, it often feels right to have another place to go. Indeed, some couples who might otherwise separate or divorce because they feel too confined in the retired relationship, because they get too angry at their mate's behavior, or because their personality simply requires a lot of alone time, discover that space is a wonderful tonic. Absence *can* make the heart grow fonder. They actually enjoy each other's company more if they also have some time apart.

When they were planning to retire from their jobs in Phoenix five years hence, Don and Julie bought a condo in La Jolla, California. They rented it out when they did not use it, and they talked about whether they should keep two places post-retirement, but they just knew that one condo in that beautiful area would feel right.

Then they downsized and moved in full-time, and they were at each other's throats within a month. The space was too small for his collections and her upholstery efforts, which she hoped to turn into a small business. They slept on different schedules and were constantly complaining about bedroom inconveniences. They got annoyed at each other's eating habits and exercise regimens. All of this came as quite a surprise after thirty years of living together, but they attributed their problems to the space restrictions.

They began to look for a house or a larger condo nearby. Then they thought that they might enjoy two climates, so they considered a place in Salt Lake City where two of their kids live. But neither of these resolutions felt right. They loved the location of their existing condo, and the weather in La Jolla was too perfect to leave.

One night Julie had an epiphany, and Don liked her idea too. They would buy a second small condo in La Jolla, and they would flip a coin to see which of them got the current place. Perhaps they could trade every year or two if one place was better than the other.

They have been in this arrangement for three years now, and it meets their needs very well. They each have a lot of privacy, but they get together for dinner almost every night—her place, his, or a restaurant. They also travel together and do things with other couples together. They have been fascinated by the reactions of their friends and family, and they're doing a survey about whether men or women like this idea more.

And when two people have children from previous marriages, some of them use the second home for more-comfortable, separate visits with their kids.

———————————

Jonah and Sylvia had lots of disagreements about how they would integrate their separate children and grandchildren into their lives. When they married in their fifties, they wanted to be one big, happy family, but after five years of trying, they hadn't been able to find the right combination. His kids ignored Sylvia when she visited their homes but disparaged her if she did not come. They insulted her by comparing her to their own mother. Her daughter picked political fights with Jonah whenever she visited their home and once told him he was stupid. Her son is a hippie type and has little in common with her new husband.

Then Sylvia and Jonah bought a condo in Sun Valley, and they often use it now for separate periods, both winter and summer, with their extended families. There was a little resentment at first when Jonah realized that Sylvia had planned a week with her kids and he was not wanted in Idaho, but they both see the value in the plan now. Having a second home has given them a sense of relief—it's like a pressure valve—and they've gotten closer to their kids at the same time.

They have talked about whether they could accomplish the same mission if they met their kids at a hotel or resort, and the answer is no. The condo affords privacy for the visits, but it also has a homey, comfortable feeling that promotes intimacy. Would it work if the nonparent were to leave their primary house while the parent visits with his or her kids? No, because the nonparent would probably feel pushed out, and the kids would be uncomfortable with that. This second home is an ideal arrangement for them.

Planning Ahead

As the number of retired baby boomers increases over the next two decades, the price of second homes may be driven higher and higher. Therefore, some smart investors are learning to lay the groundwork for their retirement plan early.

People often gravitate toward places where they have enjoyed vacations. They may have started by staying in a hotel, then rented a condo; then perhaps they buy a house. Over the years they probably made some friends there. They might have even gotten into telecommuting. It is not a big transition, then, for the couple to move to that location in retirement.

These early planners are getting a jump on the crowd. They may have to, or want to, rent out the second place while they are still working to help pay for it. But they're able to enjoy their investment parttime now and reap a lot more benefits later.

Of course, it is important to realize that that wonderful vacation place may feel quite different year-round than it did in its ideal season. Experts advise that retirees try things carefully before they pull up all the stakes. Perhaps you need to spend an out-of-season vacation in that desired location. Or you might participate in a home exchange program. In these programs, you pay a fee to have your home listed and for access to others' listings, and you do your own screening to avoid disasters. There are some risks involved, but many people have had great success with such ventures.

Making Decisions Together

It is not easy to decide where and how a couple will live in retirement. One person may want to reinvent himself in a new location, while the other does not want to budge. One may like the country, while the other insists on a major city. One may want a big house, while the other wants to conserve resources and make life easier for herself. One person may prefer two places, while the other can barely handle one. And there are many people-related questions to face as well—the importance of friends, children, and grandchildren, and the role that each will play in location decisions.

Partners make many separate decisions every day, but the magnitude matters, and decisions about where we will live need to be shared. If one partner makes the decision alone, she may love the place but resent her significant other for forcing her to take the responsibility, and that significant other may never really buy into the decision. If one partner goes along just to please the other, anger may simmer and resentments will pop up later.

If a mistake is made about where to live and the couple has to come to terms with negative consequences, it is human nature to want to blame the other person. But blaming behavior is less likely if the decision was shared.

There are no simple answers to all of the questions that retirees must ask themselves in order to resolve any differences about where to live. But there is probably no more important issue to explore than this one because only thorough discussion and compromise on both sides will result in a workable plan. The best part of this decision, as with physical attraction, is that beauty is in the eye of the beholder. People love all kinds of locations for all kinds of reasons, and the partners should answer to no one but themselves. Every retired couple should try to find the happiest solution they can.

One study by Professor Charles Longino at Wake Forest

University, based on the 2000 census, shows that only 5 percent of retirees move across state lines. Another 5 percent move within their state, but the vast majority do not move at all. Over forty years this pattern has not changed very much, but these numbers reflect the generation born during or just after the Depression years. Longino and others predict big changes when the boomers pull up stakes. "That's a whole different ball game," he says.[7]

Questions to Ask Yourself and Your Partner

1. Do I (you) want to stay put or shake things up for retirement living? Why?
2. What factors are important to me (you)? Climate? Cost of living? City versus country? Taxes? A bigger house? A smaller place? Proximity to children and grandchildren? Existing friends or new ones? Diverse-age companions or people our age? Health services?
3. How would I (you) rank these factors in importance?
4. Can I (you) afford, financially and emotionally, to make a mistake in where we live?
5. Should we have one location or two? What are the pros and cons for us?
6. How might we apportion our time if we had two locations?
7. How much do I (you) care what our children, other relatives, and friends think about our living arrangements?
8. If not yet retired, what are the pros and cons of us getting a retirement place early?
9. Which of us feels most strongly about where we should live?
10. What mechanisms will help us share the decision equally?
11. If we do not agree, how will we fashion a compromise?

illing Time: So Many Choices

At Loose Ends

Without the routine of full-time work and business-related activities in the first weeks and months after retirement, there is suddenly a lot of time to fill—more, in fact, than many of us imagined possible. We all need some structure in our lives, and most of us need to feel that we are productive human beings. Certainly there are people for whom unstructured days are nothing but bliss, but for the rest of us—the vast majority of us—we need to come up with meaningful ways to fill our time.

Retirement can cause people to think that they are on the fringes of society. They watch their neighborhood empty out each morning, imagining all the other people going off to their respective offices and errands of the day, eventually to return in the evening satisfied with goals accomplished. Without some kind of structure for the new retiree, the days can stretch ahead pointlessly. And it is easy, when this happens, to fall into depression.

Those working years may have provided too *much* stimulation, but retirement usually feels at first like too *little*. Not only is a new retiree at loose ends, but her family and friends ask the most embarrassing questions: "What are you doing with your time?" "How much are you sleeping?" "Are you bored?"

Added to the ennui of aimless days may be the feeling that you've been wrong about all this retirement stuff. Perhaps you used to feel that work was a terrible, useless rat race, and you couldn't wait for it to end. Now you're not happy in retirement either, and you wonder, "What's wrong with me?" You always hated people who thought the grass was greener on the other side of the street, but now feelings of envy about your neighbors just increase your unhappiness. You don't want to go back to work, but you can't stay in this lonely funk either.

It's complicated enough for one person to face this alone—to figure out how to stop fretting about the hours stretched ahead, to decide what exactly to do and how to do it. But it's infinitely more complicated when two people are going through it as a couple. It's *not* a good thing when both partners seem to be going down the tubes together.

On the other hand, your mate may be one of the people asking questions about your time. Certainly she will be hugely affected by the way you answer them. Many partners who thought they knew everything about one another still struggle with this new phase in their lives because both people have to face the challenges of filling time, alone and together. There may have been expectations, either voiced or unsaid, about what the other person will do in retirement, and now there may be disappointment or anger if he doesn't measure up. You both have to deal with two sets of feelings and actions in this situation. Conflict can easily arise.

Simultaneous or Separate Retirements

AARP surveys show that 80 percent of baby boomers age forty-five and over expect to continue working past the age of sixty-five—either for money or for fun.[1] That is a surprisingly large number, and the expectations are borne out by additional statistics from the 2000 census: 4.2 million people age sixty-five and older were in the workforce, up from 3.5 million in 1990. And the U.S. Department of Labor projects that the number will grow to 5.4 million by the year 2010. Indeed, 13.1 percent of retirement-age workers sixty-five and above are still on the job.[2]

The numbers do not mean that all of these people are working full time, nor do they mean that everyone who wants to stay in a job past age sixty-five will be allowed to do so. But the statistics do suggest that there is something very important about work for many of us. Whether it is for money—because older Americans often can't afford to give up their paychecks—or for psychological satisfaction, many people want to stay in the workforce as they age. Americans really are workaholics. We work longer hours in the United States than in any other industrialized country, and we get far fewer vacation days than we would in France, Germany, and other European countries. These habits do not automatically die at retirement.

There is some evidence that "mature workers" are in demand—especially if they have good computer skills. Because of demographics, there are not enough young people to fill certain types of jobs, and older people are often more dependable workers. One employer tells the story of a snowstorm during which all the older workers showed up but none of the younger ones made it in.[3]

People now at or near retirement age comprise the first generation of two-income couples; that is, both partners were probably in the workforce at some point. This is in sharp contrast to our parents' generation, where the husband was usually the sole breadwinner, and it suggests some major differences in the way that retiree couples relate to each other now versus in the past. This picture will surely continue for future retirees because a majority of all American women are now in the workforce—60 percent in 2000 versus 40 percent three decades ago.

A lot of partners manage to retire simultaneously, but it seems like fewer couples these days are retiring in the same way, at the same time. More and more couples are finding themselves "half-retired," or retiring in phases.[4] Many such couples are coping with situations like these:

- She went back to work while the kids were in college and left as soon as the family didn't need the money anymore. Now she wants to travel and have fun, but his career is still thriving.

- He wants out of the rat race early, with less income. He thinks it is time to play, but she wants both of them to keep at it in order to acquire more savings. She calls him a quitter—unrealistic, narcissistic, impatient, and egotistical.

- She is a few years younger than he, so she is behind him chronologically and motivationally. She knows that she can't collect a pension unless she works a few more years, and she wants that additional income at age sixty-five. She also wants the feeling of pride she'll have, knowing that she is contributing substantially to their retirement resources.

- She is the same age as he is but didn't really focus on her career until the kids were grown. Now she loves her accomplishments, the recognition, the camaraderie, and the money, and she's not about to give all that up.

- The company is trying to promote capable women, and she was just offered a new position, so she can't leave now. He is really proud of her but vaguely angry too.

- She was pushed out early and couldn't find a suitable job, so he must be the sole breadwinner for a few years until they both can get Social Security and maybe a pension.

Then there are people who have retired with enough resources but want a second career for psychological reasons. Liberated from the need to make a lot of money, these seniors are often looking for greater meaning and the opportunity to make a difference in the lives of others. Earlier work may have fed the body, but a second career can feed the soul. For example, a man who earned his living as an accountant always wanted to work with people versus spreadsheets. He retired at age fifty-five, and his wife thought they would relax and travel, but he enrolled in social work graduate school instead, and he is planning on a fifteen-year career. In another situation, a woman's volunteer work with adolescent girls suddenly changed when she was fifty because the board offered her the executive director's position. She was thrilled and agreed to stay in the job for ten years—long after her husband will be retired.

Sometimes the half-retired system works just great. Some men, for instance, love their first-ever experience of being home alone, perhaps pursuing a new hobby for hours on end. In fact, after a busy working life, the newly retired partner may be really comfortable with privacy and space. More often, however, conflicts arise over issues like the following:

- She wonders why he still has to bring work home on evenings and weekends. She didn't care when she was working too, but now she's been looking forward to talking with him all day.

- He wants to help out with the cooking, but he resents her expectation that he should have dinner on the table every night. Or he cannot abide any criticism of his experimental cooking skills, and she cannot restrain her insults about the way he cooks and keeps the kitchen.

- He always hated housework; he thought it was enough that he took care of the yard and the cars. Now she comes home to a very messy house at night and resents his unwillingness to keep it clean.

- She expected him to retire a lot earlier and planned for them to spend two months every year visiting their four children around the country. She became angry and mildly depressed when she realized that that could not happen for a long time.

- Because he has no official office anymore, he wants to empty out the guest bedroom so that he can set up a desk and computer there. She wants to continue using that closet for her clothes and insists on keeping a proper guest room—not just a fold-out couch.

An Australian study followed four hundred couples for three years from the day that one of them retired, and their findings are interesting.[5] The old story of him getting under her feet is disappearing because only 22 percent of the men who retired had a wife who had been a full-time homemaker. Forty percent of the partners in this study decided to retire at the same time. With the remaining 38 percent, one of them continued to work. The conclusion of this research was that the happiest relationships were those in which the husband and wife both still did some work, either paid or volunteer. People are married for a long time after retirement, and work can be a wonderful form of escape from too much togetherness.

Another study by Drs. Phyllis Moen and Jungmeen Kim at Cornell University found various levels of satisfaction for different combinations of employment and retirement.[6] These researchers looked at 534 married men and women between the ages of fifty and seventy-four in upstate New York, and their major finding was that the retired men were happiest when they went back to work and their wives stayed at home. Couples in this situation had higher morale than did couples in which neither spouse was working. Newly retired men experienced more marital conflict than nonretired men, and newly retired men with employed wives showed the highest marital conflict of all. One man whose wife continued working is quoted as saying, "The first year, I almost went nuts." Newly retired women were more depressed than long-retired women or not-yet-retired women, especially if their husbands remained employed. However, these women's satisfaction seemed tied more to having a happy marriage than to work. In fact, those who found employment after retirement were no less depressed than those who stayed in retirement.

These data show that retirement brings different rewards for different people. Even though the picture of retirement has changed in many ways over the last century, the men in these studies still seem to identify more with work, while women are more concerned about their relationships. There is evidently still a pull toward traditional gender roles, especially for the men, who are happiest when they are working after retirement and their wives are at home. It will be interesting to see whether these conclusions hold as the boomers retire, with younger women having been more committed to work and both genders having been influenced by the women's movement.

All of these findings also emphasize how complicated retirement can be. Since people usually will not—indeed, *cannot*—work forever, both partners will eventually end up at home. The couple will have to adjust at some point.

In many ways, then, one-person-retired couples are out of sync with each other. Even the partners who love it should know that a different system is coming as they get older, and they will need to make other adjustments down the line. And those who *resent* this half-retired inequality need to realize that it is temporary, and they should have patience with each other. They will probably have many years ahead for togetherness. In the meantime, both of them can make some compromises, become more independent, and think about the kind of relationship they want to have in the future.

Part-Time Work

If some work is needed for financial or psychological reasons, a part-time job can be a good solution. This allows someone who has been work-addicted to ease into retirement. It can also provide needed income until some benefits kick in or until the couple feels ready to downsize.

A *rewarding* part-time position is not easy to find, but there are ways to approach a job search as a senior. One method involves your former employer. For example, you can make yourself so valuable before your retirement day that you'll be able to write your own ticket for part-time work in the future. Or if you have already retired and decide a year or so later that you still want or need to work, you can draw up a written plan outlining what you can offer, and present it to your allies in the organization. You may have to take less compensation, but you will probably be more comfortable in—and more valuable to—the place you know well than within a totally new environment.

If you decide to search elsewhere, there are a few extra admonitions that seniors should add to the usual tricks for job hunting:

- Don't feel sorry for yourself or express any grudges toward a previous employer, or you'll be seen as angry and prone to unhappiness in the new job too.

- Have the appropriate computer skills and be open to learning new technology.

- Tout your excellent health, dependability, and respect for coworkers of all ages—even those as young as your children.

- Make sure they know that you're a spark plug rather than dead wood. Let them see that you'll remain interested even though promotional possibilities have faded. Exude a sense of joy and passion.

- Be clear about things that would motivate you, such as flexible hours or three days per week or special projects.

- Beware of giving the employer any hint that you are or might be a litigious person.

Some older people are coming up with the most extraordinary ideas for part-time work: creating and selling art, hosting in a restaurant, organizing fishing trips, painting houses, and doing seasonal income tax preparation, just to name a few. Some individuals or couples love starting their own part-time business, while others prefer to avoid that kind of responsibility.

One of the best ideas I've heard for senior couples is working in a national park for the summer season. They do it not only for money but for the camaraderie and new experiences as well. They live dormitory-style, make new friends over communal meals, and sometimes cry when they leave in the fall. National park managers evidently love mature workers and usually give them the choice of returning year after year or trying new locations.

Some other countries are also attractive for part-time or seasonal work. For example, Australia and South Africa give retirement visas and seem to welcome retirees. This can be a grand adventure for two partners who still need or want to work, but the devil is always in the details.

Volunteer Work

Many seniors are reinventing retirement by doing huge amounts of volunteer work and amazing amounts of caregiving.

AARP estimates that the volunteer work of older Americans equals 1.1 million full-time workers, and their caregiving equals 7.1 million full-time employees.[7]

Volunteer positions run the gamut from occasional hours determined by the retiree to full-time, demanding jobs about which the retiree is obsessive. You can even work online from home, at your own pace, by finding sources like www.serviceleader.org or www.netaid.org. You can take a vacation to help people in another culture, based on sources like www.globalvolunteers.org or www.earthwatch.org. You might use weekends to build houses with a group such as Habitat for Humanity; you could work at special events that raise money for a charity; or you can give a helping hand for time-limited projects like feeding the homeless during the holidays. AARP offers these ideas and many others in their publications.

There are really five steps to successful volunteer work:

1. Figure out what you want out of the experience. You may have to dig deep to understand your own motivations, but altruism is never pure giving. It will not work unless it involves some sense of pleasure or satisfaction for the giver as well as the receiver.

2. Examine what rewards turn you on, and think about how much you're willing to give in order to get those rewards.

3. Try to balance your needs and desires with those of your partner. Will you work together or separately, and why? Have you helped your partner to understand your thinking, even if she doesn't agree with your choices? At the very least, discuss the plan before you enact it.

4. Find the volunteer job that fits your criteria as closely as possible. Realize that it may take a little time to work your way into the organization, and don't expect any situation to be perfect.

5. Reexamine what you are doing periodically. Are you giving

enough to get the rewards you want? Is there something else that interests you more? Finding the right mix may take a little trial and error. Success may require further discussions with both the organization and your mate.

Balancing your volunteer desires with the priorities of your partner may not be easy. Conflicts may have been tolerated more readily when you were both working for money, but this is *volunteer work*, for heaven's sake. It's not supposed to complicate your relationship. A lot of communication and soul-searching may be necessary, as the following couple discovered:

Kevin was a gung-ho commercial airline pilot who always dreaded forced retirement at age sixty. But Anne looked forward to having him home more, traveling with his fabulous airline benefits, and persuading him to help with deliveries for her small antiques business.

The retirement party was a blast, with Anne realizing again how loved Kevin was by his colleagues and to what extent his life had been shaped by flying. She would not have been surprised if he'd tried to get a part-time position as a corporate or private pilot. Instead, Kevin signed up immediately to deliver meals to AIDS patients. He told Anne about it matter-of-factly the day after he had organized this, and when she asked him why, he said that he had been impressed last year by a speaker at their church who did the same thing. Anne felt a mixture of pride that Kevin was so caring and dismay that he was turning his back on flying. She knew that AIDS is not contagious, but she worried about the other diseases these people might have, such as tuberculosis. She said little to him, but her nonverbal communication over the next few months was loud and clear.

As time passed, Kevin did this job six days a week and seemed happy. He felt useful, quickly developing friendships with the people he met. He talked increasingly about his clients to Anne, and he seldom mentioned flying. When his pilot buddies called to arrange a lunch, he was often too busy.

After a few months, Anne's general pickiness and criticisms of Kevin increased. He was never available for things she wanted to do. He had no interest in the exotic trips she had planned. (Her antiques shop was only open three days a week, and she had trained two good, long-term employees to be able to take over when she was not there.) He seemed to care more about his volunteer job than his family.

One day, Anne suggested that Kevin should earn some money if he was going to work so hard. She mentioned other pilots who had gone on to second careers. They fought bitterly, and she eventually admitted that she felt jealous. She even wondered if he was having an affair with one of the administrators, who called the house quite often.

He accused her of going crazy. Wasn't she pleased that he had made such a great transition into retirement? Didn't she see the value in his volunteer work?

They had several discussions with their daughters, one of whom is a counselor, and began to come up with ways to solve their problems. It was quickly obvious to the whole family that Anne and Kevin's communication skills needed some work.

It was not realistic for Kevin to give up his meal delivery. He still had an enormous amount of energy and needed the structure that this job afforded him. In addition, he needed the contact with people it provided, along with the sense that he was giving back to his *community. If he were to quit, he would be restless and bored, and he would very likely resent his wife. Though Anne could provide for many of Kevin's needs, she could do little to help him with a structured, meaningful life. Both of them eventually recognized this.*

However, Anne had a legitimate point too. She had been very patient, waiting years for his retirement, structuring her own business so that she could be away at times now and eventually sell it. She felt entitled to more of Kevin's attention. She wondered why he was able to devote energy to everyone but her.

They eventually reached a compromise. Kevin altered his schedule from six days a week to three, with the months of January and July off. He asked Anne if she would come with him occasionally on his rounds, and she learned from Kevin's clients how proud he is of her and their daughters. These sick men and women had all heard about the antiques business and their daughter's wedding, and their fondness for her husband was palpable. Anne and Kevin also decided to plan a major trip twice each year, and they have worked at communicating more about their lives.

It's as if Kevin only knew how to operate at warp speed, and he needed someone to force him to slow down, while Anne needed to see the value in his work. Kevin says that his volunteer job with disabled people is even more gratifying now because he's not so frenetic about it. He knows now that it is good to focus his energies in several different directions, including his pilot friends and his family, and he is having more fun this way.

Volunteer work that we expect to be gratifying can also be surprisingly frustrating, especially for former executives, because we'll probably have little authority. Those of us who were decision makers in our paid jobs will see problems as a volunteer that we are powerless to change. But this position can also be a relief after many years of, perhaps, *too much* responsibility. At the very least, volunteer work can give form and meaning to our days. But it is also a chance to give back—to teach others the lessons that life has taught to us. And in the best scenarios, it can feed one's soul.

Tony had worked in shipyards all of his life and had always made model ships at home. After he retired, a friend suggested that he become a Big Brother, but when he filled out the paperwork, he was very tentative: "I don't suppose any boy these days would like making model ships." He asked whether all of their other volunteers were professionals, because in the pictures on the wall, all the men wore suits. He had not told Nellie, his wife, that he was applying because he thought that he might be rejected.

The organization, however, was delighted to have Tony. After checking references and giving him a short training course, they immediately assigned to him a troubled, fatherless boy, age fourteen. When he told Nellie about the boy he had just met, she asked Tony why he had to do this. The house needed so many repairs. Their grandchildren might like more of his time too. Tony explained, as best he could, why his friend's idea had grabbed him, and they talked for a couple of hours. Eventually, she raised the fact that Tony's father had died when he was only ten, and they agreed that this fact must be related to his choice of volunteer work.

The relationship was very rocky at first. The kid had no interest in models, but Tony was so proud of his work that he couldn't wait to show it off. After their first

Saturday lunch at McDonald's, Tony called his wife to say that he was bringing the boy home. Nellie, who had accepted the Big Brother idea theoretically, was furious about the intrusion into their home and worried that the kid would steal from them. But Tony promised to watch him carefully, and Nellie relented.

Tony made weekly dates with the boy thereafter, at first just suggesting that he do his homework at a table in the basement while Tony worked on his models there. Within weeks, however, the kid requested help with math and began asking questions about the materials Tony was using. Their relationship grew. Five years later, the boy got a scholarship to the state university, and they talked by phone at least once every week. Tony sent his protégé spending money regularly, and that young man is now a physician's assistant. Somewhere along the way, he also won Nellie over, and she treats him like one of her own children. The boy never really became skilled at making models, but that idea was a great vehicle for friendship. All three of these people gave something to one another and got a lot in return.

Social Activities Versus Isolation

It becomes especially apparent at retirement that people have different energy levels and needs for social interaction. One part of a couple usually wants more activity than the other; two people seldom match up exactly in this regard. A little compromise will solve most problems, but huge differences can make for angry fights.

Extreme isolation is a special issue. It could be a healthy adjustment for a little while after retirement, but it more often signifies depression. People really do need people, and relying totally on one's partner or children does not usually make for a happy life. But constant, frenetic activity is not a healthy adjustment either. These extremes can be dangerous—and people occasionally swing from one to the other.

Ron and Barbara have different views of the first few months after his retirement, but they look back on that time, almost ten years ago, with some humor. She says that the first month was scary because he never left the house. He slept ten hours every night and lay on the couch watching TV the rest of the time. She worried about depression, but he says he was readjusting his body and mind, thinking a lot and making many decisions.

Suddenly he reversed course. He got up early and had a better attitude, but he drove her crazy because he had decided to organize both their lives. He rearranged the dishes and pots and pans and spices. He criticized her cooking, and when she suggested that he do it himself, he did. He literally pushed her out of the kitchen a couple of times. She offered to do the dishes, but he said that she never had learned to load the dishwasher properly. He criticized the laundry soap she was using and bought a different brand. He decided that they did not have enough social life, so he signed them both up for dancing classes at their town's recreation department. He bought tickets for concerts and lectures, often without discussing the event with her. He kept calling friends they hadn't seen in years, even though the friends weren't always responsive. He says he had decided to become a great husband. She says he was a pain in the ass.

One day, when he started looking closely at her credit card receipts and household files, she drew a line in the sand. No more! He needed to find ways to spend time away from her, she said. He could organize his own life but not hers.

They now laugh about how he went from total isolation to frenetic activity within a few months, and they suggest that it was like a pendulum. He had to swing to both extremes before he could land in the middle. In their serious moments, they have tried to analyze what happened. It seems that Ron was really pushed out of his job as assistant superintendent of schools after a new superintendent was hired, because he and this woman did not get along. At age sixty-one he told himself that he was ready to retire anyway, but his plan had really been to hang in until sixty-three or sixty-four. He secretly wondered whether he was to blame for not getting along with a woman boss, and he ruminated about whether Barbara blamed him for changing their retirement plan. He now says that he isolated himself at first because he felt guilty and apprehensive about being chastised by his wife, although she is adamant that she never questioned him.

He says that the turning point came one morning when he looked in the mirror and realized that he had not shaved in five days. He was wearing a scruffy old bathrobe, and his appearance shocked and frightened him. He knew that he was a decent person and had done nothing wrong. He was ready for action, but the outside world was still more than he could handle, so he decided to focus on the house.

Meanwhile, Barbara, who had had an active volunteer life at the local museum, had started wondering if Ron might commit suicide, so she stayed home all of the time, becoming more fidgety herself. Neither of these extremes was the Ron she knew. Then her tipping point came with Ron's snooping in her files. She didn't want to live on pins and needles anymore. She confronted him, insisting that he find some meaningful activities, and he readily agreed.

Over the next six months Ron got himself into better physical shape, and he also met with several firms that do searches for education executives. Soon thereafter he was offered a principal's job in a nearby community, and he eagerly accepted. They both say now that his second retirement, three years later, went much more smoothly because he had practiced what not to do. Of course, this retirement was more on his terms. He takes pride now in having been resilient enough to find another job and gives much of the credit to Barbara. She would not allow him to act out his feelings through either isolation or inappropriate activity. She helped him to implement the proper balance.

What do you do when your partner really prefers splendid isolation while you want more activity? The only reasonable answer is that you must go out—either with friends or alone. Is that hard? Sometimes, yes. Might your partner be angry with you for leaving? Yes. Is it dangerous for a woman, or even a man, to go out alone at night? Occasionally. But you have to do it if you are to remain vital and engaged with life. If you need people and activities outside of the home for nourishment, you *must* do it or you will gradually die inside.

Find like-minded friends if you can. Go alone if you must—or if you actually enjoy that alone time. But find ways to keep that engaged part of yourself alive and well. If your main reason for not doing something is "My mate won't go with me" or "My partner won't like it," you have some hard psychological work to do. It's often easier, at first, to blame the other person and become a victim, but it's much healthier to come to terms with who you are and what you want out of life—and then make that kind of life happen.

Travel

Some people love all kinds of travel, regardless of cost or conditions. Others hate travel of any kind and prefer to stay in their comfortable environment. Most of us think, at first, that travel during retirement will be a no-brainer, but there are so many variables to come to terms with when there are two of you.

How Much

There are those who get in their recreational vehicles the day after retirement and travel for the next five or ten years. Some people read every travel brochure and fill their life with back-to-back tours. But one partner usually says "Enough!" at some point, and then the battle is on. "Do you want me to go with*out* you?" "Do you want me to find someone *else* to travel with?"

Where

Some people like cities, while others prefer the wide open spaces. One may want golf resorts, while the other searches for spas. Sometimes one person is eager for foreign travel, while the other feels frightened of strange places and languages, and is happy to stay where they are. Especially when the couple has limited resources, the destination for each trip takes on great importance.

In What Way and At What Price

"Should we take planes or trains or cars?" "Do we travel steerage class or first class?" In fact, these questions may have nothing to do with money. One very wealthy man, for example, hates expensive cruises but loves trips on state ferries and cargo ships, while his wife wants extreme luxury. He does have great stories of his adventures, but she refuses to go with him, so he has found a couple of buddies to share his interests.

If you don't have much financial cushion, any trip can be a cause for concern about whether those resources might be needed for something else. But even if there is money, one person may want to spend it while the other wants to economize. Travel, after all, is a discretionary expense, and it gets affected by all kinds of values—especially those that were planted in childhood.

When

Regarding time of year, one partner may want the ideal temperature and be willing to pay for it, while the other likes the savings or the lack of crowds in the off-season. Furthermore, one person may resist leaving when the grandchildren are out of school, when it is opera season, or when a favorite sports team is playing. Another may refuse to travel when golfing is at its height or during the family-focused winter holidays.

With Whom

Many couples have conflicts over whether they should travel alone, with family, with friends, or on tours with strangers. This is just one added layer of decision making, and there are truly pros and cons each way. Going just as a couple gives you a lot of privacy, and it usually forces you to interact more with strangers, which can lead to wonderful new friendships. But going with friends or family members can be fun, with shared responsibilities for decisions and, in later years, a feast of shared memories. Of course, traveling with others can also dredge up unresolved conflicts in those relationships.

Many retirees think about traveling with their grandchildren, and one hears stories about this that range from wonderful times to disasters. Two successful tales follow:

One couple, who love Europe and took an annual trip there for many years, became wary of driving on the Continent as they got older. (And most rental car companies have rules against doing business with anyone over seventy. Damn!) So they began hiring a college-age grandchild every summer to do the driving, help them with luggage, and give them assistance in any emergency. In return, they pay a small salary as well as all expenses, and the trip also provides that young person with a great educational experience. They have volunteers every summer, and even those grandkids now in careers like to fantasize at holiday dinners about taking a leave of absence to volunteer again.

A well-traveled grandmother began telling each grandchild by age two that, after the child turned twelve, she would take him anywhere in the world. She chose that age because the child is usually able to deal with homesickness but not yet obsessed with friends. She had no idea, initially, what an incentive each child would thus have to study geography and different cultures.

When the first grandchild started saying at age five that she wanted to go to Antarctica, Grandma thought that idea would blow over soon. But it didn't, and Grandpa joined them quite happily five years ago for the trip. The other grandkids seem to be choosing equally exotic locales, but the grandparents are having a ball.

They feel that they have developed special bonds with their four grandchildren this way, and their resources are being very well spent.

Of course, retiree couples who can't afford to offer the world can suggest parts of their own country to visit and explore. The impetus for the child's learning in this way is very worthwhile, as is the building of intergenerational relationships.

Decision making about all these travel factors requires some compromise. If one person always dictates the decisions, he may eventually resent having all of the responsibility—especially if things go wrong. On the other hand, the submissive partner may initially enjoy not having to do the planning, but eventually feelings of impotence and passive-aggressive actions could ruin the trip. If both partners have not taken part in decision making, that expensive trip could turn out to be just a chore.

When two partners cannot agree on a trip, they sometimes do a your turn/my turn arrangement, and they may even draw straws to see who goes first. Or they may decide at times to go on separate trips.

Travel is usually hard work, and it causes conflict in the best of relationships because you are out of your comfort zone and you may be tired. But it is so rewarding—especially in retirement, when you finally can relax and explore. You now have the time to rent a house in Tuscany and visit all the little towns you always wanted to see. You can take a class at Oxford University in England or the Sorbonne in Paris. You can go without hotel reservations and find places to stay spontaneously—a very different mode of travel from having to be at a certain place at a specific time. You can change your itinerary and park yourselves for an extra week in some lovely spot. What a luxury time gives us in retirement! Finding ways to make it fun for both parts of a couple is the biggest challenge *and* the best reward.

Sports

One hears so many people—usually women—complain about their partners' obsession with sports. Either they ski or play tennis or golf all the time, or they watch sporting events on TV constantly.

Participation in sports is usually a healthy pastime. It keeps the body toned and the mind occupied. It provides an outlet for competitive juices that may have been honed at work. It can enhance friendships. But sports can also take a lot of time and energy. In the extreme, they can divert a person from work that is needed either around the house or to make money. Sports can also provide an excuse for ignoring one's partner, other family members, and friends. Sometimes sports prevent someone from becoming a more well-rounded person. We all know people who get pretty boring when they constantly turn dinner-table conversations to brands of golf clubs or types of tennis shots.

Sporting activities can also be expensive, so one partner may use money that she really can't afford or divert resources that her partner wanted for other things. Couples need to find creative ways to address the time and money conflicts often caused by sports participation. Here are a couple of gems:

Tina and Mike made a pact after retirement that she would get whatever he spent on golf for redecorating the house, but he handles the finances in their household and likes to brag to his friends about his little games. First he convinced Tina that his club membership fee was an investment, not a cost. Then he lies to her about where he is going some days, and he gets away with this because he actually still does some consulting work. Finally, he almost always pays the fees at his course, as well as other places, with cash so that there will be no credit card receipts. When the monthly bill for club dues comes, he grandly writes out a check for the same amount to her, complaining mightily that she is getting too much because the club is really a business expense, used for guest entertaining more than his personal golf needs.

This vignette shows how one couple handles the time and cost of golf, but it also reveals a dirty little secret about how people hide money from each other. Partners do this in various ways and for different reasons—some valid, most not. But with Mike and Tina, the games suggest a dark underbelly to their marriage. Their relationship has severe limitations, and their behavior is certainly not recommended. The following anecdote is more benign because these two people are, at least, more honest with each other.

Rob and Jenny made the same kind of agreement about golf, but she is astute about the costs, and he agreed that she could use the same amount of money he spends for anything she wants. This worked fine for a year or so— especially when Jenny used her stash to take Rob out for fancy dinners. Eventually, however, Rob became aware that she was giving considerable resources to her ne'er-do-well thirty-five-year-old son from a previous marriage. Rob ranted and raved, only to be reminded of their agreement. He tried to understand, but hearing Jenny's defenses of the "kid" just made him more angry. Rob

*asked Jenny whether she gave money to her son because
she knew it made him crazy. She said no; it just made her
feel good to be able to help her son have a better standard
of living.*

*One day, as Rob was leaving for golf, he asked if she'd
rather he stay home. With a big grin, she said, "No. Go
today. Go tomorrow. Go every day. I need the money."
Rob shot the worst game of his life that day. He now plays
less often and has decided to find more things that he and
Jenny will enjoy together.*

And then there are the *addicts* who go to every game or watch
every sporting event on TV. Money for tickets can be an issue if
funds are limited. Conflict can also arise when the partner is
expected to attend as well—with enthusiasm. When the medium
is TV, there are often issues with the screaming of obscenities, the
spilling of food and drinks, or the sports addict's unavailability to
do other things. If two people are equally interested in these
games, they can enjoy the activity together. But if one simply goes
along to get along, both of them may eventually be disillusioned
by the sham.

Especially in retirement, we need to understand the great
American attraction to sports because it meets a lot of needs for
people with time on their hands. Watching two teams duke it out
can be a wonderful diversion from real-life trials and tribulations
because this is one of the few activities in life where the outcome
really doesn't matter. There is always a clear resolution at the end
of a defined time period, and your life will not really be changed at
all according to who wins. Watching sporting events also gives
people a great outlet for innate competitive feelings—without
physical involvement or possibly getting hurt. Furthermore, sports
provide a common ground for a lot of social conversations.

But obsession with sports can also cause a lot of angst between partners. Compromises need to be found, or if that is not possible, partners must learn to live and let live. The following story seems to produce knowing giggles in mixed company:

Four married men were golfing on a beautiful Saturday morning. On the eighth hole one guy said: "You won't believe what I had to do to get here today. My wife made me promise to paint every room in the house next weekend." The second fellow said: "That's nothing. I had to agree to buy my wife a new car." The third guy added: "Well, I had to agree that we will remodel the whole house."

When they got to the next hole, these three realized that the fourth guy had not said a word, so they asked him if he had to do anything to get out of the house. He replied: "No problem. I just set my alarm for five-thirty a.m. When it went off, I gave the wife a kiss and said: 'Golf course or intercourse?' She always says the same thing: 'Wear a sweater.' "

TV and Other Entertainment

People vary greatly in their preferences about the correct amount of TV watching, the programs they like, and what times of day they want the tube on or off. Indeed, it is hard to imagine how any couple manages with just one TV set. With three TVs in our house, my husband and I fought so often over who would watch the big-screen TV ("I bought it to watch sports"; "I bought it to see the details on people's faces") that we eventually had to get a second big one.

Many couples struggle over who will control the clicker—the remote control—but one wife found a clever solution. She bought an extra, which she keeps near her chair. She knows that her husband will use his remote briefly, but then he will doze off, and she will choose from then on. He never seems to know the difference.

Some fights occur because there are huge differences in how people handle noise. Some partners like to live in a quiet, serene house; others want the TV or radio or stereo blasting all of the time. And this spills over into driving in a car together—whether to listen to the radio, music tapes, books on tape, CDs, or nothing; the volume; whether to choose a radio station for news, commentary, classical music, pop, rock and roll, country and western, or whatever. It's amazing that some couples ever get to their destination with both of them fighting for control of in-car noise.

Similarly, entertainment outside of the home is a hugely satisfying part of most lives, but it can cause conflict and can cost a lot of money. Some retirees get around the cost issue by volunteering as an usher in order to gain admission to favorite events. Senior discounts on tickets also can help. But choices must always be made about what to attend, and couples who go together may have to make compromises. Movies—what kind and when? Theater—comedy, drama, or musical, and traditional, modern, or experimental? Opera? Symphony? Comedy clubs? Dance clubs?

Restaurants should also be included under entertainment. How often? What price range? What type of cuisine? Small or large? Breakfast, lunch, or dinner? With other couples or not?

None of these decisions around entertainment is critical to couples' thriving together, yet they can blow up if they're not shared tactfully and honestly between partners. With a little compromise, entertainment can enrich both of your lives.

Learning

The latest golden-years trend seems to be education—either for fun or for credit. Some retirement villages are built around colleges, and many of them require a certain number of class hours each year for people who live on the premises. The Institutes for Learning in Retirement sets up relationships between colleges and senior citizens, and they say that they are inundated with interest from both sides. Elderhostel trips, which usually include an educational component, are growing by leaps and bounds. Spurred on by medical research suggesting that mental fitness may ward off dementia, a lot of retirees want less time on the fairways and more time in collegiate classrooms.[8]

Less formal types of learning experiences are also popular in retirement—often free or at reduced cost for seniors. Museums hold painting classes. Community centers offer all kinds of activities. Groups of individuals get together to teach one another about gardening or various crafts.

Computers and Hobbies

We hear a lot these days about relationship problems caused by computers. One partner demeans the other because of inadequate knowledge and refusal to take classes. One person consistently messes up the computer and expects the other to fix it. One always wants access when the other one is online. One snoops into the other's email. One person resents the other for being totally obsessed, spending hours at God knows what. Even when they have two computers, some couples compete over which one is best.

For some people, computers really *are* escape mechanisms. They can occupy your mind endlessly, and they require no complicated, difficult, messy human interaction. They are responsive to your commands, and they demand very little in return.

But the most problematic aspect of computers is probably pornography, and older men are big users of porn. Women need to hear some of the reasons that men give for this:

- It is so easy and so available—a lot better than going to a strip club.

- We are curious—especially about young bodies, which we seldom see anymore.

- Men are hardwired to want sex, especially with the youngest and most attractive female, because we are programmed for the survival of the fittest.

- Porn is harmless entertainment, used primarily to escape boredom.

And men need to hear how their interest in porn makes some women feel:

- Dirty and discarded

- Inadequate because older women cannot compete with those young, silicone-filled, surgery-enhanced bodies in real life

- Angry about the money spent on Internet porn

- Less interested in sex with a partner who needs those fantasies

Therapists tell us that many couples of all ages seek counseling because of arguments over porn, and they say that the Internet has enlarged this problem exponentially. But the experts are divided about porn's effect on a relationship. About half of them say that watching porn is tantamount to adultery, while the other half see it as more benign—if it is not an obsession. Couples for whom porn is an issue need to talk about it carefully and come to some resolution before it wrecks their otherwise successful union.

The Bottom Line About Hobbies

Many hobbies and other activities that seem positive or harmless in moderation can be extremely divisive to a relationship if they are pursued in excess. One man, for example, who wanted to make wooden toys for his grandchildren spent thousands of dollars on equipment, then found out that he wasn't very good at it and abandoned the project after two months, leaving a mess in the family room and garage. His wife brings the subject up angrily at every opportunity. And a sixty-four-year-old woman who loves gardening has gradually lost interest in all other activities. She will not leave her home to travel, even to see their children, and she is becoming a recluse. Her husband says that she has always been inclined toward depression, but she forced herself to interact socially while she worked. Since retirement, she has gone overboard by buying hundreds of new, exotic plants. She says that this is her choice and that she needs to tend her garden daily, but her obsessive gardening is driving them apart.

It's also interesting how often the expectations of others play a role in our hobbies. As with all other activities, we love it when people praise us; indeed, that often gives us extra enthusiasm and commitment. But friends and family members may also affect us by expecting our hobby to be productive. If we're writing a book, they want to know when it'll be finished and who will publish it. If we're crocheting sweaters, they ask how much we can sell them for. If we've started running, they wonder when we'll do our first marathon. People expect even retirees' *hobbies* to be useful, and if we give them the wrong answer, we can see disappointment in their eyes. Admiration seems to be reserved for seniors who challenge their biological clocks with amazing feats of energy and accomplishment.

We'll have to be strong if we want to do things at a slower pace than others expect or just because we enjoy them. And we'll have to watch for any tendency to let a hobby push our life—and our partnership—out of balance. We need to make decisions about hobbies by looking carefully into our own heart and mind.

Questions to Ask Yourself and Your Partner

1. How do I (you) feel about working past the usual retirement age?
2. Does either of us have any interest in a second career? Why or why not?
3. If we haven't retired simultaneously, how do I (you) feel about our half-retired roles? Is either of us angry about this? When will this arrangement change and why?
4. Does either of us need to continue working part time for money? For psychological reasons? If so, for how long?
5. What is my (your) interest in volunteer work? What kind and how much? Why or why not?
6. How is my (your) volunteer work affecting our relationship?
7. To what extent are our energy levels the same? How do we resolve any differences?
8. Where does each of us want to sit on the continuum between isolation and frenetic activity? Do our differences cause any problems?
9. How much are we in agreement about travel? Where do we disagree?
10. Do we have any differences about sports? How do we resolve these?
11. What are my (your) preferences regarding TV? How do I

(you) feel about noise in the house or car? How do we
resolve any differences?

12. What kind of other entertainment choices are we making? To
what extent do these decisions meet both our needs?

13. Where does learning fit into my (your) retirement plan?
What kind of learning?

14. Do we have any problems with computers that need to be
addressed?

15. To what extent am I (are you) happy with our involvement in
hobbies? What new ones might I (you) like to develop?

7.

Managing Money Within a Relationship

Money Is a Symbol and Tool

For people who were born fifty, sixty, or seventy years ago, money is often a taboo subject—not to be discussed in polite company. But all retirees, as well as those planning for retirement, need to realize that money is a tool that is related to so many other things. This is definitely not a chapter about saving or investing or doing financial planning; rather, this material approaches money as a complicated, psychologically significant part of any relationship.

A couple's financial status at retirement is probably pretty set; it is unlikely to change drastically in the years ahead—except perhaps if you win the lottery or receive a large inheritance. Partners need to grapple with the reality that they will have to make do with what they've got, and that fact usually raises plenty of issues. Overall, talking about money can be uncomfortable, even painful, but it is also a great mechanism for facing relationship issues and working through differences between partners.

Coping with Less Income

Couples usually come to retirement with a combination of current income and savings. These have to be combined in a balanced way in order to ensure financial comfort in retirement. For example, if personal savings are small, there will have to be more work. Obviously, retiree couples run the gamut from poor to rich, but some financial adjustments will probably be necessary for most of them.

Ideally, both partners have been planning their retirement for years, but often one person has made all the decisions about money while the other feels clueless. Or retirement has come unexpectedly, and there has not been time to really think through the income and expense issues. Clearly, employers are less and less generous in funding retirements with traditional benefit plans these days, gradually shifting most of the burden to the employee's shoulders. Couples are more and more on their own.

If there are not enough resources to live comfortably, however comfort is defined by both people, there is a tendency to ask why, and it is easy to blame each other for what went wrong. She may wonder why he didn't work harder so that he could have been promoted to a higher level. He may think that he could have moved higher up the ladder if she hadn't complained so much about his traveling, if she had been better able to handle the responsibilities at home, or if she had made a better impression at his work-related social events. He may accuse her of having wanted too much freedom with her friends when she should have worked more, or of not really having invested in a career when she should and could have. One or both may also be angry with the other for spending too recklessly on clothes, cars, sports, lavish vacations, or private schools for the kids.

As difficult as these issues are to talk about, it is really important to get them on the table because, if one person is thinking these things, the ramifications will show up everywhere in their relationship. Cruel as these accusations may sound, you need to give your partner a chance to react to your feelings and perceptions. Maybe she feels bad about her actions too. Maybe she would do things differently today. Perhaps he has another take on the issue or a different point of view, which will help you come to terms with your feelings. Two partners who are blaming each other need to fight it out—to clear the air, understand the issues. Maybe they both need to give their feelings some time to percolate after the initial discussion and then revisit the issue a few days later. If they still cannot resolve their feelings about diminished income and move on, professional help is in order. The goal should be to sort out the financial past—in the context of their future together. Without this step, the monetary adjustments that must be made in retirement will not go smoothly.

Even if you both think that your retirement income is adequate, it is almost always less than before, so you now have a couple of choices:

- Keep your current lifestyle, or even escalate your expenditures, either taking money out of savings on a regular basis or finding ways to bring in more money.

- Change your lifestyle by downsizing or eliminating certain things. A few costs, such as job-related clothing and transportation, will automatically decrease, but most will not. And it is easier if both partners share the pain. For instance, one couple cut $200 per month overnight when they realized they could give up their twice-daily Starbucks stops. (They still treat each other on special occasions.) Another couple gave up the premium channels on cable TV and learned to trim each other's hair. Other money-saving targets might be limiting cell phones, magazine subscriptions, or lawn and pest-control services; lowering lights and thermostats; using more coupons; growing a vegetable garden; using a library instead of buying books; having a garage sale; visiting doctors and other professionals less frequently; and giving smaller gifts to relatives and favorite charities.

The general rule of thumb has been that expenses decrease about 20 percent after retirement, but the Savishinsky study of one-year retirees cited in a *Wall Street Journal* article found just the opposite.[1] Many people said that they never realized how many of their meals and trips had been reimbursed by the company. Other items too, such as cars, home computers, and health insurance, had been paid for by their company. And the savings these retirees *did* realize on clothing, business lunches, and commuting were often offset by increased costs for new interests, travel, and projects. These observations underline the fact that having less income and *more* expenses in retirement can often be a recipe for disaster.

Priorities

The good thing about financial priorities is that they are easier to pin down than psychological ones because money is more concrete than ideas are. But the two types of priorities are closely connected. They both reflect values, and money issues give two people key information about their relationship. Setting financial goals and figuring out how you spend money is usually a direct route to understanding how you feel about life in general. And this, in turn, will help a couple come to terms with their similarities and differences vis-à-vis future priorities. The following story describes how money can even break up a long and otherwise gratifying relationship when priorities diverge:

When they met and fell in love twenty-two years earlier, Jack was a forty-three-year-old surgeon and Tyler was a twenty-six-year-old flight attendant. Tyler quickly moved into Jack's waterfront house, and they had a commitment ceremony, witnessed by family and friends, about two years later. Over the next twenty years they traveled frequently with Tyler's airline benefits. They acquired dogs and cats together. They had a very full and happy life. But Jack always made the house payments, and Tyler thought that was only right because of Jack's higher income. Tyler was making a decent salary and he put away some savings, but they seldom talked about money.

Recently Jack decided to cut back his busy practice, and he and Tyler talked excitedly one night about moving to San Francisco, where they had many friends. Both of them were amazed when "their" house sold for four million dollars. Jack worried that he might not be able to practice in California, or not want to, so he decided that he would spend less than a million for an apartment in San Francisco, investing the rest to draw upon later.

The night after Jack had gone alone to the house closing, they went out for dinner. Tyler had been thinking for weeks about how to approach the issue of the remaining three million—or whatever was left after taxes. Most of the appreciation had occurred while they were both living in the house, and Tyler wondered if Jack would offer him half of the profit or place the proceeds in both names.

Not only did Jack not offer, but he was dismayed and hurt by Tyler's questions. From his point of view, he had bought the house thirty years ago and made the payments; it was his alone. Tyler was just plain greedy. If he was going to share this windfall with others, what about his sister? His mother?

Sadly, Tyler has now moved to San Francisco alone, while Jack has bought a smaller, cheaper house in the old neighborhood. They both wonder whether their breakup was only because of money, but they swear that there was nothing else wrong. Their sense of closeness and trust in each other was simply and irreparably broken.

When money questions seem to be coming between you, ask yourselves what each partner has spent money on in the past:

- Houses

- Cars

- Things for general display to others, or things that give only oneself pleasure

- Clothes

- Travel

- Other experiences

- Medical care or legal expenses

- Gifts to children, other relatives, or friends

- Charitable contributions

Then ask yourselves questions such as:

- Have these patterns changed over the years, or are they the same now as they've always been?

- Are we happy with the current patterns?

  Finally, examine future-oriented issues such as:

- How do we want to spend our money from now on? What material things? What activities?

- How do our financial plans reflect our values?

- How would I prioritize our wants and desires?

- What are our fantasy wishes—realistic and unrealistic?

This is the kind of exercise that a couple can have fun with on paper. Answer these questions separately, and then compare your responses. Look particularly for ways that you have changed over time and what those changes might mean. Dwell a bit on your fantasy desires, but make sure that you both get real too. Each partner will obviously have different lists, and that can make life interesting, but it's the degree of difference that can win the race or sink the ship of the relationship.

Some couples, especially in a second marriage or late-life relationship, decide not to pool their resources, so many of these issues will not apply to them. But if a couple is using the same pot of money, both people will need to find ways to understand and accept the other's decisions about spending. In some cases, they may have built up enough trust over the years to allow each other total spending freedom, but they probably still want to be kept informed. Or they might decide that each person has discretion over the spending of $500 or $1,000, but items that go over that limit must be discussed.

It's best to get these differences out in the open while contemplating retirement, but most certainly ASAP after retirement, rather than having to contend with uncertainties or passive-aggressive behavior regarding money a year or two down the line. A clear understanding of both people's priorities helps most couples as they take individual and joint responsibility for financial decisions.

Another interesting exercise for couples is to think about what you would do if you won the lottery or received a large, unexpected inheritance. This is a fun scenario that everyone envisions at some point, but retiree couples should especially consider it in terms of their partner. Lottery winnings are generally considered income, and they must be shared according to state rules and personal agreements if you are married. With an inheritance, however, you probably don't *have* to share it with your spouse. But would you give half, or any of it, to him? Would that decision change if you were not married (by choice) or if you were in a gay relationship (currently without the possibility of legal sanction)? How much would you share with other people? What portion would you save? What things would you buy? What experiences would you seek? In what ways would it change you and your relationships? Speculating about imaginary windfalls can help to clarify your own values and explicate the degree to which two partners may approach money differently.

It may be helpful to think about your money personality. What choices do you make daily that constitute your financial profile? Suze Orman, the financial advisor, offers a system based on the following issues:

- *Saving*. How and when do you save money?

- *Spending*. How and when do you spend money?

- *Bills and records*. How and when do you pay bills and keep records?

- *Giving*. How and when do you give money to charities?

- *Relationships*. How and when do you lend money or discuss it?

- *Planning for the future*. How do you handle wills, trusts, insurance, and investment planning?

Then, based on answers to specific questions, Orman says that you can quickly categorize your personality as one of the following: financial daredevil, penny-pincher, financial wreck, spend-thrift, or a person on the right track.[2]

Some retirees have been so frugal, getting their kids through school and saving enough for the future, that they have trouble enjoying life now. In fact, these habits may have originated way back in childhood and been honed by many circumstances in midlife. It's true that thriftiness in retirement can give people a great sense of security, but it can also take quality out of their lives. The goal really should be to save and spend flexibly, not rigidly.

Even with limited income, everyone needs to flip the frugality switch occasionally in order to have some of the joys of life. For example, one American woman really stretched financially to buy a cottage in France. Her friends question her judgment, but she says that the French would understand. The house is a wise investment because it feeds her soul.[3]

What matters most with a couple is the extent to which their financial personalities mesh. In what ways are they similar or different? This does not mean that they have to be the same. In fact, a conservative partner often chooses a more flamboyant or extravagant person to balance things out. That works because it is consciously or subconsciously purposeful. But every couple should understand their mix by asking:

- Do our financial priorities reinforce positive or negative qualities in each other?

- Do we balance each other out, or do we always find our financial personalities in conflict?

As a general rule, mature people aim to have balance within their own financial personality as well as with their partner's ideas and values. That is, they want to be balanced and on the right track individually as well as together. The healthy use of money usually reflects a good self-image, and agreement between partners usually suggests a positive relationship.

Regardless of whether a couple is rich or poor, there should be some room for each individual's discretionary spending. It is demeaning and humiliating for any adult to have to ask permission for small expenditures. Rather, each couple will have to work out a comfortable level for personal control—based on their financial situation, each person's spending track record, and other factors. In any case, discussion and resolution of parameters will remove most conflicts before they arise.

On the big things, however, money is usually power. In the past, the person who earned the most money may have had more power. For example, the one with the highest-salaried job may have determined when they would move, what house they would buy, what kind of cars they would drive. Regardless of the past, however, retirement should be a time for equality in financial decision making. You are both in this adventure together, and you'll have a finite amount of money for the rest of your lives. You both need to be fully responsible if this is to be a happy time— and, of course, if one of you has to make decisions alone in the future. Old habits about money and power may need to be addressed and broken in order to facilitate this new equality.

The biggest problem with all of this financial priority setting is that none of us knows how long we will live. Here's the rub: You'll probably have to spend your savings in retirement, but it must also last for your lifetime. Thus you have to think hard about what you want to spend now while you, at the same time, plan for an uncertain future.[4]

Every retired couple has to navigate, therefore, between spending too much and living too frugally. Some couples joke about wanting to die broke—spending just enough so that their last check to the funeral home bounces. But this is easier said than done. If they spend too much in the early years, thinking that they won't live beyond a certain age, they may outlive their funds. For example, they could find, at age eighty-five or ninety, that they need a lot of help to stay in their home, but they may have used up their house equity and all of their savings. On the other hand, a couple may deprive themselves of things they really want in retirement. Then they both die relatively young, their savings go to ungrateful heirs, and everyone says, "What a shame!" There are no simple answers to this dilemma because none of us knows exactly how our life will unfold, but awareness of options is the most important part of the puzzle.

Financial Division of Labor

Financial communication between partners is often done poorly or not at all. One survey, by the credit card company Capital One, showed that nearly a third of all adults have never had a conversation about finances with their spouse or significant other.[5] And communication is especially relevant to retirees because their finances have had time to become very complicated. There may have been more than one marriage. There may be benefits from more than one job. Investments may be scattered.

Before or at retirement, all couples should think about what their division of financial labor has been in the past. What were your shared and separate tasks over the years? Who paid the bills or did the taxes? Who handled investments? Who bought major items? And why did it shake out that way?

While one or both partners were working, the major determining factors for the assignments were probably time and ability. But less healthy factors may have been utilized too: a need to control everything; fears of divorce, when the partner might try to drain accounts; laziness; lack of education; and many other factors. If the issues that determined past behavior were not healthy, they need to be examined very closely.

Retirement takes away most excuses about time, and new arrangements can be considered. Ideally, both partners should know the entire financial picture because one of them could die or become incapacitated at any time.

It is thoughtless and cruel to keep your financial life in disarray and expect your heirs to pick up the pieces after your death. And it could be very costly as well. Sharing information takes a little work and energy, but the payoff is worth it.

The most common arrangement for older couples is for one person to do the bills, while the other takes care of investments. Some couples exchange their roles every year or two so that they both understand the big picture. At the very least, they should have a meeting periodically to go over major activities subsumed under each role.

If you are in a late-life unmarried relationship, a second or third marriage, or another situation in which both individuals have had well-established financial lives, you may decide to keep your assets separate. Whether it's for legal or emotional reasons, both partners will then have to do all financial tasks alone. Some couples devise elaborate schemes of who pays for what, but the system should be acceptable to both people.

Irresponsibility, Secretiveness, Dishonesty

There are a few situations in which one partner need not, or should not, be totally open about finances, but no person should take that approach without a very honest, often painful discussion of why it is necessary.

One partner may have proved to be irresponsible, spending large amounts of money or going into debt. In fact, credit card debt is growing among seniors, partly because they are living longer, but also because some people use credit cards as supplemental income when they haven't saved enough. Surprisingly, the average debt of households headed by someone over sixty-five soared from $8,000 in 1992 to $23,000 in the year 2000.[6] This is particularly troublesome because, on fixed incomes, most seniors will never be able to pay off big debts. Some of these older people don't understand the huge fees associated with credit card debt. Others get into trouble because they have no other way to pay for necessities like medications. Still others use credit to help family members. But many seniors are simply irresponsible, and the debt can eventually crush them.

Bankruptcies are growing faster among seniors than in any other age group. According to a study done at Harvard, about eighty-two thousand Americans age sixty-five and older filed for bankruptcy in 2001—up 244 percent from 1991.[7]

In other older couples, trouble may occur because one person is too vulnerable to marketing gimmicks. There is no doubt that marketers are becoming very shrewd about the rapid growth in the number of seniors, as well as the shrinking of the younger generations. The average life expectancy for the industrialized world jumped from forty-seven years in 1900 to seventy-six in 2000, and this trend is expected to continue. Currently, 42 percent of the world's population live in countries where the birth rates are below replacement levels. So retirees are a huge group, and marketers are already changing to accommodate these factors. For example, retirees are showing less interest in acquiring things, but they have much more tendency to buy experiences. And they are willing to spend money to reinvent themselves, so the markets are good for cosmetic surgery, diets, and a new class of substances called "nutriceuticals," which combine drugs and nutrition.[8] It takes some intelligence and strength for seniors to resist all of the inappropriate marketing schemes and scams that target them.

Or trouble can occur when one partner gets sucked into giving large sums of money to people or charitable causes. As some people age, they become more softhearted and softheaded—

vulnerable to sob stories from relatives, friends, or organizations. Some of them give money secretively and irrationally. For example, one older couple divorced because the woman became a born-again Christian and suddenly gave almost all of their savings to her church. Another couple went into counseling after the man gave a large amount of money to a homeless young mother he met in a coffee shop. The wife found out about it only when she got their bank statement.

There really are people out there trying to steal our money, and grifters are getting more sophisticated every day. The scams range from "free" trips to Hawaii to phony securities and worthless businesses. Stories abound of retirees losing their nest egg, and most of these cases happen because people are vulnerable and/or greedy. We like to believe good things, even when they are too good to be true. It's a pity for retiree couples to live with constant fear and suspicion, but we need to remember that there is no such thing as high returns without high risk.[9]

Finally, gambling, alcoholism, or drug abuse may be interfering with one partner's financial judgment. These are addictions for which people need treatment, but the partner also has to make sure that he is not enabling the problem. In matters of retirement finances, usually the partner of an addicted person will have to take control.

In any of these situations, the responsible partner should try hard to outline the issues and gain cooperation. Perhaps the irresponsible party can get back on track with a low-limit credit card, or by paying certain bills every month, or by getting a part-time job to pay back debts. Financial counseling can also be helpful in resetting priorities—as well as psychological counseling to get at the underlying issues.

If all else fails and financial information really cannot be shared with your partner, make sure that you give the information to one or more other people—a child, sibling, close friend, banker, attorney, or other trusted person who can be named in your will and given power of attorney. These matters are too important to be left to chance in case you die before your partner does.

Questions to Ask Yourself and Your Partner

1. What is the difference between our pre- and post-retirement incomes? How well did we plan for this?
2. Did our expenses go up or down after retirement? By how much? Why? And how do we both feel about this?
3. How would I (you) propose to make up the difference? Should we draw from savings, work for money, and/or limit our lifestyle to live within our means?
4. What is my (your) financial personality? Where did these traits originate in our backgrounds?
5. How well do our financial personalities mesh? How do we handle any differences?
6. How would I (you) handle lottery winnings or a large inheritance vis-à-vis my (your) partner and others?
7. Have my (your) financial priorities changed over time? In what ways?
8. How would I (you) list my (your) financial priorities for the future?
9. How realistic is my (your) list, based on our resources?
10. How are our two lists similar and different?
11. Where do I (you) fit on the continuum between wanting to spend now and die broke versus leave a lot of money to our heirs? Are our intentions similar or different?
12. How long do I (you) think we will live? Will our money last that long?
13. What is our financial division of labor? How satisfactory is it? How should it change?
14. Am I (are you) irresponsible, secretive, or dishonest about money? How does this affect our relationship?

15. How vulnerable am I (are you) to unscrupulous marketers? How can we help each other with this vulnerability as we get older?

here Are Many Positions for Sex

Preconditions and Biases

Society has taught us many expectations and behaviors around sex. Our family of origin has had a huge influence on how we think about it, and religion may have played a major role. Furthermore, our own sexual experience has been imprinted on our brain, and every sexual partner we have ever had has played a part in how we handle sex at this stage of life. Our current partner's behavior and expectations—in the past and in the present—are also important to the way we approach sex. So we come to any sexual relationship in retirement with all kinds of accumulated ideas and biases that younger people do not have.

Despite all of our preconceived ideas, retirement tends to raise our expectations about sexual *activity* because we are finally, suddenly, free from the stresses and strains of work. Many of us, while working, found that our energies were easily depleted. It was hard to find the time, let alone relax enough to really enjoy sex. In the past, for time and relaxation reasons, sex was often better for us during vacations, but even that could be problematic if we were rushing around to see the sights or vacationing with other people, who put demands on our time and energy.

Now, retirement suggests that we can have sex morning, noon, or night—even though it's unlikely to be morning, noon, *and* night at this age. We think that traveling will stimulate us to be more creative and interested in sex. We assume that going to more romantic, possibly erotic movies and plays will also motivate us. Just holding hands for a walk in the park may turn us on. Nothing will stop us from enjoying each other physically.

All of this is great if both people want it and have had a pretty good sex life all along. But if one partner feels less involved than the other or more angry, or if one is more physically compromised, there will have to be some resolution.

When and How

Suddenly at retirement there is time for sex, but now there may also be disinterest, discomfort, or impotence. Each couple has to figure out their own sexual comfort level, and if their individual levels are vastly different, some negotiation will be necessary.

The story of one sixty-four-year-old man illustrates the variety in sexual functioning at retirement age. His wife divorced him suddenly three years ago, saying that she was just sick of being married, and shortly thereafter he ended up marrying an old friend he had worked with for many years. He says that with his former wife, he always had to bring a lot of matches to start a fire. With the current mate, he feels like he needs to bring a fire extinguisher! She is exhausting him, but he's enjoying the change. And he doesn't think this has anything to do with the newness of their relationship. The two women evidently had vastly different levels of sexual energy all of their lives.

Studies by the National Council on Aging show that about half of Americans age sixty and over are sexually active. Other research, by AARP, says that at age seventy-five, 58 percent of men but only 21 percent of women have sexual partners.[1] This suggests that those who are not sexually active may simply lack partners. They might not otherwise choose to be celibate.

In general, people need intimacy all of their lives—perhaps more than ever as they age and receive less stimulation from the outside world. Touching and being touched seems to be a primary need, and sex can clearly be an antidote to loneliness.

But there are a variety of things that can make sex difficult for retired couples:

- Older bodies may seem less attractive to both genders.

- Shame and embarrassment about one's appearance can inhibit openness.

- Age tends to change hormones and lower libido. Lowered testosterone levels in both genders can change people's feelings about sex.

- Illness can end or diminish the desire for sex.

- Postmenopausal women may need help for vaginal dryness.

- Older men may need more stimulation or medication for arousal.

- Men who can't perform easily may avoid sex.

- Chronic physical problems such as back pain and arthritis can interfere with pleasure from sex.

- People who are afraid of a heart attack or stroke may resist this kind of exertion—in most cases, unrealistically.

The human body is still not perfectly understood, but there are exciting new developments all the time in the field of sexuality. Similarly, geriatric specialists are turning more attention to the area of sex as they research and treat older couples.

Many of the sexual issues mentioned above can be improved by the couple themselves if they have the courage to be honest and take the time to talk openly with each other. Books such as Natalie Angier's *Woman: An Intimate Geography*[2] can be useful in understanding our complicated bodies, and books like *The New Love and Sex After 60* by Robert Butler and Myrna Lewis[3] might help a senior couple see themselves more realistically.

At the same time, problems that seem to have a physical basis should be discussed as soon as possible with a medical professional—or more than one if you're not getting satisfactory answers. And other sexual issues that have a more psychological or attitudinal component can usually be helped by the right counselor.

Unfortunately, there can be very serious sexual problems when one partner has dementia. This is tricky because sexual intimacy is sometimes a wonderful touchstone for a person who is losing touch with so much of the rest of the world, but it can also be a nightmare for the partner who cannot count on the usual behavioral patterns. It is impossible to relax with someone, even a long-term partner, who could scream at you or hit you at any minute. The partner of a person with Alzheimer's or other dementia may have to take drastic measures sometimes, including locks on doors, but sex with a mentally fading partner can also help to prolong what had once been a loving relationship.

We sometimes get messages from younger people or the media that sex among seniors is strange and rather disgusting, but that image is changing fast as the boomers move toward retirement. Because this group has always expected a lot out of life, they're trying to do everything they can to continue functioning sexually at the highest quality level possible.

With good health, sex can be part of the good life for as long as we live. It may not involve the passionate, lustful feelings of our twenties and thirties, but in many ways it's better now. It can be satisfying in different ways:

- One man in his eighties says that he gets a sexual thrill by reading with his wife side by side, holding her hand occasionally, and feeling the warmth of her.

- A new retiree in her fifties says that she and her partner have had the hottest sex of their lives since retirement. For the first time since she was a teenager, she feels rested and in good shape physically. She has found new sexual energy with no job, no kids at home, and no fear of pregnancy, and her partner is thrilled.

- After a picnic in the local park, a sixty-something couple pulled their blanket over themselves to watch the sunset. They both became sexually aroused—"sunsets being what they are"—and debated about whether to have intercourse there, but they worried about being interrupted by a cop and seeing their names in the paper for indecent exposure, so they consummated the act at home instead.

- A couple in their mid-sixties decided to have separate bedrooms because he snores and she likes to stay up late. They have subsequently developed little rituals around knocking on each other's door—"four knocks for cuddling or sex; two for other things"—and they say that sex is better than before because they pretend that it's kind of illicit now, and they don't take each other for granted.

Pros and Cons of the Viagra-Type Drugs

Viagra and similar drugs have been a godsend for some couples, but they are a horror show for others. When this impotence medication hit the market in 1998, it created great optimism that male sexual decline was now treatable much more easily, and millions of men—and their partners—have found it to be useful.

One problem is that nothing comparable has yet evolved for women. Researchers were hopeful that women would benefit from Viagra and similar products too, but the studies have been negative thus far. Testosterone, the "flavor of the month" for treating lagging libido in older women, has been used for several years in Europe, but European women have not found it terribly helpful, and there are many concerns about its long-term effects.[4]

A further problem with drugs such as Viagra is that couples can hardly be spontaneous about sex. Because it takes so long for the pill to kick in, awkward sexual planning can spoil the fun. Fortunately, it looks like the new generations of Viagra-like products do not require as much waiting. This has certainly been a major goal of research.

Another issue is that many couples had settled into a comfortable groove with their sexual lives, only to be shaken up when one partner suddenly wants—and can physically have—a lot more sex. Quite a few women wish that scientists hadn't messed with Mother Nature!

Even more troubling may be the fact that these drugs seem to have encouraged some men to have affairs. They suddenly feel more sexual, but their partner may not want to accommodate them, so they look for someone else. Or perhaps they just like—and can physically have—more variety now. Or there is someone outside the committed relationship to whom they've been attracted, but they have hesitated to pursue her because impotence loomed as a possible problem. Now they needn't worry about that. In fact, it may even be easier to time the drug taking to the hour the new couple will meet at the motel than it is to the bedtime he and his usual partner might have at home.

Finally, no one knows the long-term effects of these pharmaceuticals. Some people fear that these drugs are being pushed too hard by vested corporate and medical interests without enough research. All foreign substances that we put into our bodies have some side effects, and the extent of unintended consequences is sometimes not known for many years.

There will surely be many pharmaceutical developments ahead for treating sexual dysfunction in older couples. Seniors want it, and big bucks lie on the horizon for drug companies and their stockholders. Using these products will require caution and judgment from all of us because retaining our health is more important at retirement age than ever before, yet Viagra and its clones are tools that were not available to previous generations of retirees, and they give us wonderful new options. Each couple can decide whether these drugs are helpful or hurtful for them. As with other decisions, of course, some negotiating and compromising may be required.

Fidelity or Not

Past is usually prologue to the question of whether a couple will be monogamous or not in retirement. If one or both partners have had other relationships in the past, this pattern may continue, but there are a few reasons why affairs often stop in later life:

- People get tired. Pursuing and maintaining an outside relationship may take more energy now than you want to expend.

- You become less attractive to potential sexual partners as you age—and as you lose the income and power of your career—so your opportunities decrease.

- A partner who silently suffered through affairs all of these years may suddenly get stronger in retirement, when earning power, prestige, and image don't matter as much. For example, as a high-level executive, he may have felt that the proper wife and family were important to his advancement, but now he reports to nobody, and he is fed up with her philandering. Perhaps he gives her an ultimatum to choose her artist boyfriend or him, and she won't choose, so he files for divorce.

Then again, there are a couple of reasons why retirees may be even more likely to start an affair at this stage of life than they were before:

- You have more time on your hands and more opportunity to plan.

- If your ego has been deflated by the loss of job status or other things, an affair can make you feel desirable and young again.

- There are more single women than men at this age, so men are definitely in demand.

- The excitement of an affair can be like a drug. A different body in bed can seem much more appealing than the old partner's, and your existing sexual problems with the old partner might disappear with the new one.

- There is no longer the fear of losing a job or your colleagues' respect if you are found out.

- Perhaps the thrill of possibly getting caught spurs you along like a kid in a candy store.

- Both men and women in a long-term relationship may be bored—not sure whether a divorce would be so bad.

Regardless of past or present performance, retired couples have a wide range of possible behaviors in the area of fidelity—from open marriages, where both people are free to have other sexual relationships without partner recrimination, to people who say they will kill their partner over an affair, and sometimes literally do. Some couples are honest about where they sit on this fidelity continuum; others never share their ideas with each other or anyone else.

A group of six couples in their 50s and 60s watched the movie Unfaithful *together and discussed it afterward. Richard Gere and Diane Lane play a middle-aged couple who seem quite happy with their young child and suburban life. Then, unexpectedly, Lane falls into a passionate affair with a young Frenchman. Gere misses most of the clues but eventually is forced to see the reality, and his violent reaction changes all of their lives forever.*

The group members were fascinated by the range of their reactions to the film. The men were generally more judgmental than the women about Lane's affair, but they acknowledged that they might feel differently if Gere were the one being unfaithful. Two women really hated Lane and her behavior, calling her "irresponsible" and "destructive," but two other women and one man thought that Lane's affair was understandable and potentially healthy. Most of the women saw signs in Gere's behavior of neglect and insensitivity, which the men generally did not see.

The range of values about marital fidelity among the group was explored. Some people were adamant about physical and moral commitment in a relationship and rights and wrongs, while others had quite flexible ideas. These twelve people ran the gamut from those who liked the concept of open marriage and freedom for each partner to make her own decisions to those who said that infidelity should always result in divorce, if not murder.

The conclusion was that few people talk about fidelity either before or during marriage, but we all have strong ideas about it. Each couple really has to figure it out for themselves.

In reality, there are many couples who think that they have a totally faithful relationship, swearing that neither one of them would ever cheat. But then it happens, and the partner has to think carefully about the consequences. More often than not, partners decide that the relationship is worth maintaining, but there will almost always be residual damage. And that damage will have to be worked through if the couple is to go forward without tremendous difficulty. Many people forgive, but few are able to totally forget. Couples need to know that sexual infidelity has totally ruined some partnerships, but it has actually enhanced others, making the relationship better when both people deal with it honestly and seriously.

In long-term relationships, there are particular bonds that can hold people together despite infidelity—such as children, mutual friends, fear of growing old alone, and simple inertia. But there can also be the feeling at this age that time is limited, and you don't want to spend the rest of your life with this person.

Perhaps the most difficult implication of infidelity, especially for older people who need to protect their health, is the possibility of sexually transmitted disease. One couple, for example, was never able to repair their relationship after an STD was brought home by the husband. They are still together ten years later, but they have never had intercourse since that incident.

HIV/AIDS is growing among older people. One out of every ten people diagnosed with AIDS in the United States is over age fifty.[5] Most of the new cases of AIDS or other STDs are probably single people who are openly dating, but some are undoubtedly partners who are unfaithful and lazy about protection. When one person in this situation contracts AIDS or another STD and continues to have sex at home, his partner becomes vulnerable too.

A few older men also admit that they use prostitutes—generally without their partner's knowledge. Prostitutes may be more likely to use condoms than "civilians" are, but the less careful ones do slip up, and the customer could end up with a disease.

Separate Bedrooms or Not

Separate bedrooms have saved a lot of retiree relationships. When the working world has disappeared and you are with each other most of the time, this can be a wonderful way to get some privacy. Other reasons that couples talk about for choosing different bedrooms include:

- The ability to set the temperature and airflow the way you want it. Men have notoriously higher body temperatures than women, and separate rooms can stop a lot of silly fights.

- The chance to go to bed and get up when you please, without your sleep being disturbed by your partner.

- The ability to read in bed or watch TV from bed to your heart's content, if you wish.

- The ability to stretch those old bones across the bed without infringing on your partner's space.

- The chance to get away from a snoring partner, without having to poke her all night.

- The possibility that cuddling and sex can be more romantic when it takes a little more effort.

Certainly there are many seniors who really want to sleep together. They make compromises about the inconveniences and really enjoy the closeness. The only problem with sharing is when couples feel that they have to stay in the same room because of what their kids or their friends might think. Retirement age should have earned everyone the right to make independent decisions without worrying about what others will say.

Furthermore, it doesn't have to be a permanent decision. Like many things in life, we don't always know how something will feel until it happens. Separate rooms can resolve some thorny problems in the relationship, but this arrangement may also be changed at any time if it doesn't feel right.

Anger and Unresolved Problems

Experts agree that the brain is the most important sex organ, and this is especially true as we age because we've had so much time to layer that brain with all kinds of issues.

Anger is a special impediment to good sex, and some partners are still angry about things that happened years ago. They've built up so many disappointments and petty annoyances over the years that the smallest thing will set them off. Fortunately, there are also some people who can totally separate their physical need for sex from their thoughts and grudges. They feel that good sex is their right, and they don't let anything psychological get in their way. But most people find that the physical side of life is greatly affected by the mental. One hopes that by retirement age we've learned the difference between real problems and minor annoyances, but in most relationships of any duration, there is probably some unresolved anger.

Couples who find ways, with or without help, to work through the anger issues usually come out stronger and grateful for the release—because the angry feelings have usually hurt the individual as much as, or more than, his partner. Angry comments and actions may initially be meant as revenge toward your mate, but when you prevent yourself from having good sex, you are really depriving yourself of pleasure.

Gender Differences

Most of us should also, by this age, be very aware of gender differences, but despite research that is helping us to identify the innate differences between men and women, lots of fights about sex still emanate from the mistaken perception that men and women are the same. We could learn to laugh at many of the things that used to make us angry if we would just recognize the differences in mental wiring between the genders. This subject is very complicated, but here is one research-based explanation from *The Owner's Manual for the Brain*.[6]

The male-differentiated brain has a thicker right cerebral cortex, a corpus callosum (which connects the hemispheres) that is thinner relative to brain weight, denser neurons, nuclei up to eight times larger than those of the female brain, and a hypothalamus that works on the principle of negative feedback to maintain constancy—that is, both highs and lows are moderated toward a middle range. The female-differentiated brain has a thicker left cerebral cortex, a corpus callosum that is thicker relative to brain weight, neurons that are less dense, smaller nuclei, and a hypothalamus that works on the principle of positive feedback to increase fluctuation in the system—that is, highs get higher and lows get lower, resulting in more emotionality.

The result is that the two brains are hardwired differently: the male for doing and the female for talking. The male tends to become more proficient in math, spatial reasoning, aggression, competition, self-assertion, self-confidence, and self-reliance. The female tends to become more proficient in language, sensory awareness, memory, social awareness, and relationships apparently due to the relatively thicker corpus callosum, which allows freer communication between the two hemispheres.

The factors influencing love and sex are complicated because they are based on both mental wiring and personality structure, but two of the author's most relevant conclusions are as follows. "In most male-female relationships, conflict arises when the female wants to talk and the male wants to act; the classic example is the female preference in lovemaking for greater foreplay and the male preference for immediate release." And women "tend to explain their affairs as resulting from dissatisfaction with the marital relationship: they're looking for a replacement. On the other hand, men who have affairs are as likely to feel good about their primary relationship as they are to be unhappy with it. This is all understandable from an evolutionary point of view."

The following vignette, making the rounds on the Internet, may be instructive about gender differences—that is, women as talkers and men as doers:

Her side of the story: My husband was in an odd mood last night. We had planned to meet at a bar for a drink, but I was a little late because I had been at a doctor's appointment. I thought he was upset about that, and I apologized, but he said there was nothing wrong. He knew that I was concerned about getting the results of a colonoscopy, but he never asked me about it. Then we decided to go to a restaurant, but he was still acting funny. I was getting really worried, and I asked him if he was angry at me, but he said no. In the car on the way home, I said how much I love him, but he just touched my arm casually and turned away. You know, he didn't say it back or anything. When we got home, I noticed that he had bought some new clothes, and I started wondering if he was going to leave me. I tried to get him to talk, but he just switched on the TV. Finally I said I was going to bed. A few minutes later he came upstairs, and to my surprise we made love. But he still seemed really distracted, so I just turned over and cried myself to sleep. I just don't know how to handle this. I really think he's having an affair.

His side of the story: My golf game was lousy yesterday. Bought some new clothes at the club because I'm getting fat, and I can't putt for shit anymore! Felt awfully tired last night. Got laid though!

Forgiveness and Exploration

There is a movement among some young and middle-age people to call themselves born-again virgins when they have had too much indiscriminate sex. These men and women have decided not to have sex anymore unless it is meaningful.

Older couples, who have had sexual problems in the past, might adopt this kind of philosophy about starting over. They can try to wipe the slate clean because retirement is a great time to explore their sexuality anew. Instead of wallowing in deep-seated sexual disappointments, retirement should encourage motivated couples to try again. Many seniors are very aware that the world has become more open about sex. They see more movies and plays and TV programs with sexual themes, and some of these people get curious about good sex. They develop a sense of humor about it. They are willing to drop some inhibitions and explore.

Furthermore, as they age, people usually try to achieve more integrity in their lives. Individuals try to integrate various parts of their personality, and couples attempt to bring the disparate parts of their relationship into harmony. Denial of problems no longer serves any useful role, but letting go of the past, difficult as that can be, can help a person feel more free. This, in turn, may allow the couple to move forward constructively in their sexual life. For many partners, forgiveness is at the core of relationship growth and sexual fulfillment.

Butler and Lewis say in their book that physically fit partners are the most likely to enjoy sex in their later years, and both men and women may be better lovers as they age because they take things more slowly and have more patience. Sex can be great at retirement age for those who are wise givers and take good care of themselves.

Surveys show that many older couples have great sex, while other retiree mates have no sex at all. How do couples position themselves on this continuum? One woman answered the question this way: "With lots of alcohol!" We all know that too much alcohol is a libido *depressant,* but I would add to this seventy-year-old's solution, "Whatever it takes!"

Sex for seniors can still be wonderful, especially if sex means more than intercourse. The mechanics of sex may change according to age, physical health, and desire, but couples can find sensual happiness in all kinds of ways. Touching and affectionate contact feel good at any age. Maybe they are even appreciated more with gray hair and a few extra pounds.

Some people forget how much fun it was as a teenager to kiss and touch each other endlessly, even without intercourse. That's sexual pleasure too, and it may have been sorely missed when you were a busy, middle-aged couple. Physical tenderness of all kinds can open up pathways between two people that were previously blocked.

Erica Jong, whose infamous book *Fear of Flying* was published in 1973, now says that sexual passion is overrated. It's the talking and laughing and sharing of goals that keeps couples together. We are pair-bonding creatures—like geese and swans. We need partnerships because they keep us from raw intimacy—from having to be too open too much of the time. The glue that holds two people together consists of laughter, companionship, tenderness, and sex, but we would be much happier if we changed our unrealistic expectations of marriage.[7] Overall, feelings of intimacy and friendship usually prove to be the most important elements of sex.

Questions to Ask Yourself and Your Partner

1. On a continuum of sexual activity from none to lots, where are we placed currently? Do we agree about this positioning?
2. On a scale of one to ten, how would I (you) rate my (your) satisfaction with our sexual relationship?
3. How has our sexual relationship changed over the years? Is it better or worse now? Why?
4. Do we need medical and/or psychological help with any sexual problems? Are both of us willing to seek it? Why or why not?
5. How does my (your) self-esteem about appearance affect our sex life?
6. Are we too critical of each other's appearance?
7. If we have tried Viagra or similar drugs, what has been the effect for both of us? If we have not tried them, do we want to?
8. What level of fidelity does each of us expect in our relationship? Why?
9. What was our history pre-retirement regarding fidelity? And how do I (you) feel about it?
10. How do I (you) feel about separate bedrooms? If we disagree, how can this be resolved?
11. Are anger or unresolved problems affecting our sex life? How can I (you) come to terms with these feelings and move forward?
12. How have our gender differences affected our sexual relationship in the past? Now?

13. Is forgiveness an adequate part of our relationship? How about tenderness?
14. Are we both willing to drop some of our sexual inhibitions in order to explore?

9.

Children, Grandchildren, Other Relatives, and Friends

Parenting

Parenting adult children well is not easy, and there is wide variation in how much involvement parents have, and should have, in their grown kids' lives. Some retiree couples want to remain very close to their children physically and emotionally, spending a lot of time together. Others hit the middle ground, avoiding too much dependence on their kids and vice-versa. And other people feel that they've had enough of parenting. They usually love their kids and will help out in an emergency, but they've moved on to other priorities. The crunch comes, of course, when partners do not agree, and there have been plenty of divorces over this issue.

If we assume that most couples have their children when they are between twenty-five and thirty-five, the kids of a sixty-five-year-old retiree couple will be between thirty and forty. They are usually established in a career by then and perhaps have children of their own. There are lots of exceptions to this age assumption—for example, an older man who married a younger woman may find himself retiring at sixty-five with teenagers. But in general, retirement rarely overlaps with children just leaving the nest. There has been some time for the couple to reestablish their relationship separate from their kids. And with some luck, there have been opportunities for them all to become friends on an adult level.

But sometimes retirement upsets the applecart, and the pressure can come from either direction.

The Parents' Side

Leaving the working world behind often causes retirees to reexamine every area of their lives. Among other things, they reflect on their adult children in new ways—perhaps wanting to invest more time and energy in the kid's life, maybe deciding that the child is in good shape and doesn't need them, or possibly seeing the kid as a hopeless case to whom they have given enough and from whom they must make a break. Retirement somehow empowers them to change the dynamics of the parent-child relationship.

With time on their hands and no work to think about, the parents sometimes want a lot more involvement with their young-adult progeny and any grandchildren. This can keep the parents from having to make other, more difficult decisions about what to do with their time and energy. Some parents hang on to their children because without the parenting role they feel useless. They may find pleasure and satisfaction more with their children than anywhere else—often because they have put all their eggs in the family basket. They don't know where else to put their efforts. They cannot conceive of equal joys in other areas.

This can happen especially when the partner relationship is troubled and there has been little satisfaction in that arena for one or both people. Or even if the seniors' relationship is OK, parents may really be emotionally unable to stop their involvement with the kids and may have little insight about it.

At the other extreme, some parents can be very selfish about their own needs. They may feel that they sacrificed enough when the children were young and that this is their time. They know that they won't live forever, and they're going to get and do everything they can for themselves now. Or the couple may have been driven away by ungrateful kids who want too much, financially or emotionally.

We're all aware of parents who move into a small apartment as soon as the last child goes off to college, making it clear that there is no place to come home to. We see couples who feel that they've done their job and almost never call their kids. Either they've lost interest because they're totally self-involved or talking with their children brings up such unpleasant feelings that they avoid contact. Whether the reason for the separation is justified or not, these parents make it clear that they have better things to do.

The pattern for involvement with adult children often follows gender stereotypes, with women, at the extremes, wanting symbiosis with their progeny and men wanting more separation. Women often complain that their partner has had no idea what parenting is all about—especially as the kids got older and could no longer be controlled.

But men can be overly attached also, especially if the man feels guilty about having been too busy in the past. In that case, the father often goes overboard after retirement, trying to make up, inappropriately, for all the years he was more concerned with work than his kids. Or if he has few other interests in life, his kids look like an easy focus for his retirement, without having to think about other choices.

The Adult Child's Side

Of course, grown children make this relationship a two-way street. Some of them aren't mature or stable enough to stand on their own two feet. They lean on their parents financially and emotionally, expecting a lot of help. Or in the other extreme, some adult children reject their parents in the most heartbreaking ways, and it's often hard, from the outside, to know why.

The adult children may assume that they can call on their parents more now for all kinds of help, and they know that it will be hard for the parents to refuse. (Once your child, always your child.) Sometimes these young adults are struggling to get good care for their kids while they work, and they expect their parents to babysit. Sometimes they are struggling financially. They see their parents with Social Security and a pension, a house paid off, and extra money for vacations and other luxuries, and they expect some financial help to come their way. They don't believe it when their parents tell them that there will be less money post-retirement to treat for meals or pay for the grandchildren's clothes and sports.

With every significant life change, parents and children need to have honest discussions about what they expect from one another, and retirement is no exception. Everyone's ideas about the relationship need to be explored and understood. When either side wants too much involvement, the other side needs to say, "Wait a minute! Perhaps we should have less but higher-quality time together."[1] When the kids expect more money than you are willing to give, parents need to explain that the money still belongs to the people who earned it. Any unrealistic expectations need to be handled directly and clearly—but always with love and respect.

The psychologist Carl Jung said that the most powerful influence on a child is the unlived life of the parent—our own longings, missed opportunities, or losses, which have created emotional holes in our heart. We may have wished for things in our own life that never materialized, so we put pressure on our kids to achieve what we want. For example, we may stay close so that we can help our child be the perfect parent—the one that we were not. Or our fears may be placed on our children, giving them subtle pressure to *not* take certain risks. Or we may stay overly involved because we haven't developed many resources outside of parenting, and we're afraid to tackle other aspects of life. On the other hand, for those of us who want to stay far away from our adult kids, we may do it because we have unwarranted fears about dependence—ours or theirs—or we may be repeating a pattern experienced with our own parents.

Ideally, retired couples need to find that delicate balance where they have strong, adult, mature, and loving relationships with their children. Defining these terms and making this a reality is often an area for partner conflict because people see things differently, but it can also be a wonderful benefit of being coupled at this stage of life. That is, partners can help each other achieve this balance by discussing incidents in which the picture seems to tilt in one direction or the other. If one parent seems to get sucked in too far, the other can gently point out that adult children need to lead their own lives. Or if one parent seems too selfish or cold, the mate can carefully mention the importance of those kids—not the least of which is that they may someday choose your nursing home.

It's no surprise that retired partners often have honest disagreements about parenting. That probably happened when the kids were young too, as in the following example:

Emma and Pete both were physicians who worked hard throughout their adulthood, but they also raised two great kids and had a happy family life. They thought they were exemplary in their decisions and compromises, although they disagreed about many things. For example, back when they were dating, they had one rip-roaring fight about whether children should be paid for their grades (she had been; he hadn't) and whether kids should ever be spanked (he had been; she hadn't). After a few too many arguments about these issues when the children were young, Pete says that he decided to go Emma's way. Maybe she was right; in any case, he didn't want any more fights in front of the kids.

Emma always gave the teenage kids more money than Pete would have. She demanded good grades—and the kids got them—but she didn't expect much work around the house. She says that she always loved them unconditionally, while Pete's love had strings attached.

Now both children have kids of their own, and ironically, they have very different parenting styles. The boy is just like his father would like to have been, strict and demanding; the girl is as open, giving, and accepting as her mother was.

Pete tries to hide his pleasure in his son's style, but Emma sees it, and it makes her furious. She lets both Pete and her son, as well as his wife, know that she disapproves. She accuses her son of becoming tough, and she says that she hardly knows him anymore. She has bought his children candy when he forbade it and designer-label clothes when he was against it. All of this has led to some difficult scenes between them, which Emma has "solved" by making herself scarce. From time to time Pete finds himself in the middle between his son and his wife, and he is not a very good mediator because he enjoys the rift on some subconscious level. He has tried to maintain a good relationship with their daughter too, but Emma, in small ways, pushes him out of that. Once she even said, "This one is mine."

It has been almost ten years since Pete and Emma retired, and neither of them expected the turmoil that parenting still creates for them. They talk periodically about going to counseling, but they are both too stubborn to consider any alternative thoughts or behaviors. These differences in parenting styles go back to Pete and Emma's childhoods, and their effects are now being seen in the fourth generation. They feel sad that they are missing out on the united, happy family that they worked so hard to achieve.

Two loving parents often have different styles and needs vis-à-vis their adult kids, but they have to be mature and honest about it. When they cannot, or don't want to, resolve their different approaches, they usually have three choices:

- Make compromises; meet each other halfway, essentially spending more or less time with the kids than each of you would ideally like.

- Do your own thing happily, with each of you developing a different relationship with the kids.

- Do your own thing angrily, with resentment building toward your partner. This choice is, of course, destructive to the whole family.

Many older parents long for time alone with an adult child—the core relationship that will always be special—but they are reluctant to ask for it. The son- or daughter-in-law may be terrific, but that is not your child. The grandkids are wonderful too, but you don't have forty years of history with them. Our children in their middle years are busy, and they often think that socializing needs to be done with the entire family in order to save time, but either side should be able to ask for some meetings alone. If that happens naturally and easily from time to time, a lot of hard feelings could be prevented.

One interesting communication technique is through letters.

Two men I know have written to their children since the kids were little, and one has continued throughout the years. Both of these men say that they used airplane time to write; there was something about being high in the sky—and maybe a little high on alcohol too—that made them think warmly about their parenting role. One of the men gave or sent the letters as soon as he got home; the other is saving them in a package for some future date. For some reason, fewer women seem to write letters to their kids. Perhaps it's because verbal communication tends to be easier for them than it is for men. But from either parent, letters can be a lovely gift. Now, with additional time in retirement, parents should think about writing letters to their adult children. These messages will be valued, even if they are only received after your death.

And please try to write or verbally record your family history. Many of us, at retirement age, wish that we had such a thing from our deceased parents, but few of us do. We were always too busy to videotape or audio-record the stories that we can barely remember now, and we wish that our parents had written them out for us. Well, do it for your kids now. Organize your thoughts just a little bit, and the thing will start to flow. Computers make writing relatively easy for a task like this because you can add, rearrange, and edit later. Just make yourself get started. Your kids may not thank you now, but they or their children will surely be grateful after you're gone.

Related to family history is the fun that you can have comparing memories with your adult children. Indeed, many a dinner conversation can be absorbed in this way. It can be absolutely fascinating to hear their take on an event or experience in the past because it so often differs from your own. Of course, this should be done at a calm time, not in the midst of a fight. In addition, you have to be willing to hear some negatives about your parenting role if you want them to feel safe and open up.

The reason that this sharing is so interesting is that memories are made into stories in order to organize them and remember them better, and we often need a spark to trigger a seemingly lost recollection.[2] All memories are reconstructions, and no memory is truly accurate. In many ways, what we remember is more important than what truly happened. So it's fun to compare notes within a family. Some of your most enlightening conversations with your adult children can be about their memories—and yours.

Stepparenting

It's hard enough to establish balanced relationships when both partners are the parents of those adult kids, but it's even harder when second or third marriages result in all types of blended families. Do you call all of them "ours" and try to pretend it's one big, happy family? Do you always see the kids together, as a couple? Or do you decide that the kids really have more relationship with the parent than with the stepparent and try to see them separately? Do you do both at different times, and what are the criteria? Do you feel free to criticize each other's kids or comment on each other's behavior with the kids, or should you always keep your mouth shut about that? These are all additional balancing acts in blended families, which couples have to work out with their own children and each other.

Grandparenting

It has been said that babies are like cocaine to grandparents; they want one more opportunity to love something that hasn't disappointed them yet.[3] Gail Sheehy says that grandparenting is about pure love. A whole new valve opens up, and we are given another chance at life.[4] Grandchildren soften our hearts. They even provide an opportunity sometimes for reconciliation with our children.

AARP estimates that grandparents are spending over $30 billion each year on their grandchildren.[5] Some of this is because the older generation has to pick up the slack when their kids can't manage, but most of this is for wonderful extras. Grandparents buy toys that are unconscionably expensive—and sometimes educational. They buy special items of clothing. They help pay for private education from preschool through graduate school. They sometimes pay for extras like sports fees, tutors, and music lessons. They take the grandkids on trips. They give generous birthday and holiday gifts. They may even provide generation-skipping trusts, which give the grandkids a wonderful financial cushion for education or other expenses.

But most important, grandparents give time and love. They are often more patient than the kid's parents are. For example, one man who cares for his two grandchildren after school every weekday has been teaching world capitals to the seven-year-old. She loves cuddling on his lap and looking at maps, and she now can point out almost all the world's countries and capitals. What a legacy of learning and warmth!

But finding the balance between too much and too little grand-parenting is not always easy, and partners do not always agree. What is too much time, and what is not enough? What is too much money to give, and what is stinginess? There is a lot of potential here for problems with your own children about time and money, and there is plenty of grist for relationship discord with them too. In the most difficult situations, lack of agreement between retiree partners on this subject can lead to estrangement and even divorce.

Some retirees see themselves as the disciplinarians of their grandchildren. At times the kids' parents want it this way, but more often this interference causes conflict. It is truly difficult to watch your adult child, or that child's partner, parenting in a way that you do not approve of, but grandparents really have to bite their tongue. Unless the grandchildren are clearly being abused, grandparents have to remember that they had their shot at parenting; another parent is setting the rules now.

Sometimes grandparents devote a lot of time and get enormous gratification from the little ones, only to be devastated later when their grandchildren have no time for them. The pain of this rejection is palpable in some people's stories. But in the best-case scenarios, good impressions have been made. Bonds have been formed, and memories will come back.[6] The kids will not forget you.

And this generation of grandparents is certainly changing the rules about activities. They are hiking, biking, and swimming with the kids. They are taking them for summers while the parents work. They are being sought out for advice on problems that the grandchildren won't even share with their parents.

The hardest grandparent role comes when it must be full-time. Thousands of grandparents step in every year when their own children die, go to jail, abandon their kids, or struggle with addiction or mental illness. And many grandparents rise to the occasion temporarily when their kids are called away to military duty. In situations where foster care is the only other option, most grandparents accept the responsibility. And sometimes they have to fight to take legal custody away from their own neglectful or abusive children.

Dreams of a footloose and financially secure retirement must be put aside for these retiree couples. They may have to use their savings in unanticipated ways, and they'll probably be physically exhausted. They may lose touch with their peers because they have no free time, and they will feel out of touch with the young parents of other kids.

They also have to struggle with why their own children were so irresponsible, and they often feel some guilt about their role in that. Furthermore, they are often dealing with traumatized grandchildren who will not heal or feel secure easily. But most custodial grandparents say that they have learned not to sweat the small stuff, and the kids are definitely worth it. They can be a lot of fun. They keep you young and bring you tremendous joy.

When these custodial grandparent couples forgo their own pleasures and health to step up to the plate, the potential for stress and interpersonal conflict is very high. Partners in this situation need to have a deep understanding of what's happening here and a strong commitment to helping each other get through it. If one of the partners is angry or depressed about the arrangement, the couple will probably need counseling to survive.

Aged Parents

With people living much longer these days, it is not unusual for a sixty-something retiree couple to have parents in their eighties or nineties. Caring for your own parents or supporting the care of your partner's parents can really put a lot of stress on the relationship.

Some people are willing to care for their own parent, but they refuse to get involved with their partner's, and then they hear, "You let your mother live here, but you won't tolerate mine?" Or one partner may spend money on the care of her parent without the agreement of her mate, and he becomes furious when the truth comes out. Even the act of visiting one's parent—how often, how long, with what gifts—can become a battleground.

Emotions run high in our relationships with our elderly parents partially because some of those feelings go all the way back to childhood. We know so well how to push each other's buttons. Nerves can become frayed, and exhaustion easily sets in, especially because none of us are young anymore. Any person has the right to expect support from his partner during hard times with aging parents, but that person also has to realize that it's not his partner's parent. You can't expect the same kind of caring from your mate that you feel for your parent. The decisions and responsibilities reside rightly on your shoulders. And you have to take, with or without support, the kinds of actions that you can live with comfortably for the rest of your life.

Perhaps you can elicit a little more help from your partner if you communicate your feelings well. Possibly you'll need to remind your partner that this is temporary. The money being spent or the travel being postponed will not be forever. Your devotion *can* be shown to both your parent and your partner at the same time. You may need to reassure your partner that he is loved too. But if caring for a parent is important to you and your partner does not understand, you may have to let the chips fall where they may.

Disabled Relatives

Caring for a disabled child or other relative is an even more difficult task. A retarded adult child, for example, or your paraplegic brother can be a lifelong responsibility. Divorces are common in these marriages because the stress level is so high. At retirement, when other couples are seeking fun, these couples still have a lot of unpaid work ahead.

If the patient is your child, you may have had no choice about her location earlier, but you might be arguing now about whether institutionalization would be better than home care. And you and your partner are probably struggling in very different ways with feelings of guilt, shame, and anger. If the dependent person is a brother or another relative, you may be the only couple in the family capable of looking after him, but that kind of decision can't have been made easily. For example, in a book about being the sibling of someone who is difficult or damaged, Dr. Jeanne Safer explores the far-reaching effects on the lives of those who are considered the normal ones.[7] Among these effects are survivor guilt and fear of contagion, so taking on responsibility for a sibling or other relative at retirement age—or continuing this responsibility into retirement age—is very difficult.

If one partner is unwilling to participate, leaving all of the work to the other, resentment will build up. On the other hand, if one person is too involved and too giving, there's no partner relationship left. There are legitimate questions that both of you should ask, such as:

- Are we some kind of martyrs?

- Can someone else help?

- What about us?

The key is to find a mutually satisfactory compromise that meets many needs but also allows some space for the kind of retirement we all deserve.

Friends

There is a wide range in how we feel about our friends. To some people, friends are more important than family. We choose them; they keep us whole and sane. To others, however, friends are suspect, unnecessary, never to be totally trusted.

Couples who want a lot of togetherness may have very few outside friends. They are more comfortable with each other than with anyone else. Their primary social life is with their children and grandchildren, or perhaps with their parents and siblings.

If they do have friends, it's usually couples. They seldom have the desire to go out separately, and they have little need to see friends of their own gender. If either of them did begin seeking other friends, there might be jealousy or conflict.

At the other extreme, some people want a lot of friends or a diversity of friends who are separate from the primary relationship. Life seems richer that way. You can freely pursue events and activities in which your partner has no interest. You don't have to listen to complaints from your mate about the friends you choose. You return home more energized. You might bring home some interesting experiences and stories.

Close friends have even been referred to as healers. They know our assets and flaws, and they love us anyway. They can be a safety net, protecting us against the losses that come with age. Indeed, according to a Standford University study, confiding in a friend can pay big dividends in our physical and mental health. It actually has a positive effect on the central nervous system, which in turn helps the cardiovascular and immune systems. On the other hand, when we have no close friends and both body and brain work to suppress emotions, stress hormones raise our blood pressure and dampen our immune responses. Overall, good friends are critically important to successful aging.[8]

For reasons that are probably both genetic and cultural, women seem to need same-gender friendships more than men do. And since the women's movement in the 1970s, women seem to value one another even more. They have learned to be less competitive and more cooperative than they used to be with other women.

Men often name their wife or another woman when asked about their best friend, but men are definitely gaining in their same-gender friendships because they too were helped by social movements in the 1970s and 1980s. Men have always liked to golf or play tennis or ski together, but now we also hear of things like woodworking/discussion groups and men-only gardening clubs. Men have traditionally engaged one another only around activities, but now they seem to be talking too.

Some retired men have been meeting for years in small-town coffee shops around the country. Now Starbucks and its competitors have facilitated even more gathering places. One retired group, for instance, runs together three mornings a week, ending up with long sessions over coffee. Another group of retired men commandeers a particular table at a diner every morning—even on weekends—but membership is very fluid and flexible. They say they don't complain too loudly when someone brings a woman.

Resentment and jealousy can rear their ugly heads when one partner spends more time with same-gender friends than the other does, but these couples need to realize that people have different needs. If one partner's needs are being met through friendships, the other partner invariably benefits because his mate will be happier.

This can get a little tricky when friendships are with the opposite gender, but retirees need to take some lessons from the younger generation on this issue. Young people have really mastered the ability to have friends of both genders, and their lives are better for it. If we are open to all kinds of experiences, it shouldn't matter what gender the friend is. A man may have fun in a coed golf group. A woman may enjoy going to concerts with a man she met in her music class. We all need to be secure enough to handle our partner's mixed-gender relationships because these friendships can indirectly enhance our life too. If we are too threatened or too afraid of an affair developing, we need to realize that friendship *can* be separated from sex. If our kids and grandkids can do it, surely we can too. But, of course, it never hurts for the target of jealousy to boost her partner's sense of security by noting that he is still the one!

Be a Friend to Get a Friend

Most Americans are very self-absorbed. They spend a lot of energy and money concentrating on themselves. But as they age, they often wonder whom they can depend on—whom they really care about and who really cares about them. Furthermore, because they read studies about the positive effects of having nurturing friends as a senior, they want more of that.

If you don't want to grow old alone, or with your partner as your only pal, you need to be a good, reliable friend first. You need to realize that generous people will not associate with you or be there for you if you are selfish. Forget about potential friends who are shallow, manipulative, demanding, and greedy because they will only be looking out for themselves. Try not to pick friends blindly, according to what you want them to be like; see them for who they really are. Be alert to signs of people who are emotionally damaged and dysfunctional because it's unlikely that they will change in response to you. Stay as far away from those people as you can.

If you have been a narcissistic person who thinks mostly about yourself, or if you are saddled with a narcissistic friend who is concerned mostly about himself, you need to change the dynamics and try to develop a real friendship. To test whether the relationship is worthwhile, you might apply the following ideas about a reciprocal friendship, which are proposed in *Why Is It Always About You: The Seven Deadly Sins of Narcissism*:[9]

- Each person contributes something, and each person benefits in some way.

- There is flexibility in the roles of giver and taker.

- Both parties are able to feel valued for their contributions and to express appreciation for what is received.

- Separateness and boundaries are respected on both sides.

- There is no need to keep track of who's done what and who owes whom.

Look for honest, decent, strong people, and then work like hell to demonstrate that you are a worthy friend. While looking for this kind of friendship, you may want to repair or tend some old relationships, but you might also decide to find new ones. In the process of both strengthening old relationships and establishing new ones, you must continue to develop the qualities that are respected by the kind of friends you want. This usually takes some time, thought, and action:

- Ask how your friend is *really* feeling—physically and emotionally.

- Give her magazine and newspaper articles, books, or other little gifts that will please her.

- Offer to share information about yard care, house repairs, car maintenance, doctors, dentists, and other experts when you learn that he is struggling in that area.

- Consider getting tickets together for an activity you both enjoy.

- Suggest that you plan a short trip together—with or without your partner.

- Take food, flowers, or another thoughtful gift when he is sick or has sustained a loss.

- Ask for her perspective on a situation in your life, and give your honest, thoughtful perspective when she asks you for it.

- Be supportive about his kids and grandkids; do not criticize, especially in family areas.

- Do not ask for money unless it's absolutely necessary, and be more than fair when you share expenses for something.

- Be careful about loaning or giving her money because it sets up an unequal friendship. Find other ways to help.

- Bend over backward to be a good listener.

- Offer to take him to the airport or pick him up.

- Try not to be petty about grievances, and schedule time to talk about it honestly if you need to repair your relationship.

- Try to make friends for life, because a good friend should last a lifetime.

These prescriptions apply to couple friends as well as individual ones; it's wonderful to have four-way friendships.

Questions to Ask Yourself and Your Partner

1. Do I (you) have mature relationships with my (your) adult children? If not, what are the troublesome areas, and how might they be resolved?
2. Do the children and I (you) understand one another's expectations? Do any of our expectations need to be altered?
3. Are there areas of disagreement between us, as a couple, about parenting? If so, how might these be resolved?
4. How much involvement, and what kind, do I (you) want with the grandchildren? If this is not what I (you) actually have with them, what needs to change?
5. Are there areas of disagreement between us, as a couple, about grandparenting? If so, how might these be resolved?
6. Do I (you) have any concerns about discipline with the grandchildren? How are we handling any differences with the child's parents (our children) about discipline?
7. What memories am I (are you) creating with the grandchildren? How could the quality of our interactions be improved?
8. If either of us has responsibility for an elderly parent or disabled relative, do we agree on the plan and the cost? How supportive are we of each other about this?
9. How important are friends to me (you)? Do I (you) have the

quantity and quality of friendships that I (you) desire? If not, why not?

10. How do I (you) feel about our friendships with other couples?

11. How do we feel about each other's same-gender friendships? If resentment is an issue for us, how can we deal with it?

12. How do we feel about any opposite-gender friendships? If jealousy is an issue for us, how can we deal with it?

13. Do I (you) see people as they really are? Do I (you) choose friends that are generous and strong?

14. Am I (are you) unselfish enough to be a good friend?

15. How many people do I (you) count as friends for life? Do I (you) want or need more?

ets Can Make or Break You as a Couple

Princess

Pets have been a big deal for my husband and me, as well as for several other couples I know. I have even heard of two divorces that occurred because one partner really did care more about the pet than about the other person.

Our cat, Princess, died recently at age seventeen, but we had other animals before that, and we've always argued about their care. I've refused to board them or leave them when they were ill, but Ray grew up with farm animals and saw nothing wrong with casual care. Over the years, live-in sitters have cost us a bloody fortune and once resulted in a major theft from our home. Airplane travel with the cats always caused problems because I would put the carrier on my lap instead of under the seat, some flight attendant would object, Ray would take her side, and then he and I would be fighting with each other.

We sneaked our beloved Princess into a lot of hotels,

and it was usually Ray who had to carry the litter box under a blanket, while I carried her in a black bag. One fancy resort almost kicked me out because they found her on the fourth day, and I was prepared for a Motel 6 or the backseat of our car while Ray continued the vacation. One restaurant did kick us out when they discovered her in a bag at my side. (It was too hot to leave her in the car.) One winter we rented a condo in southern California, and several friends from Seattle were invited for visits. One of these friends asked me what I would do if Princess died at the condo, and I replied that I would probably put her in the freezer until I could take her home to bury her. I learned later that my friends had shared this information among themselves and joked about bringing their own ice whenever they visited me, 'cause they never knew what might be in the freezer.

Our friends still regale one another with stories about Princess. Ray threatened to drown her a few times, and his friends always offered to help, but I never worried or took them seriously because he loved her as much as I did. We just had different ideas about animal care.

Princess gave us tremendous pleasure. All three members of our family loved her for a long time, and we miss her terribly. Ray and I would both like to get another animal, but I cannot—or will not, I guess—change my ideas about care, so pets are not practical for us at this time. Maybe when our traveling days are over . . .

Loving Companions and Salves for Loneliness

No human partner can provide the unconditional love that animals give to their owners so eagerly. A dog or cat will invariably soften your life and bring you a lot of joy, and people who have horses, birds, or other animals can go on and on about their wonderful qualities too. Even on days when nobody else thinks you're special, your pet does.

As we age and experience our share of life's losses, pets can help to soften the blows. Very often, people who are estranged from or physically distant from their children make their pets into substitutes, and for most of us our pets are like our children. When a friend or relative dies, pets remind us that we still have our animal friend. When we are sick, they let us know how concerned they are. In fact, animals are amazingly astute at recognizing their owner's moods and responding accordingly. One very active couple in their fifties talk about how much they look forward to their "sunset years" with a golden retreiver on the couch between them.

Pets also help us get some needed exercise—walking them, feeding them, bathing them, stooping to touch them, and cleaning up after them. In addition, they keep us from becoming too self-involved because they force us to realize that other beings have lives and needs too.

Obstacles to Travel and Freedom

During their working years, most people are pretty much tied to their house anyway, but retirees who have looked forward to their newfound freedom quickly realize that a pet is an impediment as well as a joy. Most mature people feel responsibility for their animals because those little creatures cannot take care of themselves, so they may have to leave a daylong conference on yoga to walk the dog. They cannot fly to San Francisco for the week without getting someone to feed the cat. If they go to Europe for a month or two, they'd better have a good backup system for their pet or they'll be too guilty to enjoy the trip.

If your partner proposes a trip or another activity when you're worried about a sick animal, you may refuse to go, and that can create conflict. In fact, you'll probably restrict a lot of your activities in retirement if you have a pet—or two, or three. Only you can decide whether your human relationship can handle it and whether the sacrifices are worth it.

If both partners agree in wanting pets and work together in caring for them, these issues can usually be resolved. But if two people have different attitudes about owning pets or taking care of them, compromises may be difficult. For example, it is hard for one person who was raised only with outdoor animals to tolerate a partner who learned to cuddle pets on a sofa in a city apartment. And when a pet favors one person over another, jealousy from the ignored person toward the pet can be a dangerous part of the equation.

―――――――――――――

Jake came into his second marriage with a six-year-old boxer named Rocky. He had just retired when his first wife died; his kids were gone from the house, and he was incredibly lonely. He bought the dog within three months "for company," and the two males were tightly bonded.

Jake and Alice dated for almost two years, but they never lived together before they decided to marry. The nights they did spend together were always at her place. A few times Jake tried to include Rocky on their dates. For example, he brought the dog for walks in the park, and Rocky was friendly to Alice at first, but she ignored him and frequently suggested that Jake leave him in the car. Alice had had dogs when her children were growing up, but they were small poodles—very different from this hulking, undisciplined animal.

They returned from their honeymoon to his house, exhausted, on a Saturday night. Sunday morning, while Jake was in the shower, Rocky bounded up the stairs and landed on the bed with all fours, straddling Alice. The dog just stood there and shook, probably surprised to find her in the bed. She made the mistake of screaming louder and louder, which seemed to traumatize the dog further. Jake finally had to lift the rigid dog off his new wife.

Sometimes Rocky would growl softly at Alice; other times he just ignored her. And Alice did little to win the dog over. Jake felt terribly uncomfortable in the middle between his two loves, but he was unable to mediate the problem. Alice hinted a few times that Rocky might be better off in another home, but that always caused a huge fight. Jake told her that Rocky would be a great watchdog in their old age, but she was unconvinced. She scheduled several overseas trips, knowing that Jake would reject most of them because he didn't want to leave the dog alone so much; then she took a friend—with Jake's money.

About four years after they were married, Rocky died, and Jake suffered alone. For the next two years, he and Alice tried to build a relationship, but frequent barbs slipped out. Outsiders wondered if their marriage had been permanently damaged by their lack of unity about Rocky, and they did eventually divorce.

Alice has little insight about how important Rocky had been to Jake, and he had no empathy for Alice's fear of the 160-pound animal. Jake says now that his son-of-Rocky replacement is a lot easier to live with than Alice was, but they are both sad that they could not overcome this impediment to their otherwise comfortable relationship.

Sylvia (the Play)

A. R. Gurney's comedic play *Sylvia* is a fabulous examination of the role that a pet can take in an older couple's life. The play long ago left the Broadway stage, but it is performed periodically by repertory companies across the country and is well worth seeing.

When the man brings home a stray dog he found in the park, his wife objects for a number of practical reasons. The audience soon learns that the wife is rather cold, very refined, and newly enmeshed in her career. The man, however, is bored with his job and at loose ends. He feels quite estranged from his uptight wife and is fascinated by Sylvia's wild, engaging ways. He looks to Sylvia for his redemption. He realizes the damage the dog is doing to his marriage, but he can't stop himself.

The wife becomes very jealous of her husband's new obsession, and it looks like their marriage might break up, but Sylvia teaches the wife a few lessons, and there is a happy ending.

With lots of laughs, this story epitomizes the troubles that can occur in human relationships over a pet, as well as the positive role that an animal can play. A pet often gives a long-term couple the honest, physical affection that they may have lost—or never had—for each other. It can even bring them closer together. But the animal can also come between partners in so many ways. One person may simply not like animals, or they may want different types of animals. One individual may have a greater need for physical touching than the other. One person may think an animal is dirty, while the other kisses pets on the mouth. One partner may believe in more discipline than the other, and one may resent having to clean up all the hair and mess. A myriad of other differences about pets can sabotage a partnership, just as differences can when two people are parenting or grandparenting.

Only each couple can decide whether a pet—with its unique, pure soul—will be a blessing or a disaster for their relationship.

Questions to Ask Yourself and Your Partner

1. If we had pets in the past, what were our areas of agreement and disagreement?
2. If we have a pet now, what are the advantages and disadvantages?
3. Which one of us needs or wants a pet the most? Why?
4. Which one of us does most of the work with a pet? Why?
5. How have our pets affected our freedom and ability to travel?
6. If our current pet dies, would I (you) want another one? Why or why not?
7. If we do not have a pet now, how might an animal soften our lives and make us happier?
8. What problems might be created by us getting a pet now?
9. What changes in our lives might make us want a pet in the future more than we do now?
10. How have my (your) previous experiences regarding animals affected my (your) attitudes about pets?

11.
Wanting Different Things

Burnout

Couples talk about relationship burnout at various stages of their lives, but retirement age is high on the list because this is the time when male and female roles often interchange. The typical picture is a woman who got more interested in work and the outside world in her forties and fifties, paired with a man who was disillusioned by work in his fifties and started looking to his family for more satisfaction. The woman wants him to support her interests now as much as she supported his career in the early years, but the man expects her to relax and do things with him. This is the prime of *her* life, while this is the time when *he* starts questioning why he is not happy. They both feel resentful and trapped—physically and emotionally exhausted. Their relationship is in jeopardy as they question why they should stay together in retirement when they feel this burned out on the relationship.

Of course, the genders can be reversed in this

scenario, with the man wanting more distance and the woman wanting more closeness, or the partners can be in a same-sex union. Feelings of burnout can be permanent or temporary; little things can sometimes come along to make the relationship more exciting again.

Charlotte and Carol had been together almost thirty years when they decided to retire from their jobs in the New York City school system at ages fifty-six and fifty-eight. Both had risen to positions of some authority, and they both would receive substantial pensions. They lived in a great house on Long Island and planned to stay put. They agreed that they should have a few splurges after retirement, but, as usual, Charlotte was the frugal one, mentioning a trip to Maine and some dinners out. When Carol announced that she wanted to buy a Lexus convertible, all hell broke loose. "Almost seventy thousand dollars for a car that you can only enjoy a few months out of the year?"

Charlotte's reaction evoked in Carol all the feelings of being controlled and criticized that had gone unexpressed most of those thirty years. Sure, Charlotte was solid and dependable and caring, but she was so boring! She had no sense of fun. She had become more and more stifling of herself and of Carol over the years. The more Charlotte said that this purchase would be foolish, the more Carol wanted that car.

They had pooled most of their resources over the years, but Carol had received a large inheritance ten years ago when her mother died. She had told Charlotte about it, but Charlotte, to her credit, never mentioned it again, and the funds were never commingled. After several heated discussions, even with Carol offering to put the car in both names, Charlotte would not budge. So Carol went by herself and bought the car.

They both had some trepidation about whether this would end their long and loving relationship. Both felt disgusted with the other, but neither of them wanted out. Charlotte started to think that maybe she was a little soured on life in general, and perhaps this car idea was not that bad. She at first refused to ride in the car, but one day, when Carol came home windblown and happy, Charlotte told her that she looked ten years younger in that vehicle. That was the icebreaker they badly needed, and they fell into each other's arms. Carol told stories about having had a red convertible when she was a teenager and how she had thought about that car ever since. It had made her more popular when she had otherwise felt different and odd. By contrast, Charlotte had been jealous of the kids who had convertibles and other luxuries, but she had never admitted that to herself until that day.

They have talked occasionally about what might have happened if Carol had taken the money out of joint funds instead of her inheritance, but they didn't have to test that. Charlotte suggests that she would have eventually accepted it, but Carol is not so sure. They have both enjoyed the convertible immensely, and they say that it has added excitement to their happy retirement together.

Comfort Levels

Two people are seldom in sync about all aspects of how they will live their lives. Indeed, it is amazing how often partners are opposites in many of their desires. Perhaps people pick their opposite in certain traits in order to achieve balance. For example, reclusive people know, on some level, that it is not healthy to spend too much time alone, and social gadflies probably know that they should be more focused and centered.

In fact, a book called *When Opposites Attract: Right Brain/Left Brain Relationships and How to Make Them Work* gives tips for overcoming the problems that arise when two people are "wired differently."[1] It isn't always the woman who is right-brain-dominant or the man who is left-brain-dominant, but that is the usual picture. The left-brain type is blunt, tenacious, and straight-forward, while the right-brain person is intuitive, spontaneous, and emotional. These two people are polarized in their ways of being, yet they were attracted to each other and have to find ways of getting along.

So we may have subconsciously chosen our partner many years ago in order to moderate our behavior, but then we came to resent the differences. And those differences became more annoying as we aged—partly because we had increasing amounts of time to think about them, and perhaps because the irritations built up over the years.

Retirement is often the turning point because, suddenly, we no longer *have* to go anywhere or do anything, and that easily spills over into "Do I *have* to live with him the rest of my life?" or "I can't stand her annoying _____ in my face all of the time!"

In order to coexist happily, retiree couples need to get pretty clear about each other's comfort levels. "Is he OK with my girls' nights out?" "Is she accepting of my obsession with golf?" "Is this a minor annoyance or a major issue for my partner?" Reassessment may be necessary now because even in long-term relationships, where attitudes have been pretty well known, comfort levels often change with retirement. For example, you may not have cared much during working years if your partner left dirty dishes around the house because you got home before he did and usually cleaned up then, but you may care a lot more when you have to face a messy house 24/7. Or if your partner is a gambler, that may have been tolerable when your incomes were high, but it may make you very angry when money is tighter.

It's easy if your wants and needs fit somewhere within your partner's comfort level, but lacking this does not mean that either of you *must* change. It simply means that you need to recognize the issues so that problems don't crop up unexpectedly, seemingly hitting you out of the blue. If you try to ignore the differences in your expectations or pretend that they don't exist, trouble will show up in ways that are not well understood, so you'd better talk about your comfort levels sooner rather than later.

If the things you both want are *very* different, you have a couple of choices:

• You may simply decide to live and let live.

• One of you may decide to change voluntarily.

• One of you may try to persuade the other, or require the other to change as a condition of continuing the union.

It's important to remember that few of us can make major alterations in our personality, and retiree couples need to accept that fact, but all of us can make small changes if we want to.

There are a few ways to maneuver around or alter your partner's comfort level. On the positive-reinforcement side, you may want to reward limited tolerance for your behavior and hope that it grows. For example, if your partner does not complain about a night out with your friends, you might suggest a special event for the two of you the following week. At the other extreme, if your partner seems extremely, irrationally intolerant, you may have to punish her in some way or even use meaningful threats. In essence, after thoughtful exploration of the issues, you will both need to know your bottom line. That is, you'll need to be clear about things you will not tolerate, but you also need to know whether your comfort levels can sometimes be adjusted—for the right reason.

Independence

A major area for disagreement is independence. How much freedom and separateness do you want and expect? Is your partner comfortable with this arrangement? Does your partner wish you were more independent, or less so? What is your range of comfort regarding your mate's independence? How much time should you spend together versus apart? If you are not in sync, what might make your comfort levels change?

Don and Abby always differed in their needs for social interaction. She loved to go out, while he preferred to stay at home. While they were both working at demanding jobs, he spent his weekends at home, reading reports and relaxing, while she had a social life with her own friends and family. Abby sometimes traveled with these people, while Don used his vacation time to veg out and catch up on his reading. Both of them were satisfied with this arrangement.

However, when they retired, their differences became much more apparent. Don began asking where Abby was going each day and when she would be back. She told him a few times, but then she began resenting her "leash" and just ignored his questions. Don hated not knowing where she was from day to day, and he also resented the money she was spending on things he considered frivolous. He even wondered if she might be involved with another man because she got so angry whenever he asked her whereabouts. They had both thought previously that he was comfortable with her independent life, but he admitted that he was not now.

One day Abby got sick of his whining and asked him: "What do you want from me?" His answer was "Stay home." He did not state any reason or suggest anything that they might do together. He simply wanted her to change.

Abby at first gave a snotty reply, but then she recognized pain in his facial expression, and she thought he needed reassurance. She listed her activities in the past week and told him why she wanted to continue. She was having fun with her friends and learning things that she had not had time for previously. She thought Don might be more tolerant after that, but it didn't work.

After he sulked for the next few weeks, she suggested things that they could do together, but he wanted no part of that either. She reluctantly agreed to stay home with him three days a week, but she quickly learned that Don wanted only a gourmet lunch and her presence while he read newspapers and watched TV. There was little conversation between them. He did seem happier, but she was miserable on those days. Eventually she talked with her friends about her dilemma. Some of them had similar situations with retired husbands, and Abby decided to resume her energetic pattern.

She explained to Don that she was not rejecting him. Rather, they had different personalities, and she had to keep moving or else. He felt threatened by this and asked her to define "or else." She said that she might explode if he continued to stifle her, and she really needed these outlets for her energy. She was not asking him to change and, indeed, she felt that he could not. But she couldn't be different either, and she refused to live only to meet his needs.

Nothing has changed much in their behavior, but Don's comfort level is quite different now because of Abby's repeated explanations over several months. Whenever he seems a bit cranky about her leaving, she reminds him again that she is not rejecting him. Her needs are simply different from his.

Don has learned to cook and now seems quite content that he has the house to himself most days. He calls Abby his "whirling dervish" and no longer seems threatened by her absences. They might both prefer it if they had more similar personalities and more shared interests, but they have accepted their differences and revised their expectations.

The ability to function independently is crucial to all of us for many reasons—including the fact that someday we may *have* to do activities alone. Meanwhile, a couple's activities can basically be put into eight categories:

- One partner's solo activities

- That partner's activities with other individuals

- That partner's activities with groups

- Both partners' activities alone together

- Both partners' activities together with other individuals, other couples, or groups

- The second partner's solo activities

- The second partner's activities with other individuals

- The second partner's activities with groups

This structure seems complicated, but the diversity of it can be very rewarding for a full life as a retired couple. Some activities can fit into several categories at different times—for example, long walks can be done alone, with a friend, with a group, with your partner alone, and together with your partner and others.

The difficulty comes when two people have very different ideas about how these lists should shape up. One partner, for instance, may get furious when her significant other fills his list with lots of independent activities, while she has only one or two. Or one partner may load up on expensive activities while the other lists only free or frugal ones. Many decisions about activities are necessary in order for any retiree to get the life she wants during those twenty or thirty years that may lie ahead. Within a relationship, however, understanding and compromise may be warranted too.

Shared Interests—or Not: The Passion Rule

It's great if you naturally share interests, but it's painful and damaging if two people are *forced* to do the same things. A lot of couples anticipate that they will love being together in retirement, but they usually find pretty quickly that togetherness feels good only when you are doing something you *both* enjoy.

When conflict occurs because interests are not shared, one criterion should be the passion rule. You might ask yourselves:

- On a scale of one to ten, what is my passion about various activities?

- What is my passion about doing it with my partner?

The second rating is, of course, more important than the first. It may create conflict if your partner's passion about a given activity takes his individual time, but it more often causes fights if he wants you along.

If your partner's passion about your involvement in a given activity is a nine or ten on that scale, you'd be wise to consider it. Some of her passion could rub off on you. At the very least, you'll understand your partner better by trying it. However, if the rating is one or two, you might want to tell your partner to bug off and stop playing games with your time.

This approach usually works for couples because the passion rule needs to be somewhat reciprocal. That is, your partner has no right to rate every activity highly unless he is prepared for you to rate everything that way too. There has to be some discrimination among passions for these ratings to be valid. Furthermore, it should quickly be understood that if you're asked to do something you hate, your partner will have to do the same. Consequently, both people should only be asked to participate in things that are maximally important to their partner.

Another strategy is to list, separately, the pros and cons of ten activities you are doing or want to do, with five of them offered by each partner. When you compare the lists, see how closely the two sets of pros and cons match. If they are similar for a given activity, you can enjoy the pros and eliminate the cons together without much conflict. If they are in that middle ground, think of creative ways to minimize the differences—perhaps going with a couple you both enjoy, or combining the activity with dinner at a favorite restaurant. But if your pro and con lists for a given activity are really far apart, you should probably both learn to live and let live. You can find someone else to go with or go alone. As a general rule, try to find things you are both passionate about, and don't worry too much about things that you might have to do separately.

The most important underlying concept about interests should be honest feedback. Individuals need to search their soul as to their real interests and their willingness to compromise. Try not to play games about this, and don't try to be too controlling, or you may miss out on a lot of fun.

Outside the Home

Differences regarding activities outside the home run the gamut from how much time each of you will spend away to whether a particular activity holds any value. The areas that seem to cause the most conflict between retiree partners are work, travel, and entertainment, all of which we have addressed in previous chapters. Also, gambling is a newly recognized danger for retirees.

Late-onset gamblers are a somewhat new phenomenon. Some experts speculate that gambling at retirement age provides people with a place to go and a little temporary excitement. It may also offer the hope of easy money to those who were forced out of their jobs or those who really need more resources. Of course, the effect is the opposite when significant amounts of money are lost rather than gained, and partners are always affected by gambling. One woman could not figure out where all their money was going until she snooped in their files and found a lot of withdrawals at an ATM in the local casino. Some partners have ended long-term relationships because their joint assets were in jeopardy.

Inside the Home

Issues to disagree about inside the home include housekeeping, drinking, smoking, food, weight, exercise, and TV. Let's focus on a few of them.

Substance Abuse

Drinking causes obvious problems when both retirees are alcoholics, and it's not uncommon for two people who previously had a small problem to fall into serious alcoholism once they don't have to show up for work anymore. There have always been a fair number of weekend alcoholics, who managed to control their habit during the week. It seems that economic survival is such a strong motivator that these people kept their drinking in check in order to keep their job. But many of these people were essentially medicating themselves to cope with depression and other mental health problems. When retirement comes, they think that more booze will make them feel better, and they start down a slippery slope. The same situation happens when the substance is a drug—in this age group, usually a prescription drug.

But the picture is even more troublesome when one person must deal with the addiction of the other. Often this too was an issue kept at bay by work but exacerbated at retirement. Luckily, there is help available from organizations like AA and Al-Anon—including help with looking at the extent to which the partner may be an enabler. The process called "intervention" can be a useful technique, with many friends and family members surrounding the abuser, telling her how the substance abuse has affected their lives, and forcefully suggesting a treatment plan. Intervention is now a skill that can be learned, and treatment programs such as Hazelden and the Betty Ford Center offer so much more help than couples could find a few years ago.

There is some anecdotal evidence that people who did not drink to excess before retirement may start after the big day comes. These are probably the people who did not think through their retirement adjustment needs very well. The lack of structure or the loss of purpose hits such people hard. They may be coping with serious problems, or the day that stretches ahead may just look boring or scary. In either case, the wine and whiskey are in the next room; it's so easy to feel a little better that way.

The partner may watch all this happening but truly be powerless to stop it. Substance abuse is enormously difficult for a couple when the two people want very different things for their lives in retirement.

Smoking

Smoking seems to be decreasing in the general population, but many older people grew up with this habit, and it is hard for them to quit. When one partner does not smoke, severe conflict often comes at retirement because the nonsmoker now has to face smoke much more of the time. Furthermore, the nonsmoker's reactions are now fortified by solid research on the dangerous effects of secondhand smoke. Both society in general and non-smoking partners are getting more aggressive.

Evelyn and Tim had been married for forty-five years when he finally retired at sixty-eight from his practice as an attorney. He says, in fact, that he worked that long because he finds her smoking intolerable. He doesn't know how he handled it so long without complaint, but his unhappiness with her habit certainly increased over recent years. Almost twenty years ago they began sleeping and watching TV in different rooms. Ten years ago she refused to go outside for her after-dinner cigarette when he requested it, so they stopped eating together. They do enjoy patronizing restaurants, especially since she can no longer smoke in most of them. And they like going to movies and plays, where she also cannot smoke.

After Tim retired, they found themselves driving much more—to visit friends and family, to parks where they would walk, or just for shopping. He asked Evelyn not to smoke in his car, but she was unwilling or unable to comply. She tried to be considerate by opening a window, but she said that driving in a car made her need a cigarette. Even when she was not smoking, the car reeked increasingly of smoke. Her limit for not smoking was about twenty minutes, and they fought bitterly. Tim tried getting her doctor involved, but she only resented his meddling, and the doctor had to admit that Evelyn's health was fine. She was lucky, so far.

Finally, a year after his retirement, Tim gave up his nagging and refused to ride in the same car with her. Now, whenever they go anywhere together, they take separate vehicles. Within the house, they live quite separately. Evelyn did concede, after another year of this, to refrain from lighting up in the house after dinner, so they do have short meals together in the dining room now. They both wish it could be different, but they are succeeding at "live and let live" as much as possible.

Household Chores

Even housework and gardening can be a source of conflict if two people have different standards and interests. For example, if one partner is a pack rat who saves everything and the other wants to throw everything away, there will be conflict. Or if one person energetically completes all of the tasks assumed to be his while the other one hates and resists all household assignments, it will be hard to coexist peacefully.

David always was a slob, but Patsy was willing to pick up after him because he made a very good living and had a great sense of humor. After they both retired and she made it clear that David had to do his share around the house, the humor became more biting and caustic. Instead of joking, as David had done previously, that his shirt looked better with a few wrinkles from being on the floor, he now said that Patsy would look better with a few less pounds, which she could shed by stooping to pick the shirt up.

Patsy nagged for weeks about picking up clothes and towels and especially about cleaning the mess David made in the shower. Then she threatened to go on strike if he didn't change within a month. Finally she moved herself and her clothes to a separate bedroom, refusing to set foot in the master bedroom. She did her own washing but never offered to do his.

After three or four months David sent Patsy two dozen roses with a card reading "Truce?" He snuggled up to her, saying how much he missed her in bed. He was obviously hoping that she would cave, but when that didn't happen, he talked about how much he had hated his mother criticizing his efforts at housework. In fact, his parents had owned a small hotel where he had worked summers and weekends as a teenager, mostly cleaning bathrooms and changing beds—which his mother never felt was done well enough. For her part, Patsy acknowledged her perfectionism about everything, and she expressed regret that it was so hard for her to change that trait.

The next night, at an elegant restaurant, Patsy and David negotiated a list of things he would do around the house. When he chose the tasks, he seemed to feel more in control. She waited a week to see whether he would follow through, then surprised him with champagne and his favorite dessert in bed. David says now that whenever he is plowing through some chore he hates, he stops any thoughts about his mother and thinks instead of Patsy that night in bed. She has also made progress by limiting her criticisms of David's efforts and results.

Food

Food choices get tricky with some older couples when one person cares a lot more about these things than the other one does, or when they have vastly different preferences. Seniors should have more time, at this stage of life, for shopping the farmer's markets and preparing healthy, fresh food. No more excuses about consuming fast food because it's fast! But when one person prefers doughnuts and cookies while the other wants broccoli, the battle is on.

Food can also be an issue when one partner suddenly gets concerned about changing her diet or taking a lot of vitamins, and the other one does not approve. For example, I know several people who began studying nutrition in their fifties and decided not to eat the hormones and antibiotics that are pumped into meat and poultry these days. They became avid vegetarians (with some still eating fish) and will no longer buy or cook meat, but their partner still longs for a good steak. When these couples go out for dinner, one of them often criticizes the other's choice of entrée, and one of them then starts a fight. The meat-eating partners complain to all of their friends about feeling deprived, and the vegetarians wonder why they can't get their mate to change. Both partners, in these cases, are well-meaning people, but food has become a difficult area for them.

Exercise

Exercise should actually be easier after retirement because there is now more time for working out. Ideally, exercise can be a joint project for couples in retirement—either done together or arranged separately with times and places convenient for each individual. But exercise ideas and regimens seldom work well if the two people have different attitudes about them.

Every person *is* responsible for his own body, and healthy living *can* be accomplished alone, but if one person ridicules the other about exercise, incentive is easily lost. Certainly, insults about weight or body shape from one's partner are not well received—especially at an age when people are often feeling more vulnerable about their appearance and health anyway.

Obesity

Obesity is a big problem in America, undoubtedly more among older couples than younger ones. Indeed, retirement is a time when many people put on weight because they are less active. Some seniors also use food as a drug to quell feelings of depression or loss.

One important point, accepted by almost all psychologists and nutritionists, is that fad diets don't work. Instead, difficult behavioral changes are our only hope for large and permanent weight loss. Dr. Phil McGraw's book *The Ultimate Weight Solution* has finally popularized the notion that losing weight is neither quick nor easy.[2] Change must come from the inside out. People who succeed at getting to a healthy weight must face their personal truths, replacing toxic messages with positive thoughts. And we also know now that one's partner has a crucial role in supporting and facilitating weight loss. For example, putting a lot of fattening, unhealthy food in the fridge is a mean and hateful message, but trying your partner's new system with him is great. Your mate can help or hurt enormously as you set reasonable limits and learn to nurture yourself in ways other than through food.

Prevention

The exciting new area in medicine is the role of prevention, and volumes are being written about that, but some of the recommendations from experts simply make common sense, such as drinking more water, limiting TV viewing, and exercising regularly. These ideas are superficial and arbitrary, but they remind older couples to think about prevention as much or more than cure.

The big benefit that retired couples have over singles is that they can help each other—nudge each other, if need be—to do all of these preventive things and more. Motivation for exercise, for example, can wane as we have less energy, but that's the time when exercise can actually *give* us more stamina, so it never hurts to be reminded of that fact. Taking a walk or swimming with your partner is usually more pleasurable than doing it alone, and involving another couple can make it even more fun.

Television

TV is often a huge battleground for retired couples, especially when one of them is obsessive about watching politics, sports, or soap operas. In most of these cases, there was no issue while both of them worked and had little time, or when one of them worked and the other was at home so that the obsession could be hidden. But now both people have time on their hands, and there is another person observing their habits.

It is really silly that couples have so many fights about watching TV, but this is such a concrete example of wanting different things.

Politics, Religion, and Other Attitudes

It is amazing how many older couples are so diverse politically that they cancel out each other's vote, year after year after year. In a long-term relationship, especially, you'd think that they would have influenced each other more, but many couples actually seem to have diverged more over time. One sometimes wonders whether this action is ideological or behavioral—that is, whether couples do this out of real conviction or from a passive-aggressive desire to aggravate each other.

There is something about retirement that also aggravates these disagreements. Certainly, the couple is spending more time together, so they have many more opportunities to get under each other's skin. Furthermore, they have more free time to ruminate unhealthily about their political positions.

Fighting about politics really has no meaning in the long run because it usually will not change any individual's life, and it needs to be put in that context. Unless two given partners are stimulated in positive ways by their political fights, they need to simply live and let live.

Religion can be another clinker, especially if one partner is evangelical about it. Usually people who hook up with someone of a different religion know that this is an issue they will have to manage maturely, and most couples do. Furthermore, over the course of a long relationship, some people get more religious while other people become atheists. These are unpredictable areas that cannot be controlled and which should be left to the individual conscience. But when one person never gives up trying to change the other, the problems will be endless. And retirement is often the time for huge religious blowups because couples have more time and opportunity to annoy each other.

Many other attitudes become grist for fights as well. Perhaps one of you thinks that your adult children should still be coddled and given money, while the other believes in tough love. One of you may always dress up, while the other is consistently casual or even sloppy. Maybe you have very different approaches to the tennis court or the golf course when you try playing together. These issues may seem minor from the outside, but they can escalate to name-calling and even physical violence if retirees let them. Couples need to remember the things that really matter in life and not let differing attitudes become too important. They also need to make sure that the particular issue they fight about most is not a proxy for something else—for example, fighting about politics or religion instead of about one partner being too controlling or drinking too much.

The Middle Ground

Older couples are known for their rigid ideas. We seem to think that because we have lived so long, each of us knows best. It can be fun to have interesting discussions with those who think differently than we do, but we need to remember that we have no right to impose our ideas on anyone. Our only real power is to change ourselves.

Anyone who has supervised people in a work setting will tell you that those who are able to change seem to succeed more than those who are rigid. It's being flexible, adaptable, and able to see a different point of view that seems to bring the most success in the workplace. And anyone who has worked with couples and families in a therapeutic setting knows that being thoughtful and open to new ideas goes a long way toward solving interpersonal struggles.

Trying something new or thinking about something in a new way will pay off in so many ways. First, your reaction may be different from what you anticipate, and it's fun to surprise yourself sometimes. Second, there may be benefits in the activity itself, and you'll probably learn something new. Furthermore, your partner relationship will be better if you can take a chance on something new.

Against our natural inclinations to be more rigid as we age, it is even more important to be flexible now, because the years ahead will hit us with many unforeseen circumstances. Surely life will be much richer if we remind ourselves that wanting different things is not necessarily a negative in a relationship. It can sometimes make life more interesting, and it can even make a couple stronger because they usually have broader coping skills through diversity than they would if they were in agreement on everything.

Questions to Ask Yourself and Your Partner

1. Do I (you) want different things in retirement than you (I) do? What things?
2. Are we experiencing any burnout in our relationship?
3. On a scale from one to ten, what is my (your) comfort level with your (my) behavior as a whole?
4. How independent is each of us? What is my (your) comfort level about this?
5. How many interests do we naturally share? Have any been forced on either of us?
6. What are my (your) five favorite activities individually or together?
7. In which of those activities do I (you) want your (my) involvement? Why?
8. What are our areas of conflict about activities outside of the home?
9. Are any of these conflicts new or particularly problematic in retirement?
10. What are our areas of conflict regarding activities inside the home, such as substance abuse, smoking, household chores, food, exercise and obesity, illness prevention activities, and watching television?
11. Are any of these conflicts new or more problematic in retirement than before?
12. How do we differ in our politics, religion, and other attitudes?
13. Are any of these differences more problematic in retirement than before?
14. On a scale of one to ten, how do we rate our levels of rigidity? To what extent do our ratings agree?
15. What can we both do to become more flexible in our thinking?

12.

Aging and Facing the Future

Styles

People have such interesting styles as they age—from completely ignoring the process to ruminating constantly about it. Neither extreme, of course, is healthy. If we ignore the effects of aging, we may miss some opportunities to improve our health or enhance our appearance. But if we focus too much on it, we will miss the moment. We will worry about things that may never happen, and we will not be really present in the fun and adventure that life offers us *now*.

The only reasonable approach, then, is to face the aging process squarely and honestly—and, if possible, with a sense of humor. For example, we might remember these four stages of life:

• You believe in Santa Claus.

• You don't believe in Santa Claus.

• You are Santa Claus.

• You look like Santa Claus.

If you stay alive, aging is inevitable, and the biggest advantage in being part of a couple is the chance to face it together. Neither of you looks the same, thinks the same, or acts the same as you did at thirty. If you want be honest about it, you're probably both better in some ways and worse in others. You're likely wiser about life, for example, and more resilient when something negative happens, but your energy level is probably a lot lower than it was in the past.

Many retired couples get into heavy criticism of each other's wrinkles, weight gain, or diminished energy, but this has only negative effects on the relationship. The goal should be to emphasize the positives and come to terms with both the good and the bad aspects of getting older. Certainly, part of the good is that you have each other to commiserate with.

Appearance

We might like to think that emotional maturity will compensate for our deteriorating appearance, but most people are still pretty affected by surface things, and the world seems to be increasingly expecting that seniors should never look their age. Youth is still what everyone wants. Few commercials feature actors in their sixties and beyond unless the product being advertised is for some illness or disability.

Another issue is that appearance at retirement age seems so wide-ranging. One has only to attend a high school or college reunion to realize that some people look twenty years younger than average, and others look twenty years older. Why is there such a variation in appearance at this stage of life, while younger people's ages are much easier to peg?

The biggest factor is undoubtedly genetics. There is good

reason why many of us look into the mirror one day and suddenly exclaim, "I've turned into my mother" or "I look just like my father." Or, in rhyme form:

Mirror, mirror on the wall,
I am my father (or mother) after all!

If our parents had lots of wrinkles, we probably will too. If their hair never turned gray, ours probably won't either. If there is a lot of hair loss in the family, we'd better plan on it. To some extent, then, our aging appearance is beyond our control.

One person in a couple can end up looking very young at sixty or seventy while the partner may look very old, and that difference can sometimes create trouble. Envy can easily creep into the relationship when the older-appearing partner has done nothing to cause that, and resentment occurs especially when the younger-looking one has unrealistic expectations for his partner to change. The best solution here is to realize that life is not fair.

Other variables for which we *do* have responsibility affect our appearance too. Attitudes and experiences seem to show up on our face increasingly as we age. The following words seem valid: "God gave you the face you have up to the age of forty, but you get the face you deserve after that." Anger, bitterness, and mean-spiritedness surely are visible on many older faces, but kindness and acceptance are too. Intelligence and curiosity can clearly be seen in a mobile face and lively, sparkling eyes. Boredom with life and disinterest in other people will show up in a dull expression. The shape of one's mouth—whether the corners turn up or down—suggests an easy smile or a ready sneer.

Illness sometimes etches lines on a face too. Certain medications, chemotherapy, and other medical treatments can play havoc with our color and facial contours. Chronic pain is often visible on a person's face. But, overall, attitudes about illness are probably more important than the illness itself. Are you in a rage or depression about it, or are you realistic and trying to do the best you can?

Sometimes, when one observes an older couple, they almost look alike, and this is probably due to attitudes shared and developed over many years together. But other times, the feelings that show up on partners' faces suggest serious problems. For example, when there has been serious abuse, the abuser often looks mean, while the victim seems sad and broken in spirit.

Something we'll call "upkeep" is the third important factor in appearance, and conflict can ensue when either partner goes to extremes. On one hand, the person who spends too much time exercising or too much money on spa treatments or expensive cosmetics can really aggravate a partner who is less self-involved or more frugal. On the other hand, conflict also occurs when one partner ignores her appearance or is lazy about it. This can be a special problem for retirees because it seems to be human nature to care how we look at work, but many of us stop caring when we no longer have a workplace to go to every day. We wear our oldest clothes around the house and seldom comb our hair. We forget that our mate is still looking at us—and making judgments about us—every day. And relationships are significantly damaged when one person is dirty or smelly and unwilling to change.

Appearance can be particularly affected by weight gain in retirement. It's easy to watch the pounds pile on when our activity level goes down, and food is especially tempting when the fridge and cupboards are so close to wherever we are in the house. There are some people who are not judgmental about weight, but there are many more who get very negative if their partner becomes obese. In fact, some people even get irate if their partner gains five or ten pounds. Cruelty is seldom a useful tactic, and it often backfires, but partners get frustrated, and battles develop. It is really funny, but also sad, how often one partner will disparage the other's weight gain while being quite unaware of his own!

Because appearance has always been especially important to

baby boomers, experts say that certain businesses and services will thrive as the boomers age. Youth-promoting vitamins and hormonal therapies will be popular, as will fitness products of all kinds. Boomers will want glasses that don't look like bifocals, and they'll demand hidden hearing aids. One-third of them expect to use psychological counselors to deal with aging. The boomers will be an affluent, wired group in old age, so financial and legal services will be tailored to fit their needs. They will continue to like adventure travel. They will be less loyal to specific religions than their parents were, but they will increasingly seek spiritual seminars and retreats.[1] All of these things, of course, cost both money and time, and one partner can become very angry when the other spends on things that seem frivolous.

Related to upkeep is the issue of plastic surgery. Some people don't really need it but want it to excess. Others could greatly benefit from it but see no reason to have it. Getting cosmetic surgery, like most other health decisions, should be made only by the individual, but one's partner usually has a lot of influence. Most plastic surgeons encourage their patients to bring their partner for evaluation sessions because they know that involvement usually presages buy-in. The partner likes to be able to ask questions and make suggestions, and she may really be needed for support later.

Surgeons also tell us that it is not unusual these days for retired couples to get face-lifts or liposuction together. Some couples have even given plastic surgery to each other as a retirement gift. These people often tell no one what they are doing, and they like being able to support each other through the process. Then they sometimes go off on an exotic vacation to recuperate and come back to compliments like "You look so rested" and "Retirement must be agreeing with you."

But plastic surgeons also talk about patients whose partners are against the surgery, even threatening the doctor occasionally and refusing to pay. These individuals either feel angry about being left out of the loop or perhaps threatened by a mate who will now look so much younger than they do.

Thus, even though cosmetic surgery is an individual decision, it would be wise to discuss it thoroughly with your partner and, thereby, try to avoid future recriminations. It is especially important to share the reasons for your decision and solicit your partner's feelings about it.

Mimi had discussed a face-lift for years with her women friends, but she announced her decision to Frank just a week before the procedure was scheduled to take place. As she had expected, he objected vociferously, saying that he did not want to see her appearance change. In addition, he objected to the cost, which would not be covered by insurance. Mimi shrugged off his concerns. He had never seemed to notice how she looked anyway, and she would rather use their savings for this than for other things.

Frank was sullen for the next week, but Mimi hardly noticed because she was so anxious about the outcome and the pain. He was dutiful about taking her to the clinic and picking her up, and he even restrained himself when Mimi said, in agony, that she wished she'd never done it. But, after the bandages were off and the ordeal was almost over, Frank presented Mimi with a letter asking for a divorce. His major reason was that they should try to find other partners who would listen better and appreciate them more.

Frank considered this incident a total breakdown in communication. He did not want a prettier wife, he said; he wanted a more sensitive one. Mimi screamed at Frank for doing this to her now, and she essentially shrugged the letter off. But Frank did move to a rental apartment the next day.

They were separated for almost ten months, and the relationship looked broken, but Mimi started talking to friends and her kids about her feelings, and she eventually saw that she had taken Frank for granted. They began having dinner together at a favorite restaurant every Friday night, and it became clear that neither of them really wanted a divorce. They wrote more letters to each other. They read books about relationships and went to seminars. Frank had a few dates, and Mimi realized that women were standing in line for him, whereas, even with her face-lift, men were not as available to her. She decided that Frank was not so uncommunicative after all. He had felt strongly about her surgery initially, he had explained his reasons, and he had been so concerned that he had acted to shake them both up. They say now that their relationship has improved 500 percent, but a face-lift almost ended it.

For many reasons, cosmetic surgery is increasingly popular. The American Society of Plastic Surgeons says that 7.4 million people had procedures in the year 2000—up 198 percent from 1992. Women currently have more than 80 percent of the surgery, but the numbers for men are growing.[2] Another survey suggests that 10 percent of American women have had plastic surgery by the time they are fifty-five, and nearly a third of the remaining women expect to get it.

Beauty really is in the eye of the beholder, and negative appraisals by that beholder can cause a lot of conflict for a couple. Your criticism can lower your partner's self-esteem, and the effects of that on the relationship are always negative because people with low self-esteem are not much fun to be around. Instead, you need to find ways to support your partner's efforts at improvement because this is a lot more effective in the long run than criticism. And separating out the appearance things that can be changed from the things that cannot is an important step in moderating your negative tendencies.

As we age, few of us are thrilled with our own appearance. Not very many of us think we look better now than we did twenty years ago. But even if we think *we* look OK, very few of us can look at our partner without noticing the effects of age. Somehow our partner—and everyone else around our age—usually seems older than we do. Somehow others look fat even though we carry extra pounds too. We need to be very careful here. Fairness about appearance may be more important than about any other subject.

Normal, secure aging is seldom the cause of estrangement or divorce. It's only when one or both people go overboard, reacting to their own or their partner's aging face and body in unhealthy ways, that serious trouble ensues. Taking extreme measures to change one's appearance can be very destructive to a relationship, but so can slovenliness and neglect. Partners can help each other to hit that desirable middle ground about the way they look.

Mental Health

Ideally, we are paying the same attention to our aging psyche as we are to our aging body, but many of us who thought that retirement will finally make us happy become frustrated and angry when that doesn't automatically happen. The author Gail Sheehy says that this is especially true for people who were very dependent on their title, status, and perks at work because they may not have developed many of the inner resources that will be needed for life after work. They probably were so focused on one scoreboard that they neglected the other ones—as son or daughter, spouse, parent, friend, colleague, mentor, community giver, and benefactor. Many of these "crippled" people have poor mental health in retirement, but those who do "get it" will reinvent themselves for a winning strategy in later life.[3]

Dr. George E. Vaillant has been the principal investigator of a landmark study at Harvard on adult development, in which 824 men and women have been followed from their teens into their eighties. The major conclusion of this research is that we are very much in control of our aging process, especially our mental health. Dr. Vaillant says that old age is like a minefield, but the ability to take people inside oneself emotionally is absolutely crucial. These four attributes are vital for mentally healthy aging:

- Orientation toward the future—the ability to anticipate, to plan, and to hope

- Gratitude, forgiveness, and optimism—seeing the glass as half full rather than half empty

- Empathy—the ability to see the world through another person's eyes

- The ability to reach out—in other words, to emotionally leave the screen door unlatched[4]

Those who cling to the memory of an unhappy childhood or negative events in adulthood are far less happy than those who develop a feeling of acceptance. We need to remain connected to life as we age, realizing that every life has its ups and downs. And we also should learn the rules of our changing world—which seems to be moving faster all the time. According to this study, a major task in the second half of life is to recover and reconnect with those we have loved in the first half. Vaillant's overall advice? "Worry less about cholesterol and more about gratitude and forgiveness."[5]

Another study, by Robert Levenson at the University of California, Berkeley, has been looking at the emotional interaction of couples in long-term first marriages as they move into middle and old age. Retirement is one of the important milestones, and these researchers have been trying to determine what kinds of couples fare well as they cope with transitions versus what kinds of couples do poorly. Their very hopeful conclusion is that while functions such as memory and motor skills decline with age, emotional functioning is usually spared. Indeed, there are often signs of continuing emotional improvement and positive development in late life.[6]

And one more study, this time in Australia, looked at what makes people happy in retirement. The number one factor was good friends, with males rating this almost as highly as females. Good health was next in importance for both men and women, and these two factors were far ahead of financial security, physical safety, seeing the world, tranquility, or having a nice home.[7] These data add to our existing research-based knowledge that it is vitally important to be able to make and keep friends as we age. If one or both partners has lost—or has never had—this emotional skill, aging and facing the future as a couple may be very difficult.

What do committed couples do when one of them has mastered these mental health abilities but the other one hasn't? There are really only three options:

- The healthy one lets the unhealthy one drag him down.

- The healthy one tries for as much separateness as possible and stays healthy.

- The unhealthy one improves, either because of the partner's influence or from professional help—or a combination of factors. This may not come easily, but it is possible if the emotionally crippled person realizes that her mental health vastly influences her physical health, life span, and quality of life.

Driving Problems

Driving is one of the first areas where deficits due to age become apparent. Not only do most of us not see as well as we did, and some of us don't hear as well, but we also don't remember directions or street names as efficiently. We may not be as sharp about signaling, changing lanes, keeping up reasonable speeds, and anticipating other drivers as we once were. We may not notice obstacles in the road or hear the noise of emergency vehicles as quickly.

Within the range of normal driving at retirement age, partners can really help each other. The passenger can point out an accident up ahead or a slippery spot in the road. But this help frequently escalates into—or is perceived as—unwanted advice. Both genders seem to resent "backseat driving," and angry reactions can result in unintended consequences, sometimes making the situation much more dangerous.

Couples need to find ways to signal their driving tips to each other in the least threatening way possible, but this is not always easy. For example, as a passenger, one woman tends to anticipate freeway exits verbally, and her husband hates that. She once asked him, "Would you rather miss the exit than have me point it out?" and he said yes. So now she plays a game. In most instances he sees the exit himself, but on the occasions when he misses it and has to turn around, she announces that she has won. She has proved that he was inattentive. But he won't let it go at that, insisting that it is he who has won because he has shown her that it's no big deal to turn around. These are childish games, but they're probably better than an angry fight that turns into an accident.

There may come a day when one partner's driving is truly dangerous. This is always hard to deal with because driving equals freedom, and it is so ego-important to most people to be able to get around independently, but partners really need to assess this carefully and honestly. It should never be a control issue for the better driver or a "gotcha" situation. Rather, the decision that one person should stop driving usually results from an accident, a traffic ticket, or perhaps not being able to find the car in a parking garage. Sometimes a compromise is possible—for example, the person should not drive at night, he should not drive on highways, or a hearing aid or special glasses must always be worn.

Sometimes the individual gives in easily, realizing the danger or feeling lucky that the other partner is still capable. However, if you and your mate cannot reach agreement, don't give up. Don't tolerate the dangerous driver, because many lives—including your own—could be at stake. You may have to engage your children, your physician, or a trusted friend to help by reinforcing your observations—telling it like it is.

Nevertheless, in this situation the more intact partner must always recognize how much he is taking away from the driver. Confronting this issue should always be approached with empathy and love, but if all else fails, the driver may have to be asked something like this: "How would you feel if you killed a child?" Unless the person has no heart for children or anyone else, this should really be the determining factor.

Questions to Ask Yourself and Your Partner

1. What is my (your) style about aging—denial, facing it squarely, or ruminating about it endlessly?
2. Do I (you) see the humor in our aging process?
3. How do my (your) genes affect my (your) appearance?
4. How do my (your) attitudes and experiences show on my (your) face?
5. What are my (your) upkeep issues?
6. How do I (you) feel about plastic surgery for myself (yourself)? For you (me)?

7. If any of these appearance issues are a problem in our relationship, how are we handling the conflict?

8. What am I (are you) currently doing to strengthen my (your) mental health? What do we need to do?

9. To what extent are we oriented toward the future?

10. To what extent do we practice gratitude and forgiveness?

11. To what extent do we have empathy for others?

12. To what extent are we able to reach out and let others in emotionally?

13. Does either of us have signs of a driving problem? If so, are we making the appropriate decisions?

14. How might we handle dangerous driving in the future?

13.
Medical Matters

The Health Care Maze

Family members at all ages should help one another through the medical system as it becomes increasingly specialized and complicated, but retirees need to pay especially close attention to each other's medical situation as they age because it is difficult to navigate the process alone.

One might think that seniors would deal better with the medical system than younger people because they have more experience with it. They know the rules. They also should have more wisdom about it, as they do in general about life. But medical care can now seem overwhelming for seniors because the rules have changed and the options have increased. If one is used to operating by the old rules of warm and caring doctor-patient relationships and hospitals that keep you until you are well, for example, it can be challenging to accept doctors who treat only a small aspect of their patients and hospitals that kick you out as soon as possible for financial reasons. Senior couples have a difficult task when one considers that most younger people also have trouble dealing with the medical maze as it currently exists.

In general, individuals should not see doctors alone when there is a serious issue. There is so much to comprehend about modern medical care that hearing complicated diagnoses and recommendations once, alone, is more than should be asked of most people. Medical terms are difficult to understand, and many doctors are not thoughtful enough to use layman's language. Figuring out what's wrong can be a lengthy process, requiring great patience as well as persistence. Surgery and other medical procedures can be amazingly complex. Malpractice is, unfortunately, a real problem in dealing with both physicians and hospitals. And overmedication or misused pharmaceuticals can be deadly. We need our wits about us in order to avoid iatrogenic medical incidents—that is, symptoms or diseases induced by a physician.

So how are senior couples particularly affected in the medical arena? First, seniors simply need to use medical care more often than their juniors do. They are going to be facing more illness in the years ahead than they did in the time gone by. Sure, there are lots of things we can do with diet and exercise to avoid illness, but our bodies break down after many decades of use, and few retirees can avoid all contact with the medical system. That's just the nature of the aging body.

Second, our culture's stereotypes about seniors cause some medical professionals to ignore or disparage them—"they won't understand, so why bother to explain?" When seniors repeat their questions or don't grasp information quickly, some providers get impatient. And there is no doubt that memory deficits make it harder for many seniors to understand the things that are happening to them.

So it is really difficult for an older individual to go it alone in the medical maze, and it is so much easier with a partner. Retiree couples need to be unselfish enough to be a second set of eyes and ears for each other. You may have to go somewhere when it is not convenient. You may have to listen to things that are hard to hear. You may have to watch procedures that make you sick to your stomach. But you owe that much to your partner. You need to be loyal and trustworthy for this task.

What can the patient's partner actually do in a medical situation? Besides listening, we can take notes. We can ask appropriate questions. We can politely ask to use a small tape recorder in order to remember the information later. This is something that secure professionals do not mind, and if that person does resist, you might want to look for a different expert. Furthermore, if an individual patient *does* have to see the doctor alone, a small tape recorder, with agreement from the provider, can be a very useful tool.

Partners can also provide comfort. Everyone knows these days that doctors spend little time with each patient and that the system is very compartmentalized. There are often long waits between the exit of one medical person and the entrance of another, and there may be stressful pauses between procedures. Not feeling alone in this foreign, frightening world of medicine can reduce stress and encourage healing for the patient. Having an advocate as one goes through the process can be a tremendous relief.

This assumes, of course, that the nonpatient partner stays appropriate and helpful—verbally and nonverbally. The patient must be allowed to take the lead. A sharp, demanding voice asking silly questions from the sidelines is more hindrance than help. And fights between the couple in front of medical professionals are rarely useful. Save your disagreements for later, if at all possible.

Of course, some people are so troubled that they signal problems in the relationship through their obnoxious behavior in the doctor's office. If the couple is not behaving appropriately, physicians and other health care providers need to be sensitive to possible signs of partner abuse (and to elder abuse if the support person is a child or caretaker). Partners can be an enormous help to the patient, but they need to stay constructive.

Incidents of medical malpractice seem to be rising, with increased demands on physicians' time and intellect, and the partner can sometimes be useful as a witness if there is a truly heinous action. More likely, perhaps, the presence of the mate can put the brakes on some rushed behavior by a doctor, or the partner might help a pharmacist or nurse by questioning an inappropriate medication.

The laws and customs are generally improving within medicine as the system becomes more transparent and the patient is seen as more of a partner to the doctor than she used to be. Patients now demand and get access to their medical records. In the past, people other than the patient have been shooed out of all medical settings, but this practice is changing fast. Family members are insisting on being present for emergency-room procedures, and they're pushing their way in even when they are not wanted. Partners are still denied access to operating rooms and anesthetic procedures, but this may eventually change too, as the rules have drastically altered for maternity delivery rooms over the past thirty years.

As hard as it is for retiree spouses to be allowed to collaborate in their partner's medical care, it is much more difficult for couples who are not married—either same-sex or heterosexual, long-term or short-term. The following chapter on legal decisions addresses the need for everyone, but especially unmarried couples, to sign health care proxies for situations in which they might be incapacitated. If there is no document available to prove the intent of the patient, he is usually denied the ability to have the person of his choice involved in his care. And, of course, even when the patient is conscious and responsive, she may have to be assertive in order to make sure that the medical staff allows her unmarried partner to participate.

In general, most medical consumers have become more assertive, more take-charge, in recent years. Their health is no longer just in the doctor's hands. They used to take orders from their physicians, but now they're only willing to take advice. Most baby boomers are already insisting on this type of control over their medical care, but many older retirees, who were raised to be polite and respectful of professionals, need to learn these new skills and this mind-set.

A partner can also encourage second and third opinions when they are indicated. According to an AARP survey, less than 25 percent of senior patients get them because of impatience, concerns about who pays, or fear of offending the doctor. But this is the only way that the patient can learn about misdiagnoses or different treatments, and research shows that second opinions truly save lives. For example, three leading medical centers recently reviewed cancer pathology reports, and they found diagnosis-changing errors in up to 28 percent of the cases. The consensus of this study is that patients especially need second opinions in four situations:

• When you want to know more about treatment choices

• When you have been diagnosed with a relatively rare condition

• When you don't fit the standard profile for your illness

• When you have doubts that need to be addressed[1]

Older patients may feel vulnerable in the midst of grinding pain or physical degeneration, but they need not be victims or unquestioning supplicants of the medical system. They should be partners with professionals. They must be the ultimate boss over their own body, and their partner can help them accomplish these goals.

Every patient needs information in order to make wise decisions, and helpful resources include books, articles, and the

Internet—although an Internet search for information can be daunting for people who are not at ease with computers. Medical libraries at universities and hospitals can also be a great help, but you may need assistance in order to get access—perhaps a friend or relative in the medical field or your own doctor if the library is not open to the public. Of course, all of this information has to be sifted to figure out what is relevant and trustworthy, and any couple may need help with that too. Sometimes adult children are happy to be asked for this kind of assistance. Friends and acquaintances can also come through in amazing ways if they are consulted.

Both the patient and the partner will benefit by understanding all of the options—which was the missing link in the following situation:

Steven was fifty-eight when his doctor told him, after a routine physical, that he needed heart bypass surgery immediately. Phyllis, his wife, wanted to get other opinions, but Steven was scared and obedient. The procedure went well, but while still hospitalized, Steven called the head of his accounting firm to announce that he would be retiring. During the following month, he went to work no more than two hours at a time, and he was not very helpful to partners who had to take on his accounts.

Over the next year, he seemed increasingly surly and withdrawn. He seldom went out, never laughed, and certainly would never attempt having sex.

Phyllis tried many times to talk about his behavior change, but he said he'd been told that this is normal after a bypass. She asked to go along to his checkups, but he insisted on going alone and said that the doctor thought he was doing very well. In desperation, Phyllis eventually wrote a letter to his doctor about Steven's behavior, adding that she would be coming to his next appointment. Because she didn't want to face Steven's anger head-on, she simply showed up at the appointed time, and Steven was too polite to explode.

The doctor tried some cursory questions, but when he got little information from the patient, he turned to Phyllis. She repeated the contents of her letter, and Steven did not deny her assertions about his behavior. The doctor seemed alarmed, and he insisted that they both go to a support group for cardiac patients.

In their very first meeting, Phyllis watched Steven's face change as other people talked about their fear of dying. That was it, she realized, and he had been unable to verbalize it! He had never asked the medical questions he should have, and he had kept Phyllis out of the process because he was afraid that she would embarrass him by taking over. Perhaps she would have also elicited information that he did not want to hear. In the next group meeting, two patients talked about concerns that their bypass surgery might have been unnecessary, and Steven seemed very shaken by that thought. The following day, both Steven and Phyllis found an Internet website that discussed this issue, and they satisfied themselves that his chest pain had warranted surgery.

Seven years have now passed, and they are a normal couple again. Steven does some volunteer accounting and tax work for a homeless shelter, they monitor his medical status together, and they have sex—carefully.

The rate of depression in heart surgery patients is very, very high. Indeed, the author of *Thriving with Heart Disease* says that coping with the psychological side effects can ravage relationships and throw a family into disarray. There can be a feeling that the patient has died, even when she is doing well, and people often feel paralyzing, all-encompassing grief. The reality is, however, that it's how you feel about the illness and not the condition of your heart that will usually determine how completely you recover.[2] As a couple, you need to understand the realities and come to terms with all of the ramifications in order to thrive— never easy to do with serious illness, but so much easier as a twosome than alone.

Preventive Measures

Good health is the key to all of our lofty plans as retirees, and couples can really help each other with preventive measures. One or both can shop for healthy food and cook healthy meals, for example, but agreement can be difficult.

Matt loved junk food and ate it every day for lunch while he was a high school history teacher. He used to have contests with his students in the cafeteria about who was eating the worst meal nutritionally, but because he is one of those people with a great metabolism, he never gained weight or felt sick. He always said that his lunches made his students relate to him better. He particularly justified his fast-food lunches and candy bar snacks because Brenda fixed healthy, almost Spartan dinners, but on some level he knew he should change.

Brenda expected the worst in retirement, and she threatened to throw out any junk food that he brought home. She was not sure that she could resist the chips and cookies if they were in the house. She had very high cholesterol and was trying to avoid taking statin drugs through diet and exercise, but she didn't trust her own willpower. Matt thought that her anxiety was escalating for no good reason in the weeks before he retired. In fact, she mentioned food so often that he began to see it as a challenge. If she thought he couldn't change his eating habits, he would show her that he could! He was somewhat concerned about Brenda's health too, but the truth is that he was mostly determined to show her that she was wrong about his behavior.

The day after retirement, Matt announced that he would be responsible for making four salads every day— two for lunch and two for dinner. In his scholarly way, he studied the nutrients in various vegetables and went about finding ingredients in out-of-the-way places. This activity has given him great pleasure, and all of Brenda's friends are trying to get their husbands to do the same. With his background, no one could have predicted that Matt would become the salad expert of Sacramento, but Brenda thinks that her nagging might have been partially responsible, while he credits his need to prove her theories about him wrong.

Retired people also have more time to exercise—and fewer excuses. In fact, one sees many older couples walking every morning in city parks and suburban malls, perhaps encouraging each other to take fifty more steps toward the reward at Starbucks. When one person is unwilling to get dressed, the other might get his jogging outfit out of the closet. When the woman says it's getting too dark out to walk safely, the man may offer to go with her. When it seems lonely to go to the gym alone, you can ask your buddy. Couples can explore ways of making exercise more fun together, and it always helps to have a sense of humor about hurting or feeling tired. In addition, if one person begins to feel and look better, the other may be competitive enough to find his own regimen.

Some experts think that we are heading toward vast financial polarities in retirement—"a Harrods-or-Wal-Mart world for seniors."[3] Lower-income retirees will not be able to afford high-tech things such as genetic therapies, but these methods may indeed work for wealthy older couples, who might eventually be able to buy themselves additional years of life. Nevertheless, no one is suggesting that any of these new ideas will be more impor-tant to the aging body than diet and exercise are.

Certainly, retired partners should encourage each other to use less medication and more natural methods because pharmaceuti-cals always have side effects. Partners can also share things that they read about preventive measures or see on TV. They can help each other remember to take the appropriate vitamins. They can even prevent some health disasters by watching their partner's behavior. As one woman advised from personal experience: "Just don't let your significant other take a sleeping pill and a laxative the same night."

For help with brain functioning, couples are being encouraged to go shopping! Indeed, there is exciting evidence that people have more influence over their own brain health than was previ-ously thought. Drs. Guy McKhann and Marilyn Albert, authors of *Keep Your Brain Young,* followed three thousand seniors over ten years and found many encouraging possibilities.[4] For example, they think there is good evidence that vitamin E helps, but *shop-ping* turns out to be a great activity because it combines three important elements: staying physically active (walking around, often carrying heavy bags), challenging the brain (making a lot of decisions), and maintaining a positive self-image (ending up feeling good about yourself because you've accomplished some-thing). Who would have known!

Mental Illness

The movie about John Nash, *A Beautiful Mind,* has made most of us more aware of serious mental illness and its toll on the partner as both people age. Living with schizophrenia, extreme bipolar disorder, severe depression, or another psychosis can be devastating for both people. Psychotic people, who are usually out of touch with reality, are an enormous drain on any partner, and institutionalization is often the only way for both of you to survive. Obtaining the proper care and monitoring the medication can be a full-time job, and neither process is easy because one must be very assertive in order to get proper mental health care in this day and age.

Very few retiree couples will face a mental illness as extreme as psychosis, but many of us will have to pull ourselves and/or our partner out of nonpsychotic depression. In some forms, one partner's depression can make a happy relationship almost impossible.

Depression can be situational—sometimes called "reactive." As we age, we realize that opportunities are closing and dreams are lost. Our body is not what it used to be, and some of our friends are dying. Perhaps we recently lost a pet or had a physical illness. Feelings of sadness in reaction to these issues are common and usually temporary. We often think of this as "the blues."

Clinical depression is more serious and long-lasting. It has been called a silent killer. Clinically depressed people are in touch with reality, but they say that they have no energy and no desire to do anything. They feel nothing but sadness and have no hope that life will ever get better. Physicians often have trouble recognizing this kind of depression in older people because doctors expect seniors to be sicker and more tired than younger patients. Also, when an older patient has had a serious physical illness, physicians may erroneously think that it is normal to be depressed. Furthermore, older depressed people may themselves be responsible for missing the diagnosis because they are ashamed of their feelings. They focus instead on physical problems, where they think there is less stigma.

Suicide is a constant, lurking fear with serious depression. The National Institute of Mental Health notes that Americans age sixty-five and over are disproportionately likely to die by suicide. That is, they comprise only 13 percent of the population, but they made up 18 percent of all suicide deaths in 2000. The highest rate of all was for white men age eighty-five and over.[5] The shame here is that many, if not most, of these depressed people could have been treated successfully with antidepressant medication and/or short-term psychotherapy if they had been properly diagnosed.

Although decisions about suicide are usually made alone, partners cannot escape involvement in suicidal feelings, and a partner gives clues to the depressed person that can be very powerful. Does he avoid the signals and pretend that suicide would never happen? Does she hang on the suicidal person's every word and follow him around? Does she constantly give reassurance that everything will be all right? Or does he dwell on the depression, avoiding all of the joy in life? All of these are poor responses. Instead, partners should watch for behavioral changes and pay close attention to a gradual loss of interest in life. And by all means, whenever a person talks about suicide, take it seriously. Talk does not always result in action, but almost every person who does the act has talked to at least one person about it.

Depending on the circumstances, you may need to run for professional help, but that may not be easily accomplished either, because internists and general psychiatrists may share society's sense of futility and nihilism about old age. You may need to find a geriatric psychiatrist or another geriatric specialist, who will be much more likely to understand the complexity of emotional factors, medical illness, interactive medications, and family needs.[6]

Of course, many people believe that suicide can also be a rational decision. Recently, retired admiral Chester Nimitz and his wife, Joan, ages eighty-six and eighty-nine, respectively, killed themselves together, and Anna Quindlen wrote movingly about it.[7] Mrs. Nimitz kept breaking bones because of osteoporosis, and she was blind. The admiral had congestive heart failure, constant back pain, and severe stomach problems. They had both lived very productive lives but did not want to go on. They left a note, which ended with: "We wish our friends and relatives to know we are leaving their company in a peaceful frame of mind." They realized that the medical system often does things because they are possible, not because they are useful, and they did not want to become shadows of their former selves. He left meticulously organized files for their daughters, and those women have since received many letters from other grown children about the indignities their parents suffered during the dying process.

Dementia of any kind can also be devastating, and the most difficult mental condition of all for a partner is probably Alzheimer's. Even when the couple has a lot of money and help, this disease is hard because it is difficult to diagnose in its early stages, it often involves belligerence and violence toward the partner, it has no real treatment or cure yet it can go on for many years, and it is eventually a death sentence. It is a draining and tragic scenario for both partners.

Hypochondria

As we age, many people prone to hypochondria seem to get worse. This is probably because we become more of who we actually are, but it's also related to the undeniable fact that we are moving closer to death. The smallest ailment of the aging hypochondriac suggests that the end is near. Normal aches and pains cannot be tolerated. Medical appointments are overly satisfying because they provide longed-for attention. Although his partner long ago tuned out his complaints, the doctors and nurses are paid to listen to them. If, eventually, those professionals tune the complaints out also, the hypochondriac is likely to go to new experts.

There are several ways for a partner to deal with a hypochondriac, but the pattern of complaints is usually well entrenched, and it often has deep-seated bases that go back to childhood. Perhaps the person only got attention from busy parents when she was ill. Maybe the whole family of origin had the same pattern. Occasionally there really was a life-threatening illness as a child, and death got psychologically ingrained as a possibility with every illness. Or maybe a parent or grandparent suffered from cancer or another terminal illness, and the lesson was learned that death always results from illness. If the partner can help in sorting some of these issues out, the hypochondriac may be able to gain some insight and ameliorate the pattern.

Change is especially worth the effort here because sometimes, when there *is* a serious problem, it is ignored because the patient has cried wolf too many times. With accomplished hypochondriacs, it truly can be hard for both the partner and the professionals to tell the difference between fact and fiction, so the partners of these patients may not easily support visits to the doctor or emergency room. Sometimes inattention really is the best course, but most partners still struggle with knowing when there is a real problem.

Caregiving Burdens and Support Groups

A serious illness can throw any relationship into chaos. Sometimes the patient has been the strong one in the past, and the two partners must exchange roles. Sometimes the healthy partner is unable to cope with the stress of illness, and the patient has to be strong enough for both of them. In the case of an emergency, the partner may have to make life-and-death decisions for which he is unprepared. In worst-case scenarios, both partners are weak physically or emotionally, and neither can really be a competent caregiver.

Partners are expected to be caregivers when the need occurs, and they usually do their best to rise to the occasion. They try to keep their loved one out of hospitals and nursing homes because few of us like those places. But safety should be a major consideration in making these decisions. That is, is it safe for the patient to be at home with an unwilling or incompetent caregiver, and is it safe for the caregiver to be alone with an unpredictable or violent patient?

Partners usually feel obligated to fulfill this caregiving role, especially if it has been a happy relationship, but self-preservation must also be considered. It is possible to have too big a sense of responsibility or, perhaps, too much guilt. Some people would rather be a martyr than say no, but the patient should not expect the caregiver to ruin her own health in the process.

Help can usually be gathered if one is resourceful and assertive. Some caregivers get annoyed that other people do not offer assistance, but they also have to be willing to ask. If people reject your request for no good reason, you may as well learn of their selfishness now and calibrate that into any future relationship.

Also, if the caregiver has the means to pay, help can be hired. Remind yourself that this is one of the best possible uses for your money—the reason that you saved all of these years. Don't be stingy now. Professional or semiprofessional help could take a huge portion of the burden off your shoulders.

Finally, support groups are more important than most people anticipate. Many caregivers say that they don't have time to go to meetings, often because they don't have anyone to relieve them at home. Furthermore, they don't need to hear other people's problems. Yet when they go, they are invariably glad they did. There is just something wonderful about sharing your pain with others who *understand,* and it is amazing how often those others can give you new ideas about your role.

Questions to Ask Yourself and Your Partner

1. To what extent do we help each other deal with the medical maze? How could we do more for each other in this arena?
2. Am I (are you) assertive enough in dealing with doctors and other health care providers?
3. What new attitudes and skills might I (you) need to learn?
4. Has either of us had a medical experience in the past that we need to understand better? Should we try to get those medical records or ask more questions now?
5. Does either of us have concerns about the other's inappropriate behavior in a medical setting? If so, why?
6. Do I (you) use books, articles, and the Internet sufficiently to obtain medical information? If we need help in using resources, whom might we ask?
7. Do we focus sufficiently on illness prevention?
8. What can we do to get better nutrition?
9. Do I (you) get enough exercise? How can we help each other to get more?
10. If either of us tends toward depression or other mental illness, how are we handling this as a couple?
11. Do I (you) feel more or less depressed with advancing age?
12. Do I (you) worry excessively about physical problems? If yes, how does this affect our relationship?
13. Do I (you) ever have thoughts of suicide? Under what circumstances?
14. Do I (you) think that suicide is ever rational?

15. How good might I (you) be as your (my) caregiver in the future? What can each of us expect if we need care at home?

16. How would I (you) most likely handle Alzheimer's or another dementia if you (I) have it?

First, a Caveat

I am not an attorney, and none of this chapter is intended as legal advice. However, over many years of clinical practice, I have often heard older clients talk about legal issues that were intertwined with psychological ones. Whether my therapeutic work is with individuals, couples, or families, I've been struck by the special, very emotional implications of legal decisions because they can be so complicated, final, and far-reaching. For example, wills hold the implication of death. Financial powers of attorney and health care proxies create the vision of being incapacitated in a hospital or nursing home. Bequests and trusts make you think about which people and what things matter to you most: "Why does one charity deserve my money more than another?" "Why does one person warrant my gift more than someone else?" And if that person is your child or grandchild, you are forced to dredge up all kinds of feelings and relationship issues. Even estate-planning decisions that were made in the past need to be reviewed periodically, so retiree couples are bombarded with these thoughts and questions more than once.

In addition to clients who come to therapy of their own accord, attorneys often refer people who are unable or unwilling to make the legal decisions that are called for. I've heard stories of crying, shouting, throwing papers, and even physical violence in lawyers' offices—which most attorneys are not trained to handle.

These client experiences, as well as stories gleaned from friends and acquaintances, form the basis for this chapter. I have certainly not tried to cover every legal/psychological nook and cranny. Instead, these are the issues that I've seen older couples struggle with most often. When in doubt, I have consulted two estate lawyers, who have given generously of their time.

The message here is that retired couples, who often have a significant need for legal help as they face and plan for the future, should recognize the complexity of this task. That is, most legal decisions are also psychological ones, and whatever affects one partner will surely affect the other. Both people should cooperate on these important decisions as never before, but middle-class retirees usually have little experience in the legal arena, and relationship issues often get in the way. Retiree couples, as well as those anticipating retirement, are challenged to make these decisions well.

Wills

Even some of the most intelligent people—one estimate is 70 percent of United States citizens—allow themselves to die without a will, and there are a lot of reasons for this:

• People fear death so much that they cannot or will not talk about it.

- They think that talking about a will with their heirs will create problems in those relationships.

- They fear that they cannot agree with their partner on the provisions of their wills, so they think that it's all better left unsaid.

- The partner seems questionable as your will's future executor, but naming an executor other than the partner could create trouble.

- They don't want to spend money on lawyers.

- They actually relish the idea of their heirs fighting about money after they die.

If you and/or your partner struggle with one of these issues, you should try to help each other. You should convince yourselves that it is an act of love to plan for the time after your death and an act of malevolence to let your loved ones figure it out for themselves. Try to remember that grieving a death is hard enough without the added burden of making sense out of a chaotic financial and legal situation.

A widowed partner and the children have a lot better chance of getting along with one another if the deceased has specified her desires financially, and surely we all want peace among our heirs. With greed being the common human emotion that it is, our heirs can get into real trouble unless we give them clear direction. For example, if one child is angry at how little she gets, it's better for her to be furious at the dead benefactor than at a living relative.

If you decide to find an estate lawyer as a couple, you can get referrals from friends, family members, other lawyers, and other professionals, but you should know that there is wide variation in hourly rates, and you will probably want to clarify the charges before you go. There are also guidance tools in books and on the Internet, which could save you some legal time. Depending on the complications of your estate, you may need a real specialist, or you may be able to do most of the work yourselves.

You can also save a lot of expensive hours in the attorney's office if you have long discussions with each other ahead of time, sorting out most of the decisions. But you may also have a lot of questions or a lot of differences in your approaches to a will, and that's largely what estate lawyers are for. The experienced ones have heard everything, so it may be worth some money to delve into that expert's legal suggestions about your differences. If you still cannot agree, you might decide to find a counselor or mediator in order to continue the discussion—probably at lower cost.

If there was ever a time to keep your emotions in check, this is it. Of course, feelings *do* come into these legal decisions, but you also need to be rational and quite clinical as you think things through. You both need to ask yourselves these questions:

- What do we really want to do with our assets—now and after we die?

- Why? (A small word but a big question.)

- What is the best legal way to accomplish our goals?

It is also important, as a couple, to realize that wills can be changed. You should do the best that you can with this immediate document, since all of us could die at any time, but circumstances change and relationships grow or diminish over time. Indeed, experts say that most people should reassess their wills every five years anyway, and there's nothing except a small cost to stop you from changing your will at any time.

Coordination of wills works best for most couples, and this helps to avoid problems after death. But the two wills of a couple can be quite different, and this is especially valid when partners have children by other marriages. Unless there is a really good reason for secrecy, you should both know the contents of each other's will. When one of you dies, the remaining partner will have a much easier time if this has been accomplished.

If, for whatever reasons, you want to complete your will and other documents but also want to keep certain hurtful provisions secret from your partner, do it privately as a last resort. Ideally, you should be able to discuss your reasons for wanting secrecy and prepare your partner for what you've decided, but if you can't, it is still kinder to your family to have a secret will, known only to lawyers and perhaps executors, than nothing at all.

As a couple, you need to be honest with each other about money in order to maximize estate planning, but, unfortunately, many couples do not fully know each other's assets—and this sometimes prevents them from doing wills. In some cases, this is because one or both of you fear divorce. Other times it's that you have a secretive personality or can't stand giving up control. Perhaps you don't trust your partner's intellect or his ability to handle the truth maturely. Maybe you have been hiding money for years, and you're afraid that the truth would have terrible consequences now. But these are all issues that you should face if you want to accomplish your financial and psychological goals—now and after death, individually and as a couple. If the two of you have not worked cooperatively on these issues in the past, you will need both courage and compromise in order to proceed successfully now.

Remember also that significant assets, such as houses and investments, push wealth up more than we sometimes realize, and wealthy couples in particular, need to take this into consideration when writing their will. It is also important to consider ways to minimise taxes imposed on your heirs

Powers of Attorney and Health Care Proxies

Powers of attorney and health care proxies (similar documents are called by different names in different countries, and are not legally binding in all countries) are also difficult for many seniors because they bring up so many knotty psychological issues: "Whom do I trust to make business decisions if I am incapacitated?" "Whom do I trust to make decisions about my life and death?" "What directions do I want to give that person about my medical wishes?" Difficult as these issues are to confront, you must execute these documents in order to avoid so much possible pain later.

You should want your power of attorney and your health care proxy to have all the necessary tools to make the proper decisions in the most difficult situations. You can seldom give specific business instructions to your power of attorney agent because those conditions are yet unknown, but you can familiarize that person with your personal and business affairs, you can specify under what conditions your power of attorney should act, and you can be very careful and deliberate about whom you name. In matters of health care, you will probably want to state your preferences regarding at least the following:

• Under what circumstances to discontinue life support

• Nutrition in an end-of-life situation

• Hydration in an end-of-life circumstance

You might want to grant more than one person to power of attorney and health care proxy status, with instructions about how they are to resolve any differences.

Sort these issues out methodically as a couple and try to resolve conflicts with each other as unemotionally as possible. But partners should also be very supportive of each other because it is difficult and complicated to contemplate one's incapacitation. These decisions may take a lot of thought and a little time. Engage other people if you have to or want to, but get these tasks done in order to alleviate current anxiety and avoid future pain.

It is typical for partners to grant each other power of attorney and health care proxy status, and it is also common to involve adult children, but there are certain circumstances in which a valued friend or a professional should be named rather than one's partner or child. For example, mental illness could disqualify family members, as could previously irresponsible behavior. If you really cannot trust your partner or child to hold power of attorney or act as health care proxy, find someone else who can substitute, but make the decision to go outside of the family *very* carefully. Blood usually *is* thicker than water.

Bequests and Trusts

Couples have many vicious arguments over giving money to their children. Indeed, this is a major reason for some parents avoiding a will. In many families, there is one child who has done everything right and another who is a rebel, perhaps a huge disappointment. Also, in lots of families, there is one adult child who has plenty of money and another who has very little.

This subject is considered in the "Managing the Family Dynamics of Inheritance" chapter of Lynn O'Shaughnessy's *Retirement Bible,* and the complications are endless.[1] As O'Shaughnessy says, families can be emotionally ripped apart by estate issues. For example, inheritances with strings attached are increasingly popular, but dictating from the grave has many perils. Children like the money, but they almost always resent their parents' interference in when and how they get it. Adult children also fight over the oddest things besides money after you die, so ask them now what they want and write it down.

How much to give each child is a complicated matter, but my experience with couples and families leads to the conclusion that, in most circumstances, children should be treated the same. That is, you help your children most by treating them equally in your will. In fact, their future relationships with one another may depend on it! After you and your partner die, you surely want your kids to be able to emotionally support and depend on one another—rather than distancing themselves or sitting in some counselor's office complaining about being victimized. If your will treats your children differently, closeness may be extremely difficult because they will probably have negative feelings about both you and their siblings. Even rich children may resent it if you did not acknowledge and "reward" them equally. If you give the rich ones *more* because their hard work merits it or because they can manage money better, they may feel guilty and defensive vis-à-vis siblings. But if you give the rich ones *less,* they may wonder why you don't appreciate how hard they've worked to become successful, or why you thought that they were less deserving than a sibling who did not do as well. With the less bright or less financially accomplished ones, your decision is equally important. If you leave them *more* money because they need it more, they may feel guilty to have received more than their share, or their feelings of greed and entitlement may interfere with sibling relationships. On the other hand, if you give them *less* than the accomplished ones, they may be angry and hurt by your lack of confidence in them or love for them. Because this issue is so complex and emotionally laden, most parents are wise to demonstrate their love through equal financial legacies.

If you are realistically concerned about an adult child's likelihood of blowing the money, you can use a trust, but make sure that the trustee is attentive enough to evaluate that child in future years so that responsible behavior can be eventually rewarded with equal treatment.

Even if you decide to treat the kids equally, however, you still have to think about questions such as:

• When will we give?

- Equal amounts of cash, or divided assets for special needs?

- How much control should we retain now, or even after our death?

- If we leave money in trusts, who should the trustees be?

- Are there any friends or relatives, besides our children, that we want to include?

These issues are, of course, related to our feelings about the kids, other relatives, and our friends, but they also reflect our own personality type and our feelings about ourselves.

Charitable decisions can similarly cause conflict between two partners:

- What if you have devoted time and effort to a particular charity, but I hate your choice?

- What if I think the amount you want to give is too high or too low?

- How might I convince you that my choice is better than yours?

- What if you want to establish a charitable trust that affects our current standard of living, while I only want to implement these gifts after our deaths?

Again, attorneys and other outsiders can help to mediate, but most of the hashing out should be done by the couple alone. It is wonderful if the partners eventually agree, but total agreement is not necessary. After arguing about charitable giving for two solid years, one childless couple eventually divided their assets in half and took different approaches with separate trusts.

When This Is Not Your First Marriage

Things get even more complicated when one or both of you have been married before, because your estate planning now needs to cover what will happen if *this* marriage is ended by death, including how the assets will be distributed to the surviving spouse, the children of your current marriage, the children of prior marriages, and any other beneficiaries.

In a thoughtful piece about estate planning in marriages other than the first one, attorney Alan S. Novick laid out the issues.[2] State laws place an emphasis on providing for the surviving spouse, but it is human nature to rebel against giving money that may have come from a previous marriage to your current partner's subsequent partners or spouses, so a lot of these couples are cautious. They want documents and trusts that don't leave too much to their current spouse. Furthermore, children do not have absolute rights to their parents' estates under most state laws, so these careful people want to address their children's bequests clearly.

It is common for people in *first* marriages to think that they will leave everything to the surviving spouse and let her, later, leave everything in equal shares to their children, but estate planners do not advise this even in first marriages, and they are especially against it in second, third, or fourth marriages, in which loyalties and motivations can be quite convoluted.

Fortunately, trusts and other legal mechanisms can accommodate your wishes for all of your ultimate heirs, but couples often argue about the specifics—partly because these decisions are so deeply personal. The attorney cited previously offers the following advice for couples who have been married before:

• Pay attention to the separate needs of the surviving spouse and children.

- Before deciding the amounts and timing of distribution from any trust, designate a trustee—and a successor trustee if the first is unable to perform his duties.

- The choice of trustee should especially be related to any powers you are giving her to make discretionary decisions and distributions.

- A life income trust can provide well for the needs of a surviving spouse while leaving the husband's assets to his children and the wife's resources to hers.

- The trust for a surviving spouse can be flexible or nonflexible. Discretion can be given to the spouse or to the trustee.

Imagine the relationship issues that you will have to confront when you make these legal decisions in a non-original marriage! You will need a lot of emotional clarity to make the proper judgments and then feel comfortable with them.

And the same types of questions need to be answered by both partners if you are leaving most of your money to charity.

When You Are Not Married—by Choice or Because You Can't Be

The 2000 United States census found that 5.5 million households—about one in twenty—consisted of unmarried partners, and most of these people are probably in committed homosexual or heterosexual relationships. Most opposite-gender couples have probably chosen not to sanction their relationship legally, but gays and lesbians do not currently have that option. In either case, effective estate planning involves thinking outside the box. There are now attorneys who specialize in same-sex planning.

Although unmarried partners *can* get most of the protections that married couples can obtain, it will require a lot of extra legal work since many laws do not give them any automatic rights.[3] These couples, at retirement age or before, should make joint decisions, and that usually requires talking about tough relationship issues—the earlier the better, however, because it's too late if one person dies or becomes incapacitated. Legal help is especially necessary if they own property together or if one is financially dependent on the other. They need to look at the worst-case scenarios in order to make the right decisions. Wills and trusts can be especially critical if either partner has children.

The two other important documents are even more crucial for unmarried couples. The durable power of attorney for finances allows you to name a person you trust to look after your money matters if you can't; this will avoid any possibility of an unwanted relative taking over or a conservatorship proceeding—which can be expensive and unpredictable for the partner. Similarly, health care directives must be used in order to make sure that the person you want will be allowed to carry out your medical wishes if you are incapacitated. These are not substantially different from the documents for married couples, but they need to be very clear for unmarried partners because medical and other professionals are not always cooperative.[4]

Unmarried couples who are reluctant to give away this authority need to be reminded that all of these documents can be revoked. Nothing is irreversible unless and until you can no longer speak for yourself.

Questions to Ask Yourself and Your Partner

1. Do we both have wills? If not, why not?
2. What factors might make us want to update them?
3. What is the philosophy behind our wills?
4. Who is the executor of my (your) will? Why?

5. Whom have I (you) named as power of attorney and/or health care proxy? Why?

6. How do I (you) feel about the plug being pulled at a particular point? What about hydration and nutrition?

7. Have I communicated sufficiently with the people I have named (executor, power of attorney grantee, and health care proxy) so that they know my wishes?

8. What bequests have been made, or should be made, in my (your) will? Why?

9. If we have children, do we want to treat them equally in our estate planning? Why or why not?

10. How will we resolve any differences between us about giving to our children?

11. How are our attitudes about charitable giving the same or different?

12. To what extent do we agree on the organizations and timing? How will we resolve any differences?

13. What are my (your) pros and cons for giving money away now versus after our deaths? Do we agree or disagree?

14. If this is not our first marriage, how are our legal issues different from those of original-marriage couples? Is this a problem for us?

15. If we are in a committed but unmarried union, what have we done to protect each other legally? What more should we do? Do we have any conflicts about this?

Part Three: Getting It Right—Together

15.
Fighting Fairly

The techniques that retirees should use to success-fully resolve conflict are not terribly different from the ways that younger couples solve their problems. However, without the distractions of work and packed schedules, many older couples find that they have to face each other in new ways. Surprising issues crop up, and problems that had been ignored in the busyness of life suddenly loom larger.

Seniors have both advantages and disadvantages in dealing with conflict and strong emotions. Certainly, older people have had a lot of time to solidify their posi-tions on various subjects, so they're often quite rigid. It sometimes seems harder for them to rethink their reac-tions to conflict than it is for younger couples. On the other hand, most retirees have also acquired some per-spective over those years. They may not get so excited so fast. They might not be as concerned about losing pride as their younger counterparts are. They know that life will not last forever, so perhaps they can be a bit more open than they used to be.

Sometimes the basic skills for fighting fairly are there, but the techniques that a couple had learned early in their relationship have long been forgotten, and they need to be relearned.

Anger Versus Withdrawal

When retired couples fight, all kinds of emotions and strategies come into play, but one of the most important determinants of resolution is their levels of anger versus withdrawal. If either individual is extreme in one of these emotions, the chances for resolution are hampered—often because the other partner is pushed into being more extreme on the other side of the seesaw. Continuing with this analogy: If *both* partners are either extremely angry or extremely withdrawn, that side of the seesaw will sit on the ground, and their relationship will go nowhere. However, if they are both more toward the middle of the anger-withdrawal dimension, there may be temporary ups and downs, but there will be a better balance in their relationship.

The two extreme positions are intense, white-hot, burning anger, on one hand, and silent, sullen withdrawal on the other. Neither is a fair way to deal with conflict, but these are very common reactions. Stereotypically, men have the anger response and women withdraw, but there are many variations within and among couples. Lots of men get very depressed and quiet at the first sign of trouble, while many women have a hair-trigger temper.

Anger, in general, seems to be increasing in modern, industrialized society. We have road rage, airplane rage, sports-watching rage, and other types—sometimes with tragic results. For customers of businesses and government offices, service has diminished to the extent that we now have to stand in long lines and wait in long telephone queues, and we often feel that we have no control over these circumstances. Many people feel pushed to the emotional breaking point, and one journalist says that there are three primary culprits: time, technology, and tension. The sheer complexity of our lives has shortened our collective fuse. It's a lot of little things that make people feel out of control, and a sense of helplessness triggers rage more than anything else.[1]

In addition, we seem to have an increased tendency to blame others for making us angry, and we, as a society, are less inclined to hold ourselves accountable for bad behavior. We like to direct our rage toward everyone in sight—especially our partner, who is so conveniently present most of the time.

Psychologists used to urge people to vent their anger—get it out. They said that it was bad for us to let anger simmer inside. They told us that we all need to get it out or we will explode like a pressure cooker. But most experts now say that it is more healthy for everyone to manage their anger. Exploding simply perpetuates the anger response by making it feel normal, so we remain comfortable with frequent anger, but this hurts our health dramatically over time, as well as our relationships.

The same experts now tell us that anger management can be learned and that it becomes easier with practice. In fact, anger must be a big problem, and anger management training must be needed, because classes and books about anger are proliferating.

So what are the general principles for taming a terrible temper? First, it's important to identify what is really upsetting you. Sometimes you are reacting to an important problem when your temper flares, but often your anger actually has nothing to do with the current situation, and you may need to get some help in examining the real issues, which frequently go back to childhood. I am not suggesting psychoanalytic psychotherapy here, where you would talk ad infinitum about the most minute details of your family and early years, but every individual *can* train himself to think about the childhood influences on his present persona: Did you get used to a lot of anger from your parents? Did you do better with your peers when you acted tough and angry? Were you forced to be angry at your older siblings because they would abuse you if you weren't? Of course, there have been five or six decades since your childhood, and a lot has happened to you over those years. Adult situations need to be searched for sources of your anger too.

Second, you need to avoid physical exhaustion and psychological overload because anger will come easily in those circumstances. In other words, if your demeanor is not naturally calm, your temper will explode through any fake calm exterior when you are tired and are losing psychological control due to overload.

Third, when you feel yourself getting angry, you must fight for self-control with every ounce of strength and every trick that you have learned. Just as people with memory problems try to associate a name with something else in order to remember it, people with anger issues usually try to find something that will interrupt the escalating feeling—counting to ten, taking a deep breath, thinking of their favorite beach, or anything else that works.

Angry fighting with your partner in retirement has special ramifications because anger will have long-term negative consequences, and there is a good chance that you will need this person desperately in the years ahead. Instead of using destructive behaviors, Professor Pepper Schwartz suggests, in her book *Everything You Know About Love and Sex Is Wrong,* that you can help the future of the relationship by asking questions such as:

- Will this issue really matter to me tomorrow? A year from now?

- Am I thinking negatively right now? How can I force myself to think more positively?

- Do I really want to let this person or situation control my mood and ruin my whole day?

- Do I really want to churn out stress hormones such as adrenaline, which will rev my body into a state of combat readiness, multiplying my risk for a stroke or heart attack?

- Can I do something, like listening to soothing music or taking a walk, that will change my mood?

- How is this situation modifiable?

- Does it really matter if I win this one, making my partner lose—with all that loss may imply for my partner's level of self-esteem, anger, and resentment?[2]

On the other side of this emotional seesaw, withdrawal was also once thought of as an effective technique for managing a fight. If he seems unreasonable, leave the room or the house. If she is screaming at you, refuse to engage until she calms down. More recently, however, many experts believe that withdrawal is wrong too. It connotes an air of superiority and tends to escalate your partner's anger. We have all had situations in which we want to sort things out but the other person turns her back on us, and that usually feels terrible. It's a rejection when that other person refuses to engage, and withdrawal is seldom an effective technique for calming us down.

Unless the fighting with your partner is turning into true abuse—in which case you should withdraw and escape—you need to try to resolve things by responding to the core of the issue, not the anger per se. You should verbalize your take on the situation. You might suggest a solution or a compromise.

The crux of the matter is that you usually need to have the fight in order to resolve the conflict, but in a reasonable way. You are thereby modeling behavior that your partner might gradually pick up on, allowing her to save face while calming down.

Fighting fair, then, requires that both people hit the middle ground between anger and withdrawal. Monitor your feelings and words. When you find yourself moving toward one psychological extreme or the other, you might even say out loud, "I've got to stop myself from getting really angry here" or "I feel like withdrawing now, but I'm going to try not to." Verbalizing your own feelings may have some influence over your partner's demeanor as well.

Limit the Time, but Get to the Core

Fighting fairly should also have some time limits because exhaustion never improves your chances at resolution. You can simply say that you are too tired to continue now, suggesting a time that you would be willing to talk about it later. Or you can say that you want to give this issue some thought and talk about it when you have more perspective. It is often a good idea to make an appointment for planned conflict resolution because both people will probably give it more importance that way, thinking about the issue beforehand and putting aside other concerns and distractions to focus on it. Then, most of the time, you'll either forget about the fight or resolve it more easily later, when you've gotten some psychological distance and your emotions are not running so high.

If an argument goes on and on, some people try to resolve it superficially just to get the fight over with. But this is a mistake because the problem will usually just crop up later. Instead, agree that you both need to stop now. This decision will not only acknowledge that your routines are important, but it will allow you to put this fight in the context of your overall relationship. What seems important at one moment can either look very insignificant later or be seen as part of a troubling pattern that must be dealt with in a more comprehensive way.

The Bedroom Is No Place to Fight

Professor Schwartz examines various myths about relationships, including the one about never going to bed mad. The idea behind this common dictum is that people should not let problems simmer without addressing them, but Schwartz says that sleeping on a problem is actually a pretty good idea. Anger will usually dissipate with time, and it is amazing what solutions your subconscious mind may come up with during a good night's sleep. Maybe you'll realize that it wasn't such a big deal after all. But even if you're still mad the next day, you and your partner will probably be in a more rational mood about it.

Reserve your bedroom space for relaxation and more pleasant activities. You want the bedroom to be associated with peace rather than war. You both need your sleep anyway, and it's better to move to separate rooms, if need be, than to argue in bed.

Jealousy

Jealousy is one of the most unfair elements in fights between partners. This emotion usually emanates from feelings of insecurity, but it is almost always disguised and presented with an air of righteous indignation. If either person is not very strong psychologically, jealousy can be very damaging to the weaker partner—whether he is the perpetrator or the recipient of those emotions. Jealousy can actually kill an otherwise healthy alliance.

This was a relatively new relationship of five years for Geoffrey and Michael when they almost split up. Each of them had had a couple of three- or four-year committed alliances in their thirties and forties, but neither of them had felt any need to settle down permanently with one person—until they met each other in their mid-fifties. They were by then tired of changing partners, and they strongly verbalized their wish to grow old together. They had a lot of similar interests, and they both looked forward to retiring by age sixty-two—"to travel and have a lot of fun."

Michael had a history of being jealous with his partners. He actually thought of it as a game—a sign of caring. Some of his partners had seemed flattered by his constant questioning about other men and the times that he surprised them at home unexpectedly. Only one person had ever really disliked it strongly. Michael was also the more dramatic and volatile personality of the two men, and he liked himself that way.

Geoffrey was the calm, cool, and collected one. He had a fast-track career, and a lot of his colleagues did not know that he is gay. He had a lot of restaurant meals with other businesspeople, as well as a great deal of travel, while Michael did neither for his job as a hospital lab supervisor, so Michael worried almost from the beginning about Geoffrey finding a younger, richer, better-looking man.

Michael always had amusing ways of asking his questions, so Geoffrey didn't mind at first. Indeed, he did feel a little bit flattered. But after only six months, he told Michael to cut it out. He was faithful, and it was unfair to imply that he wasn't. Midway into their five years together, they found a couples' counselor for six sessions of useful dialogue about this, during which Michael talked about his insecurities, and after that Michael controlled his jealousy a little more. But he slipped back into old patterns, and this time it was not a game to him. It was deadly serious because he felt that he was losing

Geoffrey. Furthermore, retirement was looming in a couple of years, and he was jealous of Geoffrey's accomplishments, feeling that he had done less with his life.

In reality, he was losing Geoffrey's love and respect. Geoffrey stopped carrying his cell phone because he was too annoyed at Michael's interruptions. He spent less and less time at home. At the four-year mark, Geoffrey asked Michael to move out—a devastating blow. They discussed how wonderful their life had been together except for this one glaring problem. Michael got really serious this time, asking to stay while he went into individual therapy and tried to figure this out. He found a great therapist, who probed the lack of acceptance Michael had felt in his childhood and adolescence. His family had never supported his gay lifestyle. Despite the bravado he showed to most people, he felt alone and vulnerable in the world, and as he began feeling older in his fifties, Geoffrey had been like a lifeline. His fears of losing that relationship made him both vulnerable and angry at his own dependence.

Over the next year Michael and his therapist role-played a lot of situations—both real from his past and imaginary. Michael tried on different emotional responses to various events. He found out how much better he felt when he shut off his jealous feelings. The therapy was a combination of talking about Michael's past, trying to understand some of his insecurity, and behavioral training—forcing a different response without necessarily understanding the source of the feelings. The therapist said that it's like controlling what you eat: You may want that candy bar, and even reach for it, but you stop yourself because you know it's not good for you. It will make you fat, and that will surely screw up your self-esteem. So because Michael's jealousy was really toxic to both Geoffrey and himself, he had to stop allowing himself those thoughts and actions.

Things are not perfect between them, but they have recommitted themselves to a lifelong relationship. When they fight and jealousy begins to reappear, Michael has asked Geoffrey to cue him by saying, "Remember the J-word." Michael is still training himself to control his thoughts, and he is taking painting classes—an activity he loved as a child and is pretty good at. He says that art gives his life added serenity and meaning.

Feelings of jealousy are familiar to most of us because we seldom feel totally secure in our relationships with others. Deep down, we wonder if we are smart enough, rich enough, good-looking enough, or socially adept enough to hold the person we love or the friends we like. Even if we don't worry about our partner actually going away, we may wonder, deep down, if we could lose that person's respect or time or devotion. And that threat of loss could come from almost anywhere. We are basically afraid of being hurt.

Typically, however, jealousy is expressed with none of these insecure feelings. Instead, it comes out with anger and accusations and bravado. It's your partner's fault. He is making you feel this way. That is why jealousy is so unfair. It usually comes from inside but is projected outside of yourself.

So what should the jealous person do? Rather than allowing this feeling to consume us, we should heed the oft-heard maxim that if we love someone, we must set him free. If the relationship is meant to be, he will come back; if not, he was never ours anyway. It takes a secure person to live by this credo, but freedom really is the only way to strengthen a partnership, and jealousy will almost always diminish it.

In situations where there really is a threat, such as an ongoing affair or another relationship that excludes and demeans you, the correct response is not jealousy. Instead, look at it as a problem to be solved—with feelings, but in a rational way.

Criticism

Criticism is another obstruction to fighting fairly. It too usually evolves from a damaged and fragile ego, but it is projected on the partner. It seems to be human nature for some people to feel happy and important only when they put others down. Some of these people would never criticize their friends, but they think that they have the right to constantly put down their partner.

In the extreme, criticism undermines the confidence of your partner, diminishes your own self-esteem, escalates anger, and eventually drives couples apart. This is not an easy trait to change, but awareness is the first step. Many people are in denial about their own critical tendencies, and it is especially hard for them to accept that these issues are based in insecurity. They are sure that they're right; they're just trying to help. But with dedication and practice, the negative effects of criticism can be understood, and it can be modified to some extent.

Using the Past

Past is truly prelude to everything we do. This is usually a good thing because older couples find great comfort in family ruts, especially those that have offered reassurance or shortcuts through the hard times. For instance, the author of a piece called "The Same Old Love" says that couples who have been together many years often have communication codes and language patterns. They can say things to each other without words or with very few words. They enjoy telling stories about the past, and they can finish each other's sentences. In these relationships, predictability is a plus. Acceptance has grown like a delicate fruit.[3]

But past can also be prelude to a lot of conflict. When the past includes serious problems, or even just annoying ones, some partners cannot or will not let it go. They consider every current situation in light of the past, and every opportunity is used to keep the negatives of the past alive. This rehashing may meet the psychological needs of some resentful partners, but it is not fair fighting because people cannot change if the past is a constant, immutable factor.

In general, we need to minimize the past, learning from it and seeing patterns in our relationships, but never ruminating endlessly about it or letting it interfere unduly with the present. We need to live in the present as much as possible. Surely we can do nothing to change the past, and we will miss the best parts of now if we are not able to put the past in perspective. Most people hate being reminded of negatives anyway; that only seems to make them defensive and rigid about change. Instead, what all couples should want for themselves is to be more open to new possibilities, with a sense that the future can be different and that they can both make psychological progress.

Pressing Those Buttons

After even a short time together, couples know each other so well. It doesn't take long for us to figure out each other's weak spots and vulnerabilities. And it is so tempting, in the midst of a fight, to go for those jugulars. But partners need to control these impulses to inflict pain if they are to have a strong and close relationship.

Most of us have a natural longing to be open with our partner, to really share life's ups and downs, but it is painful to be too vulnerable if you live with a person who uses your weaknesses against you. After that happens a few times, most people tend to shut down emotionally and protect themselves. So partners need to realize that they only hurt the relationship by pressing those buttons of vulnerability.

Gender Issues That Affect Fighting Styles

In the past twenty years, several authors have popularized the notion that both men and women go through distinct stages in life, and we know that there are some gender differences. For example, Gail Sheehy says that couples often find themselves out of sync with each other after age fifty, when men become more nurturing and women seem more ambitious. In *Understanding Men's Passages,* Sheehy asserts that the first half of a man's life is all about crafting a false self, which he uses to earn approval, rewards, and recognition. But the second half is the time for more authentic roles. This is the time when a man moves from competing to connecting, thereby redirecting his life.[4]

Many men don't really embark on this journey of change until retirement forces it upon them. Thus there can be a tremendous letdown, almost a sense of betrayal, when the man realizes that he has worked really hard and made many sacrifices, but the rewards are not as satisfying as he thought they would be. This can be a time of real pain and turmoil as the man tries to reinvent himself, discarding societal expectations in order to look inward and follow the dictates of his own heart. If he is to thrive at this age, a man must find meaning in his life.

But this process can also make a man more vulnerable to his partner, and women need to resist the impulse to dig hard into these fragile male egos. Both women and men should try to analyze and be tolerant of conflicts that emanate from a man's search for meaning. It remains to be seen whether more women will have these feelings of betrayal now that they are so much more invested in careers than they were a few years ago, but most people believe that women are wired differently.

People *can* learn to react honestly rather than defensively when their mate hurts their feelings. Instead of responding with anger and counterattack if their partner hits a soft spot, they can force themselves to name their feeling—that is, to *say* that they are feeling belittled or angry or jealous rather than acting it out. Then, if the partner cares at all about the damage being done to the relationship, he may well apologize.

Normal Fighting Versus Abuse

Partners need to learn the difference between normal fighting and abuse—both the physical and emotional kinds. Of course, the definition of normal fighting can vary significantly by culture and experience. Certain groups, perhaps the Greeks and Italians, seem to enjoy loud, volatile interactions, while people of other ethnicities may raise their voices much less often. Nevertheless, most of us know instinctually when we are being abused. Any physical fight is usually abuse, and constant verbal put-downs can be equally destructive.

Living with an abusive person, and the stress created by his or her behavior, can make you physically and/or mentally sick, so you need to protect yourself. There are bottom lines for you to figure out for yourself, but physical abuse should never be tolerated. The abuser in these situations usually says that it will never happen again, but the victim has little choice but to leave because abusers rarely change. Despite their promises, abusers seldom stop.

On the other hand, some fighting is normal in every partnership, even necessary if a couple is to work through the differences that invariably occur. In fact, relationships without fighting are rarely healthy because one person is probably doing all of the giving, and none of us should ever be a doormat. Seemingly perfect relationships are usually deceiving, and many therapists note that the couples getting divorces are very often the ones who never fought previously. Instead, those "perfect" partners usually buried their differences and their feelings until one of them couldn't take it anymore and wanted out.

Life would be pretty boring if couples never disagreed. Arguments can be stimulating. You can learn a lot about yourself and your partner by really working something through.

In essence, we teach people how to treat us. At retirement age, a long-term couple should have already established their guidelines for resolving conflicts, but because so many new issues come up at this stage of life, partners may have to establish new rules or reestablish old ones in order to fight fairly:

- Control tendencies toward anger or withdrawal in your fighting style. Try to stay balanced between these two powerful emotions.

- Minimize any feelings of jealousy. Realize that jealousy usually comes from insecurity, and it is more likely to destroy a relationship than improve it.

- Curb your criticisms of your partner. Try to be mostly positive.

- Limit your fighting time. Make an appointment to continue later if necessary.

- Get to the core of the conflict. Don't focus on peripheral issues.

- Try not to fight in the bedroom. Use that space for more pleasant things.

- Know the difference between normal fighting and abuse, and do not tolerate abuse.

- Stop pressing your partner's buttons of vulnerability.

- Be sensitive to feelings that spring from difficult life transitions.

- Learn to manage your emotions rather than letting them run wild.

- Stay in the present. Try not to dredge up negatives from the past.

- Give respect to your partner and expect it in return.

Some of us may have given our children powerfully damaging messages in the past if we have not followed these guidelines—especially if one of us has been an abuser and the other has accepted that abuse. But retirement can be a great time to correct the messages. Many older couples have observed problems in the relationships of their adult children and suddenly realized, or been told, that their children had no adequate models for fighting fairly. After all, our children tend to do as we do, not as we say, and sometimes they are not even aware of our influences on them. If we, as a retired couple, can change the way we interact about our differences, it is never too late to show a better model to our adult kids.

Revenge Versus Forgiveness

Revenge is a powerful drive in most human beings, and there are a few situations in life that cannot, indeed should not, be forgiven. But the old adage is true that when you seek revenge, you should dig two graves, one for your enemy and one for yourself, because the desire for revenge is usually very self-destructive. And wanting revenge is especially damaging to a retiree couple's relationship, just at a time when they will be needing each other more and more.

There are probably a few scars from any long-term relationship. The bad things build up, but the good things do too. Rather, at this stage of life, we need to let things go. Water under the bridge! Spilt milk! Don't sweat the small stuff!

Of course, there are differences between accepting, forgiving, and forgetting. All of these processes are not always possible. Niceness has a range. Some people find it easier to forgive and forget than others do. But we all need to realize that our focus should be forward, and therefore forgiveness and acceptance are the goals, even when forgetting may be impossible.

Older couples need to reexamine their predictable patterns of interaction. Sometimes problems have festered for years and wounds have been constantly reopened. In some cases the original incident is barely remembered, but the feeling is still intense. To put these hurt feelings into perspective, and to fight fairly about inevitable couple conflicts, you need to:

- Look at your own behavior as well as your partner's. Fights should be two-way streets, and both partners should be introspective about their roles.

- Change the interaction simply by changing your words. We tend to be very accusatory in a fight, but a sentence that begins with "I feel . . ." is much more effective than one that begins "You are . . ."

- Try to walk in your partner's shoes; develop empathy. Narcissism and selfish attitudes cannot coexist with fighting fairly.

- Lower your expectations to whatever you would expect from a friend. Even though we want the best from everyone, we don't always expect it from outsiders. We seem to tolerate lapses in our friends more easily than in our partner.

- Value even a small payoff for what it may bring in the future.

Change is hard, especially as we age, but good things build upon one another in a relationship.

• Realize that forgiveness of your partner gives you strength because you break free from being controlled by someone else's actions. You do not have to forget, but forgiveness usually feels good.

In the words of many self-help groups, we need to change the things we can, accept the things we can't, and seek to know the difference. In a committed relationship, we often wish that our partner would significantly change, and some people never stop trying, but that is such a total waste of resources. By retirement age, we really need to heed the dictum attributed to Mae West: "Don't marry a man [or woman] to reform him [or her]. That's what reform schools are for."

Furthermore, the concept of being right or wrong in a conflict should automatically become less important as we age. The stronger and more mature we are, the less it should matter whether we win any particular fight. Time is shorter now, and winning every struggle should be so much less important than keeping our relationships loving and close.

Questions to Ask Yourself and Your Partner

1. When we fight, where does my (your) style fit on the anger/withdrawal seesaw?
2. If anger is an issue for me (you), how can it be managed better?
3. If withdrawal is an issue for me (you), what can we both do to help us reengage appropriately?
4. Do you think I'm a jealous person? Are you?
5. Has jealousy been destructive to our relationship? If so, what can I (you) do to change?

6. Am I (are you) overly critical? How can I (you) become more positive?

7. Does either of us dwell too much on the past?

8. Are we able to limit the time frame of a fight?

9. Do we try not to fight in our bedroom?

10. Do we engage in normal fighting, or does either of us sometimes feel threatened by the other's intensity?

11. Do I (you) ever feel abused, physically or emotionally, in this partnership? Why?

12. Does either of us try to get revenge on the other for past problems?

13. Am I (are you) able to forgive most of the time? Forget?

14. To what extent do we accept each other as we are?

15. Do we fight often enough?

16. Do I (you) fight fairly in most instances? What are our worst offenses?

16.

Communicating Well During This Stage of Life

Listening

Listening sounds easy, but it's really common for couples to tune each other out, especially in long-term relationships. Seniors often think that they've heard it all before. Their eyes glaze over. They're bored or disinterested in the content; they're annoyed with the same old style. They are more focused on themselves than on their significant other.

More important, partners often fail to listen with that "third ear"—the one that searches for context and meaning. Corporate trainers teach this trick in order to enhance business communication, and couples' therapists try to inculcate it into their clients. In order to listen in this way, we have to constantly ask ourselves these questions:

- *What do these words really mean in this context?* When she says, "I'm tired," does she mean (a) physically tired because she did some gardening today; (b) mentally exhausted from worrying about the biopsy she had last week; (c) overall, fed up with life; (d) mad at me because I left her to take out the trash today; or (e) something else? The only way to get further clues is to ask some questions.

- *What is he or she really trying to say?* He just said, "We have to get more exercise." Is this (a) an innocent, innocuous remark; (b) a recognition that he has gained weight; (c) a concern about his weight because he is having an affair; (d) a sign of worry about his health; (e) a dig at me for being a couch potato and gaining a few pounds; or (f) something else? Ask some relevant questions.

- *What has been assumed in this conversation?* She just said, "We're overdrawn at the bank again." Since she has made this comment many times before, following bill paying at the beginning of the month, her partner might logically assume that this is an innocuous remark—expressing her frustration with this task. He assumes that she really means, "We're spending a lot, but it's OK because I'll take some money out of savings to cover the checking account." But with other assumptions, this remark could signal financial disaster.

- *Are any of these assumptions faulty?* This time (a) she might be seriously worried because the bills have been unusually high this month; (b) she might be implying that my pension is too low to meet our needs and that I am not a good provider; or (c) she might be suggesting that the expensive cruise we're planning for February needs to be canceled. The partner needs to ask some questions.

- *What has been left unsaid?* He said, "I have an appointment with the lawyer tomorrow to change my health care proxy." Is he leaving unsaid that (a) he talked to someone at his club whose mother just died a horrible death, and he's decided that he'd rather have nutrition and hydration, even if life is prolonged, than to starve and dehydrate to death; (b) he thinks I'm failing fast mentally, and he's chosen our son to make these decisions instead of me; (c) he's worried about whether the document was written properly when it was executed years ago, and he wants to make sure that our new attorney puts in the current legal language; or (d) something else? The partner needs to ask questions in order to understand the meaning.

Human communication is such that we don't always say what we mean, and we don't always mean what we say. No person can be a mind reader, but older partners often *think* that they can because they have so much "wisdom"—and perhaps so much time together.

Listening with this third-ear style is necessary in order to maximize every relationship—with children and grandchildren, friends, bosses and coworkers, siblings, shopkeepers and restaurant staff, and just about everybody else. But it could be the most important quality of all in our closest personal partnership. Older couples often say that their friendship is the thing that keeps them together, and real friendship is rare without strong listening skills.

Why does listening matter now more than ever? First, because we are together a lot more in retirement, and if one of us is disinterested in the other, one or both of us may be miserable. Second, because both of us have interesting things to say and discuss as we go through these retirement transitions and try to finally become whole. And third, because facing the future at this age can be frightening, and we need to be able to talk about it. As we both experience more illness or have to deal with deaths among our friends and family, it would be nice if we could really listen to each other.

One might think that retiree couples, with many years of both relationship and worldly experience, would be experts at this. They know their partner so well. They're aware of all the vulnerable areas. They understand the other person's hopes and dreams.

But these couples are also very experienced at tuning each other out, and familiarity can sometimes breed contempt—the feeling that certain aspects of the partner are so distasteful that they will simply be ignored. Nevertheless, there are a lot of benefits for the relationship if both people have an awareness of hidden, complex meaning within their interaction.

Frame the Issues

Examples abound of what happens when people do not frame their communication. Perhaps because of their age and some change in brain functioning, or perhaps because they're taking each other for granted in the relationship, this is a common phenomenon among older couples. The process goes something like this: one person starts talking, finds that the partner is not listening, gets the partner's attention somehow, goes on without recapping, encounters irrelevant questions, feels frustrated, and then ends up angry because he has not been understood. All of this occurs because the issue has not been framed properly and the other person doesn't know what you are talking about. Very often, if you start the discussion again later with more of a frame around it, any disagreements will be resolved quickly.

When we start speaking, *we* know the context, and so we often assume that our partner will also, but that may be too much to ask. She has probably been focused on something else, and our comment may seem like it's coming out of the blue.

Communication would go much more smoothly between partners if the speaker could think about context initially and establish it firmly with a couple of conversational tricks. These are a few of the ways that you might frame an issue:

- "You remember that concert I told you about last week?"
  (Pause for answer.) "I'd like to get tickets for . . ."

- "I've been thinking a lot about Jim's problem at work." (Pause for some sign of recognition.) "What do you think about suggesting that he . . ."

- "I've really been missing Rudy lately." (Pause for some sign of connection.) "What would you think about getting another dog?"

Some couples also find that verbal communication works best when it begins with the other person's name. Apparently, hearing their own name at the beginning of a sentence helps some people to focus their attention.

Pick Your Battles

This is another crucial communication skill. If we're alert and have opinions about life, there are so many things to argue about in this world, yet most of us don't fight about everything with our friends. We accept them pretty much as they are. Why, then, do differences matter so much with our partner? Why can't we accept her ideas and attitudes more easily?

The explanation is that we don't have such complicated relationships with our friends. We aren't so enmeshed in power struggles with them—always wanting to score points or even the score. However, a close personal partnership is always a balancing act, so the need for control gets played out in these battles, often with significant negative consequences. The expression of emotion in this close relationship is always multilayered, including both what the words mean *now*, on the surface, as well as their further meaning in the overall context of the relationship.

There are a few couples who seem to enjoy fighting, but for most of us, constant bickering is useless and destructive. It tears us up inside and causes the relationship to suffer. Most of us know intellectually that we want peace in the relationship, but it's hard to put that into practice sometimes. We realize that most of the stuff we argue about doesn't really amount to much and that most of our arguments are of the petty kind, but it's very hard to change.

How do we teach ourselves the difference between important conflicts and petty complaints? How can we learn to control our verbal communication better? One older couple, for example, spent months in counseling, asking themselves questions and thinking long and hard about the danger signs for them—the things that they need to avoid in order to improve their communication. At the last session, they arrived with a large, framed, calligraphy-styled set of five rules titled "Conditions for Communication." These rules would not apply for every couple because communication styles are unique in every twosome, and they needn't always be written and put on the wall. But these ideas suggest that a customized set of prescriptions could help many couples. This couple's rules are:

- Pick only one fight a day; a second one will have to be postponed until tomorrow.

- Fight only after 7 p.m. and only after one glass of wine. (More than one drink could be dangerous, but a little wine usually makes our aggravations seem less important.)

- Fight only in the family room or kitchen—and never in the car.

- Ask ourselves, before the fight escalates: Will this matter next week? In five years?

- Ask ourselves frequently: Is this a battle I really want to fight? What might the consequences be?

Be Sensitive to Egos and Gender

John Gray's book *Men Are from Mars, Women Are from Venus* and Deborah Tannen's book *You Just Don't Understand* popularized the notion that many of our differences are gender based. The science on all of this is still in development, but many relationships have been saved in recent years because we're thinking about all of this much more openly: "Is he really a jerk, or would most men rather watch a football game than have an emotional discussion?" "Is she really a crybaby, or is that a typical reaction when women feel hurt?"

In her book *An Unfinished Marriage,* Joan Anderson tells of the year-long sabbatical she took from her marriage to sit by the sea and think about her troubled, stale partnership.[1] She eventually returned, recognizing the rewards of mutual reliance in midlife, but Anderson has sparked a cottage industry serving women seeking to reflect on their lives for a weekend by the sea. Many of their group discussions focus on gender problems and the fact that roles change as we age, with women gaining ground in the second half of their marriage and men becoming more dependent on their wives.[2]

Making gender one "screen"—one assessment tool—in our communication efforts can help us see things in a different light. Most of us decide, then, that it's useless to ask, in the words of *My Fair Lady,* "Why can't a woman be more like a man?"—or vice versa. This gender tool helps us to laugh at many of the communication issues that made us angry before, and we sometimes even appreciate the balance that gender differences can provide in a relationship.

Some people have incredibly sensitive egos, and this too is an important factor in communication. With such a vulnerable ego, this kind of person sees slights where they do not exist, and she always takes things too personally.

Where do these ego issues come from? Is it nature or nurture?

Again, the science is still in development, but one wonders about the heritability factor because whole families often seem to have either very strong or very weak egos despite differences in their life experiences. It is puzzling to observe that some people who have suffered great assaults to their ego are self-confident and successful, while other people with this background are "damaged goods." Nevertheless, whether a sensitive ego comes from genes, childhood experiences, hard knocks in adult life, or something else, that person's partner has to put up with it and deal with it. It helps if both people can learn to recognize the effect that the fragile ego has on their communication.

In general, we can all enhance our communication skills if we really live by Thomas Harris' idea, originally published in 1967, that "I'm OK; you're OK."[3] This is a simple cliché for many of us now, but it is truly profound—especially for couple communication. That is, it's pretty hard to really believe that another person is worthy unless and until we feel that way about ourselves. And we can build a much stronger, more loving relationship with our partner if it is based on our own security and good self-esteem rather than a grasping neediness.

Accusatory Versus Feeling-Based Styles

In an argument, most of us are adamant that we are right. We're sure that we only want the best for the relationship; we don't want to hurt our partner. We wonder why our wisdom is being so misunderstood and demeaned. Of course, our partner is equally certain of her own infallibility, and there is the rub!

In the long run, resolution usually depends more on the communication style of both people than the content of their argument and position. If we are accusatory, our words come across as an attack, and we can end up saying things that hurt deeply. We can even make the relationship irreparable that way. But if we base our statements on our own feelings, we are less likely to encounter resistance, and the damage is usually much less.

The simple act of starting a sentence with "I feel" versus "You are" can change everything! The difference underlying the words is a mind-set based on how you are affected by something versus what your partner did wrong. If your mate has any empathy at all, she will respond to your troublesome feelings and will want to make you feel better. Your partner can then look at her own behavior less defensively.

Our tone of voice can be a problem too. Some of us need to work on how we come across—too loud, too passive, hateful, or condescending. We need to recognize the signals that we give via the words we use *and* the way we speak.

Negotiation

Volumes have been written about negotiation, but the two most important elements for senior couples are compromise and knowing your bottom line. Compromise is always required in a partnership, and no two people can live happily together without this trait being present on both sides. But the ability to compromise is especially important at retirement because many adjustments are required during this stage of life.

Individuals should also have limits beyond which they will not go. That is, compromise should never mean a total cave-in. Sometimes our bottom lines are well known before the negotiation begins; other times they become apparent to us as the process is progressing; and occasionally we're not sure of our limits until after the negotiation has ended—maybe not even then. Or perhaps our limits waffle, and we want to renegotiate the outcome much later.

As a general rule, the more we know ourselves and our bottom lines, the stronger we will be in any negotiation. And this is usually one of the assets of age—having many decades of negotiations under our belt and knowing pretty much what we want out of life. Above all, we should know ourselves well enough to recognize when the core of who we are is being threatened. That is, when the other party insists on something that will damage our soul—our sense of all that is right—the negotiation should be over.

Most couples could stand to sharpen up their negotiation skills because there is always some conflict in life, but the health of the relationship should always be more important than who wins— especially at this age, when we need each other more than ever.

Of course, not all disagreements have to result in an argument—especially if you can separate out the actual issues from the personalities involved. You can try to put yourself in the other person's shoes and see both sides. You can attempt to overcome your own personal stumbling blocks and understand your own biases. You can take responsibility for your own feelings and get a grip on them. You can learn to express yourself without sarcasm or hostility. You can clearly ask for what you need and want rather than expecting your partner to read your mind.

Very smart people sometimes have an advantage in business negotiations. They think quickly on their feet, have an ability to convolute arguments, and are able to pounce effectively when they see vulnerability on the other side. But in the relationship area, emotional intelligence, or EQ, is much more important than IQ. People with high emotional intelligence are more successful at relationship skirmishes because they are good at reading their partner's feelings and understanding the big picture of the relationship.

Win-win solutions are always best, and United States Secretary of State Colin Powell, one of the world's best negotiators, offers seven laws for gaining the power you want without alienating the other person.[4] Powell's principles can be applied to senior couples as appropriately as they are to world leaders:

- Dare to be the skunk. Be honest even in tough situations. Being responsible sometimes means pissing people off.

- You want to encourage arguments among equals. You want straight talk—even ideas that you don't want to hear.

- Share the power. Everyone needs to be responsible, and everyone needs to know the valuable role that they play.

- Know when to ignore your advisors. Other people often possess more data than judgment. You need to make your own decisions out of your own hard-won experience.

- Develop selective amnesia. Things change. Never let your ego control your position, because if you do, when your position goes, your ego goes too.

- Come up for air. You need a full, well-rounded life in order to do negotiations well.

- Declare victory and quit. Negotiation is not rank, privilege, title, or money. It's responsibility.

Find Humor

Humor is largely a gift. This is obvious because we so often see the same type of humor in several members of one family—even when they have been separated early in life. Humor must be somewhat inbred because some people who have had awful lives objectively are still able to see the world as a wonderful, happy place, while other people who have had every advantage can be totally humorless.

When at least one part of a couple has a fabulous, noncaustic sense of humor, they can weather storms so much more easily than when there is little humor at home. These fortunate partners seldom blow arguments out of proportion. They enjoy life and see the absurdities in it. Even when the more serious one starts to drag the relationship down, the humorous one can cut the mood quickly with a deftly funny remark. One couple told me that in the midst of their worst conflicts, they try to think about how this experience will make a funny story later.

Humor can, to a certain extent, be learned, and all of us need to work at that. Usually, if one partner can defuse a tense situation in an appropriately funny way, the other person will respond positively. It is a challenge for most of us to "think funny" while we are feeling angry or sad, but we should make it a test of our own creativity, and our humor can build. At the very least, we can vow to be open to new ways of looking at things, and we can respond when our partner tries to be funny.

Questions to Ask Yourself and Your Partner

1. Do we have any problems listening to each other?
2. How and when do our listening issues manifest themselves?
3. Have I (you) developed a sufficient "third ear"? How well do I (you) listen for context and meaning versus the literal words?
4. Does either of us tune out a lot in our communication? Why?
5. Am I (are you) good at starting verbal communication by framing the issue well?
6. How successful am I (are you) at picking our battles wisely?
7. How much does either of us enjoy our conflict? What are the payoffs?
8. Do we need to set any rules, specific to us, for when and how we should fight?
9. To what extent am I (are you) able to compromise appropriately?
10. What are our differences in communication style that might be due to gender?

11. Which of us has the more fragile ego? How does this affect our communication?

12. To what extent have I (you) mastered the ability to feel "I'm OK; you're OK"? How might we work more toward that sensibility?

13. Do I (you) have a feeling-based, nonaccusatory style? How can we help each other to do this better?

14. At what point in an argument do I (you) usually feel clear about my bottom line?

15. Do I (you) buy into the fact that win-win outcomes are better for our relationship than win-lose ones? To what extent do I (you) work at this?

16. What issue in our relationship do we most need to negotiate, and how might we use this for practice in the near future?

17. Does either of us have a good sense of humor? How can I (you) develop a better one?

17.
Getting Outside Help When You Can't Do It Alone

Education

It is never too late to learn about relationships, and retirees can gain a lot of knowledge from friends, books, classes, seminars, educational videos, TV, and radio—the kinds of things they seldom took time for before.

Sometimes, in fact, people accept change faster in the context of education than of counseling because professional help might seem too invasive or intense. Or they may think that strong people solve their own troubles; the world of counseling is for people with *real* problems. While many couples see an advantage in having the counseling tailored only to them, it is a threatening disadvantage for other couples when the counselor hits too close to home or is not sufficiently skilled to make them comfortable. Some of those people can accept the same principles and advice more easily in an educational setting. And in many cases therapy will follow.

The good news is that at retirement age, many people become more willing to share their problems with friends. Indeed, there is something about aging that frees many of us up to be more open. Maybe there is less to lose now that work and vocational competition are over. Perhaps we care less now about what others think of us because we are more comfortable with who we are. Or we might simply be getting more curious about how other couples relate to each other. Whatever the reason, we usually discover that when we *do* open up to friends, it is amazing how often they share their struggles with the same issues. Sometimes they have found very creative solutions, and we can learn from them. At the very least, we can usually laugh about it together.

Books can also answer a lot of questions and give us new ideas. For example, John Gottman, Ph.D., wrote *The Seven Principles for Making Marriage Work* and *The Relationship Cure* based on three large research projects, and he claims that he can predict with 91 percent accuracy which marriages will end in divorce—after only five minutes of observation.[1]

Gottman is very interested in a couple's style, and his team has found two distinct patterns of dysfunctional interaction—with implications about divorce:

- Couples who openly contest and fight with each other in an attack-and-defend mode, with escalating conflict, often divorce early in the marriage.

- Many couples whose marriages are marked by coolness and the suppression of emotions split in midlife. These couples are alienated and avoidant. They realize that their marriage is empty. They stifle too many things. They have few positive emotions toward each other, and they suppress negative ones. They have a passive and distant relationship with no laughing, love, or interest in each other. They often feel intense loneliness.[2]

Therapists often dread dealing with hot relationships and angry, battling couples, but it is actually easier for them to work with the fire than with suppressed emotions and avoidance. When a couple is fighting, they are at least engaged with each other, and the therapist can possibly help them come to terms with failed dreams and a pattern of blaming each other for their problems.

Another author who is widely read in the field of relationships is Harville Hendrix, Ph.D., and his most helpful book for senior couples is *Keeping the Love You Find*.[3] Hendrix focuses heavily on childhood issues and their connection to current relationship problems, so his books can assist a couple who want to be quite analytical about themselves.

There are hundreds of other books available on the subject of personal partnerships, as well as TV programs like *Oprah* and *Dr. Phil,* and seminars and classes galore, so there is no shortage of educational information on this subject. The challenge is to find the sources that give you what you want and need.

Marriage Mending

Many churches do a masterly job of helping couples without getting too intense via a method they usually call Marriage Encounter. (The Catholic Church sometimes calls it Retrouvaille, which means "finding and joining again.") This is a loosely organized campaign to lower the divorce rate through education and to enrich existing marriages. Most of these churches, of course, are especially concerned about marriages that involve young children.

The American divorce rate appears to be twice that of European countries and three times that of Japan. Many couples get married for the wrong reasons and then get divorced for equally wrong reasons. Marriage has been oversold in our culture, but many people think that divorce has too. So many churches are answering the question: What can society do about it?[4]

These encounter sessions usually take place over a weekend at some kind of retreat. They do not focus on either partner individually, and they do not talk much about love because that emotion can wax and wane over the course of a marriage. They *do* talk a lot about commitment and the need to work through problems, even in the midst of our consumer-driven, throw-it-out culture. They take the position that conflict occurs partly because our society is too focused on happiness, making us more critical of our partner and setting the relationship up for lots of negativity. When that happens, partners get more polarized, depressed, and anxious to get out of the marriage. Instead of focusing on happiness, therefore, these marriage encounters teach couples how to communicate better. They emphasize that many troubled couples are not wrong for each other; rather, the two people are behaving badly. These church-sponsored sessions usually put high value on staying together.

Other, more secular seminars are also available, and these tend to have less moralistic emphasis on keeping the marriage intact. The leaders of these groups may be more willing to recognize issues like drinking, drugs, and emotional abuse as good causes for divorce.

Certainly, all couples could learn from many of the techniques that these Marriage Encounter or marriage improvement groups use, but there is a range of reactions among attendees, from finding these weekends a waste of time to saying that it saved their marriage. Reactions seem to stem from the seminar's content, style, and leadership, as well as the individual attendee's mind-set.

The most effective part, which people mention repeatedly, is the exercise in which one partner answers a given question and then the other must repeat back what he has heard. This procedure demonstrates how often one person does not communicate clearly and/or the other person does not hear either the correct words or the emotional content. Many attendees are shocked to learn that "paraphrasing" what your partner says could be this meaningful as an educational technique.

The other helpful exercise seems to be writing letters to each other on a given subject. This is surprisingly effective because some people express themselves better in writing than they do verbally, and they also know that they will not be interrupted. On the receiving side, reading the other person's thoughts, versus hearing them, seems to give the partner time to react more rationally and less emotionally. But there is nothing magic about doing these exercises within a seminar. Couples can try it in front of the fire on a cold Saturday evening at home.

Many of these seminars find ways to minimize group process because of privacy concerns. They structure sessions so that partners are dealing just with each other. But my feedback from attendees suggests that couples wish there were more group interaction—more opportunity to learn from other couples. In my opinion, the best marriage workshops combine individual partner time with same-gender sessions and larger couple groups.

When to Get Counseling or Medication

Although many couples go all the way through a divorce without even considering outside help, counseling is appropriate whenever the problem-solving techniques that a couple has tried are not working or are making things worse. Sometimes two people get so bogged down in their own issues that they can't see much light at the end of the tunnel. Sometimes they are unrealistic and can't see the big picture of what a relationship should look like. Certainly most of us have trouble being objective about ourselves, and our friends and family can't be objective about us either. A professional, then, can offer us objectivity, along with his training and experience with many other couples.

Ideally, partners should go for help together. Even when one of you thinks there is no problem, both people should go because when you are in a committed relationship, whatever affects one person will certainly affect the other. But many couples do not go together because one person refuses to participate—out of fear of emotional exposure, from unwillingness to divulge secrets, or for some other reason.

In that case, the person who wants help should go anyway. Sometimes you can later engage your partner by explaining the process or pleading for involvement. Even if that never happens, one of you may be able to make a difference in the relationship by going alone because a change in one person's insight or behavior almost always causes some response from the other. But even if nothing changes in the relationship, the individual who went for help has usually learned a few things.

Psychopharmacology is another form of treatment. It is most useful in cases of depression, severe anxiety, bipolar illness, phobias, and drug or alcohol abuse. At times psychopharmacological help is *necessary* for one or both members of the couple before they can make use of counseling services. This kind of treatment *can* be fast and can work well, especially with the many new drugs coming to market. But pills can only be prescribed by a medical doctor; many health insurance plans do not allow much time between patient and doctor; and quick diagnoses are often wrong. Finding the proper medication and dosage often becomes a matter of trial and error. In the antidepressant category alone, there are many different drugs to choose from, with different reactions from different people and very different side effects for each user. For example, Prozac is said by some patients to cause weight gain and loss of sexual desire and/or potency. It also requires four to six weeks before noticeable changes occur. So finding the correct drug formula for any individual may take many months.

The side effects of drugs can also mask problems and/or create new ones, and older people often have more puzzling side effects than young people do because there are other things going on in older bodies. For example, one woman found that when her partner took an antidepressant to help stop his heavy drinking, he suddenly became belligerent and aggressive.

Couples surely should deal with medication issues together as they age. They can help each other monitor the side effects and persist until the right drug combination is found. Or they can encourage each other to do the psychological work that might help them avoid—or get off—medication because every pill has some side effects, and the medication may be a big expense as well.

Learn How to Shop

There is a huge range in the training of people who call themselves therapists or counselors, and there is great variation in cost. Even the terms *therapist* and *counselor* are confusing because they tend to be used interchangeably. The educational background of these people can vary from many years of graduate training to little or no high school, although the ones with little education are usually charlatans. There is no right or wrong set of credentials, but every client should ask questions and perhaps check the answers. Many counselors now advertise heavily, and it is not easy to sort out the good from the bad. One should be prepared to spend some time and money on the search process.

In general, the professionals in this business can be categorized as follows:

• *Psychiatrists.* M.D. degree and three or more years of specialty training. Physicians are the only therapists who can prescribe medication, although other professionals often have relationships with physicians for this purpose.

- *Psychologists.* In most cases, a doctorate (Ph. D.) in psychology, counseling psychology, or educational psychology, or a master's degree in one of these specialties. Research psychologists may also work with clients at times.

- *Clinical social workers.* An M.S.W. (master's degree in social work), including clinical training in therapeutic work. The letters LCSW (licensed clinical social worker) may appear after a name. Occasionally, social workers with expertise in research or community organization may also work with clients.

- *Counselors.* Usually a bachelor's or master's degree in marriage and family counseling, drug and alcohol addiction, psychology, sociology, or nursing. People with a divinity or other religious degree also work as counselors. Sometimes graduates of holistic health programs or institutes also do counseling with clients.

This list is not exhaustive because just about anyone can hang out a shingle as a counselor. Occasionally a counselor without formal training is competent—perhaps an educator who has a knack for helping people. But beware of the crystal-ball-gazing variety.

So how do you start looking for a counselor or therapist? First, you need to decide whether to go alone or as a couple—the partner approach being preferable though not always possible. You may *choose* to go alone if you feel that you can't be honest in front of your mate. This decision comes first because some counselors are narrowly focused on individuals versus couples, but most of them will work either way because clients who begin individually sometimes want to bring in their partner later, or vice versa.

Next, ask your personal physician(s) and your friends, if you trust their judgment, for suggestions. Call your mental health association and organizations such as AARP, describing the kind of person you think you'd like to see. For example, you might be more comfortable with a man or a woman. You might want someone younger or older. You might prefer a certain type of background and training.

Natalie struggled with depression most of her adult life, but it was kept under control with medication. She married Bill when she was twenty-four and had two children by the time she was thirty. Her depressive episodes, up until that time, had been treated by the psychiatrist her mother had seen for years. Then, while doing volunteer work at Cedars-Sinai Hospital in Los Angeles, Natalie met a psychiatrist whom she really liked, and she began a professional relationship with him that lasted twenty years.

When she was in her late forties, Natalie's father began to talk about selling his thriving business, which supplied the film industry, because he had no heirs to take it over. Natalie said, "What about me?" and he admitted that he had never thought about his only child, a daughter. She was intelligent and motivated, with some business experience by this time, and the next six years enhanced their relationship as he taught her the ropes. When her father died and Bill was looking for a career change anyway, she brought her husband into the business.

They were so busy for the next decade that they hardly noticed Natalie's depressions. She had stopped seeing the former therapist long ago, for lack of time; she got antidepressant prescriptions from her gynecologist. Bill and Natalie had their relationship struggles at home, but it was clear that Natalie was in charge at work, and they were committed to each other.

Then, in their early sixties, they started thinking about what their exit strategy might be. Neither of their kids had any interest in the business, and there were two possible buyers. Bill was hot to sell and do other things, but Natalie's major impediment was her fear of a major depression once she had "nothing" to do. As she hesitated about the business, their relationship and Natalie's health began to deteriorate. Bill too felt more depressed and anxious, and he insisted that they find a therapist to work this out.

They spent three months with a highly recommended psychologist, who helped them in certain ways, but this woman had little tolerance for Natalie's insistence that her depression was biochemical and for Natalie's extreme fears about what she would do in retirement. One day Natalie said that she wished they could find someone more like her former shrink, and Bill said, "Let's call him." He would be in his seventies now, and they wondered if he would still be in practice—or alive.

This man did not usually see couples, but Natalie convinced him that their marital relationship and business issues were totally interwoven with her depressions. Even in the first session, they saw that he was the ticket to their future. When Natalie worried aloud about what she would do, this man said, "Really? You are an expert in dealing with depression, and you are a talented, compassionate, educated human being. I can think of at least four places where Cedars-Sinai could use your volunteer help with patients." And the key sentence: "I could open some doors for you."

In short order, Natalie found the perfect buyer for the business, and everything else fell into place. She and Bill saw the shrink together for about two years—through the transition. They feel that he saved not only Natalie's

*sanity but their otherwise happy marriage as well. Of
course, they know that they did most of the work. They
talked about shared dreams and goals, as well as separate
ones. They did it in a neutral, supportive setting in
which they both felt less defensive than they did in "real
life." They did the work, but the right therapist was key.*

Then there is the issue of cost. Psychiatrists charge the most;
religion-based counselors generally charge the least. Because
there is still some stigma in segments of our society about therapy
and counseling, and because medical records these days are far
from private, many clients choose to pay the bills themselves
rather than have an insurance record. But this is less an issue for
retirees than it is for workers, who are often concerned about
their image and promotions.

Most insurance policies provide some coverage for mental
health care, but you will have to find out which therapists are
included, how much is covered per session, and how many sessions are allowed. Insurance seldom pays it all. Medicare usually
pays nothing for counseling.

Next, call three or more professionals to talk briefly on the
phone. You can glean a lot of information in a short conversation.
You will probably want to ask about cost and whether that person
offers a first consultation, perhaps fifteen or twenty minutes,
without charge. If things click on the phone, you can schedule an
appointment.

Always remember that you and the counselor are choosing
each other. You both have to feel right about working together. Ask
about education, and look around the room for diplomas—ideally
from schools whose names you recognize. After describing your
problem briefly, ask how many sessions the counselor would initially recommend, at what cost, and then if you wish to proceed,
come to some beginning agreement. Perhaps you'll make an

appointment with this person right now, or you might tell her that you have introductory appointments scheduled with other counselors and you want to think about it. You might agree to call by a certain date.

You will probably get tired of telling your story more than one time, but it is worth the effort, and it may even help you to crystallize the issues as you verbalize them repeatedly. Counseling usually takes time, and personal rapport is very important. You will see that you get different feelings and approaches from different people. Some counselors talk a lot, some very little. Some use the analytic method, based on Freudian principles, in which the patient-therapist relationship is examined as well as the presenting problems. Most now use some version of cognitive-behavioral techniques (CBT) in which the emphasis is on rationality and behavior modification. For example, with an older couple who are frequently in conflict with each other, the cognitive component might include changing pessimistic attitudes, while the behavioral aspect would strive to increase pleasant events that they can enjoy together. The goal would be to increase their quality of life through better methods of problem solving and conflict resolution.

And then there is a seemingly endless assortment of unique and often weird methods that counselors are sometimes pushing. Each professional should be able to clearly explain her orientation to you, and you should ask a lot of questions if you are not comfortable. There are many things to look for in the interaction process: style matters; personality counts; the feel of the office is important. Trust your gut reactions.

Have the courage to leave at the first sign of serious trouble. Beware of anyone who makes you too dependent and prolongs the treatment unnecessarily. Do not tolerate any kind of physical or verbal abuse. This does *not* mean that you should escape when things get uncomfortable for you emotionally. You will have to tolerate some discomfort in order to work through the problems and get help, but you will also have to monitor the process. This person must be your collaborator, not your master. Anyone who orders you to do something or tries to control you should be suspect. You want a stable, mature professional with whom you may work for a long time.

As a couple, you may disagree with each other at any of these steps—who calls for the appointment, what you divulge, which expert seems best. And you'll have to come to terms with these differences, even while trying to solve your other problems. But don't let these differences stop you from proceeding. Do your shopping and come to a compromise decision if need be. You can always make a change in therapist later if this person doesn't work out.

In fact, if enough money is available, the best of all worlds for a heterosexual couple is to find two counselors—male and female—who work together. I consider this the gold standard for couples because it allows gender to be less of an issue, and it gives an additional professional perspective. It can even be instructive for the client couple to watch the two therapists work out their differences.

Although the usual gender issues will not surface with gay and lesbian couples, they too may want to pick and choose the mix. For example, one male couple wanted two gay male therapists, and they ended up appreciating this arrangement. Their primary reason was that they wanted to minimize any possible feelings that their therapist did not understand them or was taking sides with one of them against the other. They also liked getting more than one "expert" opinion in each session, and they found that the four-way alliances that developed were very interesting. However, the biggest benefit to this arrangement, which they had not antic-ipated, was that they could periodically split up for individual therapy.

Advice Only in Your Context

Vulnerable or insecure clients like to get a lot of advice. They are needy and feel good when an expert tells them what to do. They like a counselor who gives them a lot of nurturing and doesn't ask too much of them. Thus they may initially prefer someone who comes up with a lot of suggestions.

At the other extreme, some clients just want to ramble on and on about their own issues without much interruption from the therapist. They resent being challenged or prodded into another way of thinking. If any advice does come, they like to prove that it is wrong. It's a game they play with the professional: "I know better than you do." Or it's a way of playing the victim and avoiding responsibility: "See what you did to us by giving us poor advice?"

Retiree couples should generally avoid both of these extremes and look for a counselor who will hit the middle ground, giving some advice but forcing them to make their own decisions.

As the client in a therapeutic situation, each person should look at, turn over, and examine every piece of professional advice in the context of who you are and what you want. You must realize that the professional is just a trained person with a particular background and certain biases. He can help you greatly, but only if you have a major role in the process. You must not let anyone pressure you to do something that doesn't feel right—that doesn't fit into your sense of integrity. There is no shortcut for the psychological work that is necessary before you should really act upon anyone's advice—even that of the most degreed, highly paid, qualified professional. Good therapists realize this and help their clients to become stronger decision makers. Stated succinctly, they help people learn to help themselves. Watch out for therapists who give you too many directions.

Questions to Ask Yourself and Your Partner

1. What kind of educational efforts would I (you) like to try that might enhance our relationship?

2. What books might I (you) read about relationships, especially at this stage of life?

3. Have we shared enough with our friends to benefit from their relationship issues and solutions? If not, why not?

4. Would I (you) like to try a Marriage Encounter type of weekend or retreat? Should it be church based or secular?

5. How would I (you) define the point at which we should seek outside help?

6. Do I (you) have a psychological problem that might benefit from medication? How should we seek the best source for this?

7. Does either of us take too much or unnecessary medication? If so, how is it interfering in our relationship?

8. How can we help each other solve the problem in a better way?

9. If we need counseling now or in the future, what educational background do I (you) want the person to have?

10. What type of personality would I (you) want a counselor to have?

11. If we need professional help, would I (you) prefer to go for counseling alone or together? Why?

12. If you (I) refuse to go together, would I (you) go alone?

13. Am I (are you) vulnerable to a therapist who gives too little or too much advice?

14. Am I (are you) good at taking advice only in my (your) context?

18.

Handling Divorce, Dissolution, or Death with Dignity

Divorce Statistics

Retirement may be an even more powerful cause of midlife divorce than children leaving home is. Suddenly one or both partners may realize that there are no more buffers between them—no children, and now no work either. The dynamics of their marriage may have changed because retirement has ruined most of the mechanisms that they had for avoiding each other. Now they are face-to-face with a person they have not gotten along with for years. They may have no desire, at this late date, to learn to take each other's feelings into account. The chickens have come home to roost. Both partners have come to the stark realization that they do not enjoy spending time together. Their working years had simply postponed the inevitable.

You have a choice to make in this situation. Do you try to find ever more complex ways of avoiding each other? Do you attempt the hard work of creating a lifestyle that you will both enjoy, trying to meet each other's emotional needs and finding real pleasure in your companionship? Or is this the time for divorce?

Maybe there is a serious problem that only divorce will solve, but more often two people just don't feel passionate about each other anymore, and that triggers a sense of emptiness and loneliness. Perhaps that feeling was really triggered by losing the passion for life that the individual once had, but it's much easier to blame it on the partner than to search inside one's often bankrupt self, so divorce just happens.

Data from the United States Census Bureau show that divorce has been rising significantly for people over age fifty-five from 1980 to 2000. This is especially important because people fifty-five and over numbered about fifty-nine million as of 2000—21 percent of the population—and these numbers are growing as the boomers advance in age. The divorce statistics for the boomer group will be interesting to watch.

The percentage of *all* adults who are currently divorced shows the following upward trend:

1970:	3.2%
1980:	6.2%
1990:	8.3%
2000:	9.9%

For people fifty-five years and above, the statistics show a similarly rising pattern (data for 1970 were not available):

	Divorced men	Divorced women
1980:	936,782 or 4.8%	1,726,814 or 5.2%
1990:	1,376,732 or 6.1%	2,262,055 or 7.6%
2000:	2,427,880 or 9.4%	3,611,990 or 10.9%[1]

These numbers do not include the category "married, spouse

absent," which would push the percentages considerably higher. The numbers above are quite shocking enough.

These statistics show that although divorce rates for all age groups have been rising (from 6.2 percent in 1980 to 9.9 percent in 2000), the rates for older people have risen even more rapidly: 4.8 percent in 1980 to 9.4 percent in 2000 for men, and 5.2 percent in 1980 to 10.9 percent in 2000 for women.

The numbers also are in contrast to what one might expect. One would think that when we look just at people over fifty-five, the divorce rates would be much less than for all adults. Older couples would be thought to divorce less often than younger ones because relationships at older ages should be more stable. Common sense tells us that couples should have worked out the kinks in their relationship before the age of fifty-five.

This does appear to be the case in 1980, when the rates for divorced older men and women were 4.8 and 5.2 percent, respectively, while the overall rate was 6.2 percent. But in 1990 the rates for divorced older people were climbing vis-à-vis the general population (6.1 percent for men and 7.6 percent for women versus 8.3 percent overall). Then by 2000 the rates are *higher* for people age fifty-five and over than they are more generally—9.4 percent for older men and 10.9 percent for older women versus 9.9 percent for the overall population.

The actual *number* of divorced women would be expected to be higher than that for men because women live longer than men do, but the *percentages* are higher too, suggesting perhaps that older women are more active than older men in seeking divorce.

Do these rising divorce statistics for people fifty-five and over have anything to do with retirement? I'm pretty sure they do. If the seven-year itch is the first big divorce cohort and children leaving home is the second, retirement appears to be the third. This is a time when couples experience big changes and stop to reassess their lives. They ask themselves questions like "If I now have enough money, shouldn't I think more about my own happiness?" "Do I really want to spend the rest of my life with this person?" "Are we really compatible?" So retirement is a significant divorce-danger time for couples.

One interesting cultural comparison is a study reported in 2000 from Japan.[2] For many years, Japanese people took great pride in having a lower divorce rate than Western countries, but a sharp increase in divorces among older Japanese couples is changing this perception, and it is often blamed on decades of postwar, single-minded devotion to work. Between 1973 and 1997 the number of divorces among couples married more than thirty years jumped eightfold, and the divorce rate is rising faster for older couples than for any other group.

The Japanese researcher calls the major cause "husband-at-home stress syndrome," with the husbands hating being under their wives' control and the wives developing all kinds of psycho-somatic physical problems—and thinking of suicide. As Japan's centuries-old rules are changing, older wives complain about still having to do all of the housework. Because their children no longer accept the tradition of caring for aging parents, many elderly couples feel very lonely together. Women initiate most of the divorces, but both men and women are no longer willing to just grit it out—as the Japanese value called *gaman* used to require.

More and more of these Japanese couples are seeking counseling, looking for common interests, and trying to communicate better, but it is very difficult to change. For many, it's too late.

Sort It Out Carefully

Some divorces—or dissolutions of unmarried relationships— are good because they end years of suffering and free both people up to grow in new ways. For example, some late-life divorces result from abuse, cruelty, chronic substance abuse, or chronic irresponsibility, and ending that can be a great relief. In fact, no marriage can survive unless both people want to save it. Lots of things *can* change in an unhappy marriage, but nobody can make two people want to stay married.

Nevertheless, the whole process of divorce is ugly. It hurts both members of the couple psychologically, even if they really wanted it, because divorce is always a kind of failure. At the very least, people wonder why they chose that person, and divorce shakes their self-confidence about decision making. Children of divorce are always affected too—even adult kids who are living their own lives. Holidays are no longer the same for them. They now have to choose between their parents in a variety of ways, and communication becomes more difficult because they now have to watch what they say to each parent about the other. Grandchildren are hurt too because their world can no longer have the semblance of one big, happy family. And last but not least, divorce is, in most cases, financially nasty and expensive. Few couples can separate their assets without a lot of bickering, and even the richest couples will suffer because each person will have less money after a divorce than they did together.

The stakes can get really high and complicated for retiree couples when one partner has been a high earner. Many of these superachievers hate giving a lot of "their" money to an about-to-be-ex-spouse, and behavior like hiding assets or lying about money can really escalate the anger level.[3] It seems clear that great success can be just as hard on a divorcing couple as limited resources are—sometimes harder. Partners with these "success issues" need to talk about them in the process of a divorce and not be overwhelmed by the financial implications of them. Even couples who had prenuptial agreements are not home free because the contract can be nullified if the poorer spouse isn't treated fairly.

Unrealistic expectations are one of the major causes of dissolutions, so it would be wise for divorcing couples to consider whether they might have been crippled by these kinds of unrealistic ideas:

• There should be constant and passionate love.

• There should always be good sex.

• There should be similar interests.

• There should always be considerate behavior.

• There should be few fights.

The fact is that most people react to the way they are treated in a relationship. When they are treated well, they are usually content in the relationship. During most courtships, of course, people treat each other nicely, and the loving feelings are strong and natural. Then the excitement wears off, and your partner seems to change. She is preoccupied with work or children or friends or other interests. He may have a short-term or chronic physical problem. In most long relationships, there are many times when consideration seems to disappear, and love has little reason to stay.[4] We all need to understand and accept that.

Wanting a divorce or dissolution, therefore, can be caused by "hard reasons" such as abuse or "soft reasons" such as unhappiness, poor communication, or boredom. If both partners are not really tuned in to what realistic relationships look like, these soft reasons can be exaggerated, eventually blowing up a marriage. But they can also be talked about and worked on and improved.

What most people want, especially at retirement age, is someone to count on for better or for worse, and if two people have any possibility of achieving that together, they should try to work things out. At the very least, people can usually learn to tolerate more from each other and understand each other better.

Together Versus Side by Side

Many people assume that there are only two extremes in a marriage: closeness or divorce. In fact, many couples have found ways to coexist quite happily in side-by-side arrangements. Here is an example:

Tom and Denise always looked forward to pursuing their passions in retirement. He is a collector of many objects, especially old electronics, and she does a lot of volunteer work with animals. Over the first five years of retirement his collections grew exponentially, while she adopted several dogs and cats and worked long hours at a shelter. He hated the hair of the animals getting into his precious antique electronics, and he filled the living room and bedrooms so full of his stuff that she had to make aisles to navigate the rooms. Of course, they could never invite people into this mess, and they became quite socially isolated except for visits with their children.

They also became very cross with each other, and Denise spent less and less time at home, returning only to sleep and care for her beloved animals. Finally she raised the possibility of a separate condo for herself. They agreed that that would be a real hardship financially, and they settled instead on a small remodeling project, which would give them separate rooms with separate entrances. Tom never cooked anyway, so he got a mini-kitchen in the living room, while Denise got the appliances. Their adult kids thought they were crazy and started to blame one or the other, but they proceeded anyway.

Tom and Denise are now seventy-five and seventy-eight, and this arrangement works fairly well. She has some friends over from time to time and is a lot happier.

> *He is pretty grumpy, but he has always been a curmudg-*
> *eon, and he refuses to change. They go out for dinner*
> *together once or twice a week, but they seldom see each*
> *other in the house. They visit their children and grand-*
> *children both separately and together.*
>
> *They have promised to be there for each other if one*
> *needs medical help, but it is hard to envision how they*
> *will be able to work this out. They joke about praying*
> *that each of them will not be the one to become depend-*
> *ent. He fears that her dogs would be licking his face, and*
> *she is terrified that he would put her bed in the middle of*
> *his mess of antiques. In spite of this less-than-ideal*
> *arrangement, they do not want to divorce, and they do*
> *seem relatively happy—even Tom in his irascible way.*

Side-by-side arrangements don't have to be this drastic, but couples can find innovative ways to get a lot of what they want in life without resorting to divorce. One couple, for instance, found that they were fighting because she liked to do her craft projects with total silence in the house, while he liked to watch sporting events on TV and scream at the players. They had difficulty resolving this difference until she realized that she is naturally a morning person while he is instinctively a night owl. They had been compromising by getting up together at about nine-thirty each morning, but she began rising about five every morning and going to bed quite early, while he has become even more of a night person. This gives her the quiet time she craves and elicits only minor irritation from him.

Handling Divorce Lawyers

Nothing seems to escalate the rancor in the process of divorce as much as attorneys. Sometimes it is hard to know whether blame for this turmoil belongs more to the clients or the lawyers, but even couples who try to part as friends often find themselves alienated from each other after an hour in court.

Most divorce attorneys say that they never make the process more difficult than it would otherwise be, but one needs to remember that they benefit enormously from conflict. Increasing billable hours is the only way that their income goes up.

If two partners and their progeny are to retain any benefit—both financial and emotional—from the love that they once shared, both people need to get a firm hold on the legal process. Both of them need to realize that their lawyers work for them, not the other way around. A good attorney can be a great asset in the divorce process, but if one individual's lawyer tries to escalate the conflict, a phone call to your about-to-be-former spouse probably should be made to communicate directly and minimize misunderstandings.

Based on my clinical experience with lots of couples, the best-case scenario is when two people do most of the paperwork themselves, negotiating the terms and even filing the documents directly with the county or another legal authority if possible. This not only minimizes cost, but more important, gives the couple most of what they want with a minimum of lawyer-driven angst. Without young children to worry about, the financial settlement is usually the main issue. If finances are complicated, you might have to engage an accountant or real estate expert, but the two of you can remain clearly in charge this way.

The next-best arrangement is to deal with a professional mediator. This person may be either an attorney or another trained expert, but a mediator's main task is to treat both participants fairly. There is little incentive for him to take either side, especially if the fee is a fixed amount, and both parties must agree before there is any dissolution of the relationship anyway.

Only in the most complicated or nasty of circumstances should a couple need the full legal complement leading to a divorce trial.

Don't let your anger push you into this unnecessarily. There are better methods of revenge—including living well thereafter. One should always try to achieve a fair divorce settlement, but in general it is better to focus on a sane process than to tear up your gut for months or years with hatred and angst.

Death Is a Different Kind of Loss

Divorce is a loss for which people bear some responsibility and over which people have some choice, but the death of a partner is different. It can make the survivor feel lost, frightened, and out of control. One positive aspect is that other people do not blame the survivor of a death, as they often do with a divorced person, but widows and widowers still find that they are out of sync with their coupled friends. And widowed women, particularly, complain that they are no longer invited to some parties because their women friends are afraid that they will attract the husbands.

It is hard to say whether a sudden death is more difficult than a prolonged one or vice versa. When one's partner dies suddenly, there is no chance to say the things that you may want to communicate, and there may be many regrets. On the other hand, a prolonged death usually requires great sacrifices from the caregiving partner, during which social interaction with friends is often lost and exhaustion sets in.

Death is also a loss that can never be regained. Divorced couples have been known to remarry each other, but even if that never happens, divorced spouses with children usually maintain some relationship for life. People who are not married, whether heterosexual or gay and lesbian, are less legally attached than married partners are, but they may eventually reconsider, and they too have the possibility of reconciliation after dissolution. But the death of a mate is final.

The effect of a partner's death should not be minimized, but there is some fascinating new research suggesting that there may be positive aspects too. In an article cleverly titled "Grieving Over What's His Name," we learn that many widows and widowers show no signs of mental anguish or need for counseling.[5] Some people report being more satisfied with their life *after* the death than before it. The researchers found that about half of those who were depressed had felt that way before the death and were no worse after it. Those who suffered the most seemed to have an "anxious neediness" personality trait. One reason that most older adults recover quickly is that they've usually had experience with death. It is also likely that, in almost any long marriage, parts of one's personality are put on hold or fall into the background of a relationship. That hidden, private part of yourself can now be rediscovered. Most people grieve and move on.

Moving On from Divorce or Death

Moving on *can* take a long time, and other people are often impatient. After a divorce or the death of your partner, your family and friends will usually be compassionate for a while, but they get annoyed when you don't seem to recover quickly. They fail to recognize that every person has to grieve in his own way, in her own time frame. For example, friends and family members may suggest a trip or a change of residence, becoming upset when you don't take their advice. In these cases, the divorced or widowed person has to tell others politely to back off.

The real key for moving emotionally forward is to accept the cards that we are dealt. We may never fully heal. We may be stained by the loss. But these imperfections can make us more interesting and in many cases more beautiful. Eventually, most emotionally intelligent people come to the recognition that problems do enrich life. From life's struggles we learn about self and others. A perfectly even-keeled existence sounds attractive, but it would really be quite boring. The depth of life comes when we experience all the darkness and all of the light. Only then can we understand the true nature of people and things, and only then can we really have compassion for others.

Alice Walker, the author of *The Way Forward with a Broken Heart,* says that people should not fear the broken heart because that kind of heart gets bigger: "The broken heart opens as never before."[6]

Questions to Ask Yourself and Your Partner

1. Since retirement is a dangerous time for divorce or dissolution, what factors in our relationship could lead us in that direction?
2. Are these problems "hard reasons" or "soft reasons"?
3. What would be the pros and cons of dissolution for us at this age?
4. If at some point we couldn't live in real togetherness, can I (you) imagine us living in a side-by-side arrangement? What might that look like for us?
5. If we ever do decide to divorce, how might I (you) handle my (your) lawyer?
6. Do I (you) think that we could divorce without any lawyers involved? Why?
7. In what ways would your (my) death be difficult for me (you)?
8. Would these feelings differ if the death were sudden or prolonged?
9. What kind of caregiver might I (you) be with a long illness?
10. What coping mechanisms would I (you) use to move on from dissolution or death?

19.

New Relationships Are Different Now

The Differences

Hearing seniors talk about the new world of dating is sometimes a riot! They often seem both resentful and excited about being forced into the dating game after a divorce, dissolution, or death. Older singles need to be aware of the emotional potholes in this brave new world of relationships, and it doesn't hurt for even current couples to think about the pros and cons of what might lie ahead.

The author and humorist Judith Viorst compares dating rules past and present this way: 1963, Niagara; 1999, Viagra.[1] From fantasy romance to sexual performance in thirty-six years!

It appears that everyone is more aggressive these days about romance—especially women.

Chuck had just retired from his job as a local TV news anchor when his wife of thirty-five years succumbed to ovarian cancer. They had had a good marriage, but the last year of her life had been hard on everybody. He had been a dutiful caregiver, but after her death Chuck sank into a mild depression that lasted almost two years. His two married sons propped him up, and his grief counselor was very helpful because she gave him permission to grieve in his own way. He found it hard to be in "their" house, so he traveled a lot with various groups during those years.

Eventually, Chuck began to get interested in the real world again. He redecorated the bedroom they had shared and the family room, and he suddenly felt comfortable calling it "my house." He began accepting dinner invitations from friends, and many of those included a new woman. Even his son introduced him to a woman he knew at work.

Chuck's plan was to invite each woman to have coffee on their first date. That way he wouldn't waste a whole evening and a lot of money if things didn't work out. Imagine his surprise when most of the women were flirtatious, refusing to end the date quickly. They invariably invited him back to their house for a meal or suggested that they'd like to see his place. They asked for his phone number. One woman took her shoes off the minute they got to Starbucks and started massaging his leg with her toes. Two women wore low-cut black dresses—to Starbucks!

When Chuck did go to bed with a woman for the first time after his long dry spell, he confessed that he was nervous, but the woman said that she just wanted to have fun. She doesn't get emotional about these things. Chuck asked if she wanted him to use a condom, and she replied that nobody does. She's too old for pregnancy, and STDs are unlikely in "people like us."

Chuck has been dating for two years now, and he says it's just weird. He often feels like women are judging his sexual and social performance—which he never imagined years ago. The sex is nice when all systems are working well, but he longs to feel a real emotional connection to somebody. The one time he did fall pretty hard for someone, she told him that she had no desire to marry again, and that turned him off. Another woman with whom he felt he might be developing a relationship told him that he'd better hurry up and decide or she would move on.

He often feels confused and mentions a widower friend who has become extremely withdrawn, but he also knows that he should keep looking for that special woman who will make him feel whole, as his wife did. With a wicked smile, he says that he is learning a lot.

Sex is usually expected these days by both genders, but many older individuals have complicated rituals around what they do and don't want in bed. And, of course, disease is a factor that few of us had to consider when we were young. AIDS is a fact of life that seniors are not immune to, and other sexually transmitted diseases are common as well. You surely are sleeping with every person your partner has ever had sex with, and people don't always tell the truth. A few older people insist on seeing test results, as many younger couples do, before they have sex with a new partner.

Paying for dates is far from clear either. The new dating etiquette among young people seems to be that both individuals should pay according to their means, but some older women still expect to be taken care of, and many senior men feel awkward about "going Dutch." Other rules are changing too. For example, men of older generations don't know whether they should open doors and hold coats for women; some females expect it, while others consider it old-fashioned, and some even resent it.

One question that plagues some older single people is whether they could—or should—ever fall head over heels in love again. Their answer seems to be totally variable, from absolutely yes to definitely no. While some people would give anything to experience those intensely passionate feelings of love again, others see themselves as more analytical now. Life has taught them to examine everything and never totally trust anyone, so it would be impossible for them to love as they did when they were young. In the words of one handsome seventy-two-year-old man: "If you think you have fallen totally and instantly in love, give yourself six months, and that feeling will pass."

Perhaps it *is* unwise, at this age, to think of love in the same way that we did at twenty, because horror stories about senior relationships abound. There are lots of con artists out there, and single seniors with money are frequent targets. It is not uncommon, therefore, for older people to hire private detectives when they don't know a great deal about a potential mate. It is also common to involve lots of friends and family members in the courtship so that various opinions are elicited about the newcomer.

While some single seniors are quite matter-of-fact about the dating process, many older people have learned that their heart is not as resilient as it used to be. They thought that they could handle just about anything by this age, but rejection is still as hard as ever—and maybe harder. Mending your heart seems to take a longer time now, even though age should have developed a little shell around it. And love at this age can seem like a last chance; losing it can be very painful.

But there is humor in the senior dating process too, and the name game at this stage of life can be amusing, especially in committed relationships. *Boyfriend* and *girlfriend* don't seem to fit, but no definitive replacement has caught on, so some people are using "my S.O." (significant other), "my L.P." (life partner), or "my P.A.P." (permanently attached person).

Also, by the time we reach retirement age, many of us have had more than one spouse or lover, and the mind is not what it used to be. We should be able to laugh about slips of the tongue, but we know that many new partners would become furious if they hear the name of a previous lover uttered unconsciously, by mistake. The perfect solution was offered by an attractive, twice-divorced woman who seems to have lots of beaus: "Don't focus on anyone's name. Just call them all honey."

Cohabitation

The 2000 Census Bureau data show that about 230,000 households contain two unrelated male and female adults, one of whom is age 65 or older. That's up 60 percent from 1990 and 71 percent from 1980.[2] Some experts believe that the number is actually higher, and it will surely increase because people are living longer and social mores are changing fast.

There aren't many trends where grandparents are imitating their grandchildren, but cohabitation is one of them, and the reasons may be financial, psychological, or both. Some seniors avoid marriage because of a desire to keep their finances separate. Many older singles would have to do a lot of legal and financial work before they could sensibly marry, and others would lose alimony payments or Social Security income if they remarry. Also, older people bring a lot of baggage to a relationship, and it takes time to figure out whether you want to coexist with your partner's previous spouses, children, and bad habits. Furthermore, living together without marriage seems to meet the needs of many adult children, who worry about their inheritance and, rather selfishly, prefer not to have their other parent replaced.

Prenuptial Agreements

If two older people *do* decide to marry, there is the issue of a prenup. These are regularly enforced in America, but are not legally binding in countries such as England and Wales. In such countries, although the court may take them into consideration when it comes to the dissolution of a marriage, they are under no obligation to honour the agreement. I personally think that all couples should have one before they marry. Even young people with few assets need to think about how they will share their life. For instance, if one of them makes it big, with millions in income, both should think rationally now about whether they will share the wealth equally or not. If one of them expects to benefit from a trust or inheritance in the future, the other should probably know about it. This way, they can avoid the bitter divorce contests we hear about when one person is surprised. People of all ages also come to understand through a prenup that marriage is a business arrangement as well as a love match.

If a committed couple chooses *not* to marry or if they are gay or lesbian, these documents may be called by different names— cohabitation agreement, domestic partner agreement, or relationship contract. But any two people who commingle assets, live in each other's property, or share expenses would be wise to consider a legal document of this kind.

Almost every older about-to-marry couple needs a prenup because they come to marriage with a lifetime of financial and psychological history. Hard as it may seem to sit down with separate lawyers and negotiate the terms, it is really worth the effort because this process will flag potential problems, and it could help to avoid a lot of conflict later.

Sometimes the partner with fewer assets resents being asked to sign a prenup, but that person should want to get everything on the table. This is especially true if there are children from previous marriages because those kids will support the union more if they feel that their mother or father is being smart about business. Again, the message to both parts of the couple is that they are getting into business together, as well as into bed.

May-December Issues

Second, third, or subsequent marriages often involve partners of considerably different ages. This is especially true if the older person has wealth because money, even more than power, is still the biggest aphrodisiac in the world. In many cases, money *can* buy love—or at least a reasonable facsimile thereof.

It seems to be human nature to like younger faces and bodies. Indeed, we seem to be hardwired to want the healthiest, most attractive mate for survival-of-the-fittest purposes. A younger partner may seem especially appealing after a difficult divorce or death, when one's own self-esteem might have been shaken. That person makes the retiree feel younger by association. The older person is given a new lease on life.

Men, and a few women, sometimes look for a younger partner as their potential caregiver. That can be an advantage because it is quite likely that a person our own age or older will die before we do, while a younger person would probably be there to pick up the pieces. It might be wise to have this in writing, however. Many wealthy older people, with legal advice, tie caregiving to an inheritance in their will because younger partners have been known to disappear when the going gets rough.

Overall, the major impediment to May-December relationships is probably differing levels of physical and psychic energy. For example, two people who get together when the man is fifty-five and the woman thirty-five may have no problem with energy at the beginning, but fifteen or twenty years later, the man just won't be able to keep up.

And the other difficulty is trust. Despite what may have been said about love, the older person usually knows on some level that money or security is a factor, and he cannot trust in the same way that an older partner might have made possible.

Questions to Ask Yourself About New Relationships

1. Am I excited or frightened to be in the new world of dating for seniors?
2. Who should pay for dates in this era? Why?
3. What other rules of dating etiquette have changed? How do I feel about them?
4. What are my sexual rules and mores in a dating situation?
5. Could I ever fall head over heels in love again? Should I? Why?
6. How should I learn about a new potential mate?
7. Should I hire a private investigator?
8. To what extent should I involve family members and friends?
9. Would I marry again? Why?
10. What would be the pros and cons for me of living together without marriage?
11. How do I feel about a prenuptial or cohabitation agreement? What are the pros and cons?
12. What would I want in my prenup or relationship contract?
13. What would be the pros and cons of marriage to, or cohabitation with, a much younger person?
14. What would be the role of my children in making decisions about a new relationship?
15. What might I do if my kids object to the person I love?

20.
Growing Whole—Individually and Together

Last Chance

Most retirees have not accomplished all that they had hoped to do in life. They may have faced some of their own failures, but often they have put the blame on obstacles that others placed in their way. Well, this is the time of life when we need to take responsibility for our own mistakes and missed opportunities. We have to *own* our own reality in order to be happy, and this is the last chance to do it.

Life is all about making choices and then living with the consequences. Some of us are benefiting as seniors from good choices that we made many years ago, while others are still struggling with the effects of poor choices in the past.

One of the most poignant depictions of retirement regrets is the 2002 movie *About Schmidt*. Jack Nicholson plays the title character, who has carefully filed and labeled a lifetime of insurance company records, turning them over to his much younger replacement. But when he returns to the office a few weeks later, where he was told that he would always be welcome, the young manager has no time for him, and Nicholson finds his record boxes on the trash heap. Furthermore, he is nasty to his wife, who is trying to ease him into retirement; he only appreciates her after she is dead. This character's choices—expecting too much on his return to the office, relating to his wife in such a demeaning way—leave him with a multitude of regrets. Because of his choices, he is unprepared to face life alone, and he has to learn some very hard lessons.

Most of us waste so much precious time and energy wishing that things were different. Instead, if we accept the simple premise that we are responsible for most of what happened in our life, it is not too late to make many new choices now. For example, if a man is sorry that he didn't follow his passion for music in college, he can take lessons or find a group to play with now. Or if a woman never bought that red convertible she always wanted because she was too practical to splurge on it, she can get it now.

Our Passions Are Precious

Too many of us were too prudent for too many years. Now, before our passions are completely gone, leaving just an empty feeling inside, we need to take the risks that we didn't take before. Think about the following statements:

- Make your heart race a little.

- Don't be too careful.

- Don't let yourself wallow in regrets.

- Seize the day.

- Don't let the music die in you.

- Rewrite your agreement with life.

- If we change our mind, we can change our life.

These are all clichés, but they are valid sentiments.

Our caution may come from habit, but it also comes from fear at this age that we are losing our edge and might look foolish or make a mistake. We worry that we may have nothing more to contribute to the world. Advertisers no longer seem to target us. Technology is getting away from us, and social mores are changing so quickly. Younger people are passing us by. But the difference between being frightened by these circumstances and being challenged by them comes from the attitudes we bring to life.

Even though the world sometimes feels like it's spinning around older people, passions about technology do often develop. Retirement is really the ideal time to come to terms with rapid change because we finally have fewer distractions and worries. It really can be fun, for example, to master the computer—printing photographs, emailing old and new friends, and getting huge amounts of information on anything that interests us. We have time to take classes now and learn new things. We can ask intelligent questions and find the answers—even when the "expert" is younger than our youngest child. We can overcome our caution by developing the attitude that this brave new world is really pretty exciting.

Letting Go of Hopes and Dreams

In order to be realistic and open to the future, we need to let go of some hopes and dreams—especially the impractical ones, like being a multimillionaire or a famous ice-skater or a champion tennis player. We may even have to give up our hopes of having a perfect, loving marriage or a wonderful, close relationship with our child.

When we suffer the loss of these hopes and dreams, even though the loss is purely in our mind, we sometimes have to grieve hard. Even though these dreams may seem silly to others, they may have given us psychological warmth and comfort for many years. Now we will have to go through life recognizing that they will never come true, facing the sadness of that psychic loss, and finally coming to terms with reality.

Couples have such an advantage over singles because they can help each other cope with this process. By contrast, the most difficult partnership is one in which your hopes and dreams are demeaned.

When one person does decide to give these ideas up, sensitive partners resist the impulse to say "I told you so" because they would not want that said to them. They realize that letting go of unrealistic hopes and dreams can be a constructive process that will eventually benefit the relationship.

One example of what we should be *happy* to give up at this age is our rigid ideas of masculinity and femininity. New retirees indicate that this can be a problem at first, with both people trying to establish their territory. But in most cases couples work things out by becoming more androgynous—each expressing *both* masculine and feminine qualities, and each becoming more nurturing in a variety of ways. By all accounts, this is a happy state of being for many older couples and a best-case scenario.

One of the hardest dreams to give up is the one about total happiness in retirement together, but this too is necessary for moving to the acceptance step.

Teresa thought that they would finally have time to talk when she and Chip retired. He thought that he would finally have time to relax with the TV and computer. In their separate visions, they would be a deliriously happy couple.

When they realized, after the "honeymoon" period was over, that the perfect dream was unlikely to ever happen, they felt let down and angry. Petty annoyances grew. Fights escalated. And then they both became quiet and sullen.

They were shaken out of their unhappiness by their son's suggestion that his dad should have a "cave." Teresa thought that was stupid and unnecessary; she was sure that they would talk even less this way. But their son convinced her to clean out his old room and give it a try. They put the old computer in there, and Teresa was thrilled when Chip suggested that she should have a new one. They put the old TV in there too, and Chip insisted that she should have the newer one in the den. Then they went out to buy a new recliner for the "cave," and Chip even asked her if she would like a similar one for the den.

Teresa's assumption that they would talk less with this arrangement has not been realized. There's not a whole lot more talk either, but that's OK. She tries not to go into Chip's special, sacred place very often, but he calls her in to see something periodically, and they do meet frequently in the other rooms. The fact that they worked out this "cave" idea so cooperatively seems to have given them both hope. Teresa has let go of the dream that they would have a lot of togetherness, and that is sometimes sad for her, but being realistic about their personalities has lots of rewards. One of those rewards for Teresa is that she has some new appreciation of her relationships and discussions with her friends.

Finding New Hopes and Dreams

I like the plaque that says "Dreams are whispers from your soul." Sometimes we don't even know why we dream about things at night or think about them repeatedly during the day. But if we sit with these ideas for a while, we can usually figure out the sources. They may be remnants of childhood fantasies, or they may give us a glimpse of who we want to be, but they are always worth listening to.

Then, as we let go of some of our old, unrealistic hopes and dreams, couples can support each other in developing new ones. In this way, our relationship can really have a renaissance. Old passions can be reawakened, and new passions can be found— even when everyone thinks we're crazy. After all, age earns us the right to be a *little* eccentric. We only have to please ourself and our partner now.

We retirees should always make adventure a big part of our life because it keeps us alive and kicking. New experiences, especially scary ones, are good for us because they stretch our psychological resources and make us stronger emotionally. In fact, one sixty-six-year-old woman said that her last thought before she goes to sleep most nights is: "Did I do anything new today? Did I scare myself a little in the past month?"

Seniors should still look for opportunities to overcome obstacles—like the donkey in this fable, who demonstrates how to "shake it off."

One day a farmer's donkey fell down into an abandoned well. The animal cried piteously for hours as the farmer tried to figure out what to do. Finally, the man decided that the donkey was old, and the well needed to be covered up anyway. Furthermore, it just wasn't possible for him to pay the cost of a crane to pull the donkey up, as well as a vet to treat the injured animal. Instead, he invited several of his neighbors to come over and help him with this task. Reluctantly they all grabbed a shovel and began to pour dirt into the hole. Quickly the donkey realized that he would be buried, and he cried louder than ever.

Then, to everyone's amazement, the donkey quieted down. A few shovelfuls later, the farmer finally had the courage to look into the well, and he was astonished at what he saw. With every load of dirt that hit the animal's back, he was shaking it off and taking a step up.

Pretty soon everyone was thrilled as the donkey stepped up over the edge of the well and trotted off.

Very few couples have gotten to their retirement years without realizing that life is going to shovel all kinds of dirt on us. But we can learn, even at this late stage, to shake most of it off and meet life more on our own terms. We can be more resilient. Instead of fighting life and each other, we can search for the humor in every situation. We can stop taking ourselves and the world so seriously.

Figuring It Out

Individually and together, wise couples strive to grow whole at this stage of their lives. Individually, each person tries to be the best that she can be. She realizes that she invents herself every day by the choices she makes—and so does everybody else. He figures out what really matters to him and what he really wants out of the years that are left. He finally accepts the fact that it's not about being right; it's about being happy. They both try to integrate the various parts of their personality into a whole. And together they attempt to integrate the various parts of their relationship into a cohesive picture.

It is never too late to get some of this emotional stuff right. Productive years lie ahead if we really figure things out, asking questions such as:

• Who am I?

• Who are we together?

• What do I want the rest of my life to be?

• What do we want for ourselves as a couple?

These questions are more important for senior couples than ever before because, as retirement ages decrease and life spans increase, they will have a long time to enact their sense of purpose.

Some people predict that the boomers will have an especially hard time with retirement because they have always wanted to shape every stage of life, but they will find that there is no short-cut to fulfillment. *Things* will not bring them happiness, but the examined life might. They will have to get their inner lives in order if they are to thrive in the outside world.

The singer Barbara Cook uses words from a song to express this goal of finally understanding oneself: "It's not where you start but where you finish." She says that it takes courage to emotionally undress yourself—to show who you really are, but that is the only way to communicate with another person "core to core."[1]

Realism

The people who age well are realistic—neither overly optimistic nor unduly pessimistic. They are honest about the problems they can't solve, but they work on the ones they can. They manage misfortune by being flexible and creative. They can tolerate unpleasant feelings. They moderate their expectations so that they don't constantly compare themselves with others. They don't need more and more things to make them happy.

It's pleasant to be around people who have a consistently sunny outlook, but all of us will someday face ill health and adversity, if we haven't already, and the difficulty with always being positive is that sometimes the sky *does* fall on us. We need to be able to cope with real issues when they come, and not pretend that everything is fine. Coping strategies that may have worked really well at fifty may not be very useful at seventy or eighty. We need to be prepared to see things as they really are.[2]

We also manage best when we are realistic about what we want to do with our time. There is great pressure on retiree couples now to be superseniors, and our generation has a new anxiety: Are we active enough? One writer, in fact, suggested that people should not allow themselves to retire until they have committed to six activities that their partner approves of. Wow! That prescription leaves no time and space for figuring it out as we go along—for letting life wash over us a bit as we move into this important transition period.

Most of us want to stay engaged in life, with activities that we *want* to do. However, the pressure leads some of us to try too hard to look younger, to be fit, to seem important, to recapture the exhilaration of youth. Being busier isn't necessarily better. Some of us need the courage to say that we're relaxing—not doing much of anything. We're slowing down as opposed to speeding up. We're not joining any more groups or doing any more volunteer work for now. We're spending this time thinking rather than squandering it on meaningless activities. We're deciding what is realistic for us.

Real Self-Esteem Versus Facades

One of the most wonderful things about retirement age is finally feeling free to drop some of our facades. Once we no longer have to think about work and all that the working world entails—including an upwardly mobile social life—we can drop some of the masks we show to the world. Some people find it difficult to let down these defenses, but many others welcome letting go of superficial measures of worth, such as beauty and financial success.

Their life up until retirement has often felt like they were pushing a boulder up a hill, only to have to push it up again the next day. Finally they can relax and try to claim their authentic self. It's not that retirees will ever relax totally or be without guile, but they certainly can focus more on whatever makes *them* happy versus worrying about what other people will think.

Of course, whatever makes them happy may not be any easier to figure out than the facades were! In some ways they had those down pat. The world expected certain things of them, and they expected certain things of the world. Those facade behaviors and attitudes were well practiced over many years, becoming comfortable and routine.

But this is a lot more fun. It may take some time, but it feels really good to eventually gain the kind of self-esteem that nobody can ever take away from you. It can be tremendously exhilarating to really know that you are OK just as you are.

The process for achieving that kind of self-esteem is illustrated in *The Velveteen Rabbit*, the classic children's story by Margery Williams.

"What is real?" asked the rabbit one day when they were lying side by side on the nursery floor. "Does it mean having things that buzz inside you and a stick-out handle?"

"Real isn't how you are made," said the skin horse. "It's a thing that happens to you. When a child loves you for a long, long time, not just to play with, but REALLY loves you, then you become real."

"Does it hurt?" asked the rabbit.

"Sometimes," said the skin horse, for he was always truthful. "But when you are real, you don't mind being hurt."

"Does it happen all at once, like being wound up," he asked, "or bit by bit?"

"It doesn't happen all at once," said the skin horse. "You become. It takes a long time. That's why it doesn't often happen to people who break easily, or have sharp edges, or who have to be carefully kept. Generally, by the time you are real, most of your hair has been loved off, and your eyes drop out, and you get loose in the joints and very shabby. But these things don't matter at all because once you are real, you can't be ugly, except to people who don't understand."[3]

Giving and Receiving Emotional Nourishment

The ability to receive and give love is what motivates most humans to get out of bed in the morning. It gives purpose and meaning to life, and every piece of research on aging shows that people who stay close to other people are stronger and healthier because of it. Nurturing old relationships and making new ones surely takes some effort, but it is very much worth it.

Unfortunately, some of us are good at giving emotional nourishment and love but not very good at receiving it, or vice versa. Many retiree couples have, in fact, spent many years perfecting a pattern of one-sided nourishment, but this is the time to break that model. Some people may think that it's fun to get all the emotional goodies and have to put out very little in return, but both partners will really benefit if they are on both sides of this equation. Mature people want to both give and receive nourishment because real joy is possible through both.

At the time of Katharine Hepburn's death, her family said that her motto was "Listen to the song of life." The happiest people seem to have a good handle on the ups and downs of life. They realize that it is useless to expect life to be fair because it's full of both good and bad, and the distribution is not equal. People cannot separate good times from bad, and perhaps there's no need to do so.

Gratitude

In this day and age, gratitude is an underrated quality. No one teaches it to us in school, and today's world does not encourage us to value what we have. But the ability to be grateful and content with our life and relationships takes us a long way on the road to happiness.

Growing old is not for sissies, but it's so much easier within a good partnership than it is either alone or in a problematic relationship. For that reason, retired couples should feed the best parts of their lives together. Every personal partnership could be better, but we're lucky if we have a decent one. Couples should travel retirement's journey with a spirit of adventure and gratitude.

Nellie is in her early eighties, and when she recites this line from the Robert Browning poem, "Grow old along with me. The best is yet to be," she laughs melodically. When she was young, she thought that this poem was nonsense. What could possibly be good about growing old? And what could get better if one is getting older? And who cares about relationships anyway when you are old and possibly near death? But she understands the words now. She feels incredibly lucky to have a sentient, sensible partner with whom to face the years ahead. And life is getting better all the time for them, largely because they appreciate each other more.

If you are lucky or resourceful enough to have a good—or good enough—partner, find ways to make it work.

- Be realistic.

- Pay attention.

- Try to calm down—be quiet inside.

- Have realistic expectations.

- Take a gratitude inventory.

- Be intentional and thoughtful about the future.

- Be lovable and able to love.

Remember: If you want your ship to come in, you usually have to build a dock.

Questions to Ask Yourself and Your Partner

1. What was I (were you) like as a child? What were my (your) hopes and dreams then?
2. What have been my (your) best choices thus far, and what were my (your) worst?

3. Have I (you) been too cautious or not cautious enough?

4. If I (you) carry any bitterness from unrealized hopes and dreams, how can I (you) get rid of it?

5. What dirt has life shoveled on me (you)? Have I (you) learned how to shake it off?

6. Do we give each other enough support in accomplishing our hopes and dreams—even when they are not shared?

7. What do we want the rest of our lives to look and feel like?

8. Do I (you) know the difference between optimism and realism?

9. What facades did I (you) have in the past? Why?

10. Have I (you) dropped them, or do I (you) want to drop them now?

11. How close am I (are you) now to my (your) authentic self?

12. Am I (are you) psychologically whole? In what areas could I (you) improve?

13. Do we give enough nourishment to each other?

14. Do I (you) know how to ask effectively for the nourishment that I (you) need?

15. What are the top five items in my (your) personal gratitude inventory?

References

Chapter 2: Retirement Is Wonderful

1. James Payton, "Happily Ever After? How Baby Boomers Envision Retirement," www.bizmonthly.com/11_2001_focus/f_17.html.
2. Kelly Green, "How to Survive the First Year," *The Wall Street Journal*, June 9, 2003.
3. Mary Williams Walsh, "So Where Are the Corporate Husbands," *The New York Times*, June 24, 2001.
4. Charles McGrath, "Live Fast, Die Old," *The New York Times Magazine,* February 21, 1999.
5. Tracy Thompson, "Action Aging," *The Seattle Times*, October 25, 1998.
6. Anna Quindlen, *A Short Guide to a Happy Life* (New York: Random House, 2002).

Chapter 3: It's Also Difficult

1. *Dateline,* NBC-TV, July 29, 1997.
2. James Payton, "Happily Ever After? How Baby Boomers Envision Retirement," www.bizmonthly.com/11_2001_focus/f_17.html.
3. Jack Welch, *Jack: Straight from the Gut* (Headline, 2001).
4. Sharon Begley, "The Brain in Winter," *Newsweek: Health for Life,* fall/winter 2001.

Chapter 4: Variations on the Theme of Relationships

1. Kim Wallace, "How Your Child Benefits from Play," www.parentcenter.com/refcap/fun/games/5607.html.

Chapter 5: Deciding Where to Live

1. Rosanne Knorr, *The Grown-Up's Guide to Running Away from Home* (Berkeley: Ten Speed Press, 2000).
2. Shirley LaFollette, "Empty Nesters Look for Easy Maintenance, Big Closets," *The Mercer Island Reporter*, October 13, 1999.
3. Francine Russo, "Buddy System," *Generations: Time Bonus Section*, January 2002.
4. Wendy Cole/Palmetto, "Being Out at 65," *Time*, June 30, 2003.
5. Marina Kowalski, "Gay Retirement Communities," www.toosquare.com/archives/issues/july2002/gay/index.php.
6. Mindy Cameron, "A Booming Market for Boomer Retirees," *The Seattle Times*, September 2, 2001.
7. "Census Data May Reveal New Retiree Migration Preferences," www.retirementliving.com/Rlart68.html.

Chapter 6: Filling Time: So Many Choices

1. William D. Novelli, "As We See It," *AARP Bulletin*, February 2002.
2. Barbara Hollingsworth, "Retirees Who Don't," *The Seattle Times*, November 10, 2002.
3. "Older Worker More in Favor," *The Seattle Times*, June 17, 2001.
4. Rebecca Winters, "Half-Retired," *Time*, November 22, 1999.
5. Adele Horin and Amanda Morgan, "Let's Call It Quits—and Spend the Rest of Our Lives Together," www.smh.com.au/articles/2003/02/13/1044927740459.html.
6. "Retirement Brings Different Rewards for Husbands and Wives," www.apa.org/releases/retirement.html and "Retirement: Planned or PotLuck," www.globalassignment.com/10–22–99/retirement.htm.
7. Elizabeth Larsen, "The Occasional Volunteer," *Modern Maturity*, January-February 2001.
8. Peg Tyre, "R Is for Retirement," *Newsweek*, June 10, 2002.

Chapter 7: Managing Money Within a Relationship

1. Kelly Green, "How to Survive the First Year," *The Wall Street Journal*, June 9, 2003.
2. Suze Orman, "What's Your Money Personality?" *O: The Oprah Magazine*, July 2002.
3. David Rampe, "The Piggy Bank Chronicles," *The New York Times*, May 3, 1998.
4. Joseph Nocera, "Are You Ready for This?" *Fortune*, August 16, 1999.
5. Ellen Hoffman, "When Couples Clam Up," *AARP Bulletin*, June 2002.
6. Pamela Yip, "Like Quicksand, Credit Can Slowly Pull You Under," *The Seattle Times*, July 14, 2002.
7. Christine Dugas, "American Seniors Rack Up Debt Like Never Before; Medical Expenses Often Feed the Cycle," *USA Today*, April 25, 2002.
8. Bill Morton, "The Age Avalanche," *The Costco Connection*, January 2002.
9. Erick Schonfeld, "They're Out to Steal Your Money," *Fortune*, August 18, 1997.

Chapter 8: There Are Many Positions for Sex

1. Marsha King, "Golden Years for Intimacy," *The Seattle Times*, December 9, 2001.
2. Natalie Angier, *Woman: An Intimate Geography* (Virago Press, 2000).
3. Robert Butler and Myrna Lewis, *The New Love and Sex After 60* (New York: Ballantine Books, 2002).
4. Marilyn Elias, "Who Wrote the Book on Love?" *The Seattle Times*, January 31, 2002.
5. "Sexuality in Later Life," National Institute on Aging, www.niapublications.org/engagepages/sexuality.asp.
6. Pierce J. Howard, Ph.D., *The Owner's Manual for the Brain* (Austin: Bard Press, 2002), pp. 217–21, 251–54.
7. Erica Jong, "The Zipless Fallacy," *Newsweek*, July 30, 2003.

Chapter 9: Children, Grandchildren, Other Relatives, and Friends

1. Stan Hinden, "Good Relationship with Kids, Grandkids Is Key for Retirees," *The Seattle Times*, August 18, 2001.
2. Stephanie Dunnewind, "Which Holiday Memories Stick?" *The Seattle Times*, December 22, 2001.
3. Mark Rahner, "Here's a Hot Comedian Alert," *The Seattle Times*, September 15, 2001.
4. Gail Sheehy, "It's About Pure Love," *Parade*, May 12, 2002.
5. William D. Novelli, "As We See It: Reinventing Retirement," *AARP Bulletin*, February 2002.
6. Stephanie Dunnewind, "Summer with the Grandkids," *The Seattle Times*, July 6, 2002.
7. Jeanne Safer, Ph.D., *The Normal One: Life with a Difficult or Damaged Sibling* (New York: Bantam Dell, 2003).
8. Rebecca Stowe, "Friends," *Modern Maturity*, September-October 1997.
9. Sandy Hotchkiss, *Why Is It Always About You? The Seven Deadly Sins of Narcissism* (New York: Free Press, 2003).

Chapter 11: Wanting Different Things

1. Rebecca Cutter, *When Opposites Attract: Right Brain/Left Brain Relationships and How to Make Them Work* (New York: Plume, 1996).
2. Phil McGraw, Ph.D., *The Ultimate Weight Loss Solution: The 7 Keys to Weight Loss Freedom* (New York: Free Press, 2003).

Chapter 12: Aging and Facing the Future

1. Marilyn Elias, "Boomers Generate New Business," *USA Today*, February 28, 2001.
2. "Vital Signs," *The Seattle Times*, September 23, 2001.
3. Gail Sheehy, "Racing Toward Midlife," *Men's Health*, May 1998.
4. George E. Vaillant, M.D., *Aging Well: Surprising Guideposts to a Happier Life from the Landmark Harvard Study of Adult Development* (Boston: Little, Brown, 2002).

5. George E. Vaillant, M.D., quoted in Lou Ann Walker, "We Can Control How We Age," *Parade,* September 16, 2001.
6. R. W. Levenson, "Expressive, Physiological, and Subjective Changes in Emotion Across Adulthood." In S. H. Qualls and N. Abeles, editors, *Psychology and the Aging Revolution: How We Adapt to Longer Life* (Washington, D.C.: American Psychological Association, 2000).
7. Val Kupke, "Relocating for Retirement, or What Makes for a Happy Retirement?" Sixth Pacific Rim Real Estate Society Conference, Sydney, January 2000.

Chapter 13: Medical Matters

1. Susan Jacoby, "Help Yourself to Seconds," *AARP Bulletin,* February 2003.
2. Wayne M. Sotile, Ph.D., *Thriving with Heart Disease: Line Happier, Healthier, Longer* (Newleaf, 2003).
3. Marilyn Elias, "A Generation Rewrites the Rules," *USA Today,* February 28, 2001.
4. Drs. Guy McKhann and Marilyn Albert, *Keep Your Brain Young* (Hoboken, N.J.: Wiley, 2003).
5. "Older Adults: Depression and Suicide Facts," National Institute of Mental Health, www.nimh.nih.gov/publicat/elderly/depsuicide.cfm.
6. Peggy Eastman, "Restoring the Inner Self," *AARP Bulletin,* March 2003.
7. Anna Quindlen, "In a Peaceful Frame of Mind," *Newsweek,* February 4, 2002.

Chapter 14: Legal Decisions

1. Lynn O'Shaughnessy, *Retirement Bible* (New York: Wiley, 2001).
2. Alan S. Novick, "After the Marriage Is Over," in *Estate Planning,* King County Journal Newspapers, September 2003.
3. Eileen Alt Powell, "Unmarried Money: Non-Traditional Couples Need Old-Fashioned Money Management," February 27, 2003, www.lexisone.com/balancing/articles/ap030003h.html.
4. "Unmarried Couples and Medical Decisions," FindLaw for the Public, www.public.findlaw.com/family/nolo/fag/A0D144C7-BF8E-4F5F-B3290CDFEE2FF363.html.

Chapter 15: Fighting Fairly

1. Dianne Hales, "Why Are We So Angry?" *Parade,* September 2, 2001.
2. Pepper Schwartz, *Everything You Know About Love and Sex Is Wrong* (New York: G. P. Putnam's Sons, 2000).
3. Carolyn Scott Kortge, "The Same Old Love," *Hemispheres,* October 1997.
4. Gail Sheehy, *Understanding Men's Passages: Discovering the New Map of Men's Lives* (New York: Random House, 1998).

Chapter 16: Communicating Well During This Stage of Life

1. Joan Anderson, *An Unfinished Marriage* (New York: Broadway Books, 2003).
2. Kathy Balog, "Renewing a Marriage Is 'Unfinished' Business," *USA Today,* March 19, 2002.
3. Thomas A. Harris, M.D., *I'm OK—You're OK* (Arrow, 1995).
4. Oren Harari, "Behind Open Doors: Colin Powell's Seven Laws of Power," *Modern Maturity,* January/February, 2002.

Chapter 17: Getting Outside Help When You Can't Do It Alone

1. John M. Gottman, Ph.D., and Nan Silver, *The Seven Principles for Making Marriage Work* (Orion, 2000); John M. Gottman, Ph.D., and Joan DeClaire, *The Relationship Cure* (New York: Three Rivers Press, 2001).
2. "Predicting Which Marriages Will Fail—and When," *A & S Perspectives,* University of Washington, autumn 2000.
3. Harville Hendrix, Ph.D., *Keeping the Love You Find* (New York: Pocket Books, 1992).
4. Bruce Chapman, "Marriage-Mending," *The Seattle Post-Intelligencer,* February 23, 1997.

Chapter 18: Handling Divorce, Dissolution, or Death with Dignity

1. United States Census Bureau, Table 34 for 1990 and
   www.factfinder.census.gov/servlet/DTTable?_ts=51113220468
   www.factfinder.census.gov/servlet/DTTable?_ts=51113529125
   www.factfinder.census.gov/servlet/DTTable?_ts=51122192906
2. Joji Sakurai, "Divorce Rate for Japan's Elderly Couples Is Growing," Smart Marriages Archive, Divorce Statistics Collection, www.divorcereform.org/mel/rolderjapan.html.
3. William C. Symonds, "Divorce—Executive Style," *Business Week,* August 3, 1998.
4. Fran Henry, "Marriage Movement Aims to Keep Those Knots Tied," *The Seattle Times,* September 13, 2001.
5. Benedict Carey, "Grieving Over What's His Name," *The Seattle Times,* June 22, 2003.
6. Alice Walker on *Charlie Rose,* PBS-TV, November 14, 2000.

Chapter 19: New Relationships Are Different Now

1. Judith Viorst in Barbara Mathias-Riegel, "Intimacy 101," *Modern Maturity,* September-October 1999.
2. Genaro C. Armas, "More Seniors Are Living Together Without the Benefit of an 'I Do,'" *The Seattle Times,* July 30, 2002.

Chapter 20: Growing Whole—Individually and Together

1. Barbara Cook on *60 Minutes,* CBS-TV, December 2, 2001.
2. Susan H. Greenberg and Karen Springer, "Keeping Hope Alive," *Newsweek: Health for Life,* fall/winter 2001.
3. Margery Williams, *The Velveteen Rabbit,* originally published in 1922, now in the public domain.

Index

Resources (UK)

Useful websites:

www.retirement-matters.co.uk
This is a UK website which gives details of retirement and over 50's related products, services and information and is interesting, informative, and easy to use.

www.statistics.gov.uk
This is the website for National Statistics online. It details all the official UK statistics regarding Britain's economy, population and society at national and local level.

www.saga.co.uk
The Saga Group focuses exclusively on the provision of high quality, value-for-money services for people 50 and over. These include holidays, an award-winning magazine, insurance and financial products, and radio stations.

www.citizensadvice.org.uk
The Citizens Advice service helps people resolve their legal, money and other problems by providing free information and advice from over 3,200 locations.

All Piatkus titles are available from:

Piatkus Books, c/o Bookpost, PO Box 29, Douglas, Isle Of Man, IM99 1BQ

Telephone (+44) 01624 677237
Fax (+44) 01624 670923
Email; bookshop@enterprise.net
Free Postage and Packing in the United Kingdom
Credit Cards accepted. All Cheques payable to Bookpost

Prices and availability subject to change without prior notice. Allow 14 days for delivery. When placing orders please state if you do not wish to receive any additional information.